1992
24.95

FILM MUSIC

FILM MUSIC

A NEGLECTED ART

★★★★★★★★★★★★★★★★★★★★★★★★

A Critical Study of Music in Films

SECOND EDITION

Roy M. Prendergast

W · W · NORTON & COMPANY

New York · London

MUSIC PERMISSIONS

Elmer Bernstein (with Sylvia Kaye), for:
  The Man with the Golden Arm. Copyright 1955 by Dena Music, Inc. Used by permission—pp. 113–18
Leonard Bernstein, for:
  On the Waterfront. Copyright © 1954 Mills Music, Inc. International Copyright Secured. Used with permission—pp. 132–38
Scott Bradley, for:
  The Cat That Hated People. Copyright © 1947 by Loews, Inc. Rights throughout the world controlled by Robbins Music Corporation. Used by permission—p. 194
  Heavenly Puss. Copyright © 1948 by Loews, Inc. Rights throughout the world controlled by Robbins Music Corporation. Used by permission—pp. 192–93
Aaron Copland, for:
  The Heiress. Copyright © 1949 by Famous Music Corporation—pp. 90–94
Hugo Friedhofer, for:
  The Best Years of Our Lives. © 1946, Samuel Goldwyn. All Rights Reserved—pp. 74–79
  Broken Arrow. Copyright © 1950 by Twentieth Century Music Corp. Rights throughout the world controlled by Robbins Music Corporation. Used by permission—pp. 218–19
  Joan of Arc. Courtesy of Madrigal Music Company, ASCAP—p. 230

Continued on page vi.

Printed in the United States of America.

The text of this book is composed in Times Roman.

Library of Congress Cataloging-in-Publication Data

Prendergast, Roy M., 1943–
Film music : a neglected art : a critical study of music in films
/ Roy M. Prendergast.
p.   cm.
Includes bibliographical references and index.
1. Motion picture music—History and criticism. I. Title.
ML2075.P73   1991
781.5′42′09—dc20   90–21393

ISBN 0-393-02988-3
ISBN 0-393-30874-X (pbk)

W.W. Norton & Company, Inc., 500 Fifth Avenue, New York, N.Y. 100110
W.W. Norton & Company, Ltd., 10 Coptic Street, London WC1A 1PU

1 2 3 4 5 6 7 8 9 0

For my sons, David and Martin

Contents

Part IV: CONTEMPORARY TECHNIQUES AND TOOLS

Preface

This book is the first attempt at a comprehensive look at the history, aesthetics, and techniques of film music. Seldom in the annals of music history has a new form of musical expression gone so unnoticed. While the use of music to accompany film is a relatively new phenomenon, beginning in the last decade of the nineteenth century, its relatively new appearance should not have precluded a body of intelligent and perceptive writing on the subject.

The fact remains, however, that there is no such body of critical literature on film music, with the notable exception of a few penetrating articles by critic Lawrence Morton. The remainder of the literature on the subject of film music has been done by so-called aficionados. For the most part, these writers have little or no musical background and the depth of their musical perception seldom ranges beyond such superficial matters as whether or not music for films should be performed without the accompanying visuals. These writers have also been responsible for the propagation of several myths concerning music in films, some of which, hopefully, have been dispelled in this book.

What are some of the reasons for this dearth of illuminating literature? One reason certainly is the idiom composers writing for films chose: namely, the late nineteenth-century symphonic style of Strauss, Wagner, Verdi, and Puccini. This fact, coupled with the incorrect assumption of many musicians that twentieth-century music represented some sort of human condition in as powerful a way as possible. Music can add to the film's impact. Music of a more dissonant nature can have the same sort of jarring effect on the viewer/listener

as starkly realistic visuals. Economics, too, play a role in the musical idiom
employed in documentaries. As documentaries are seldom made with much
profit motive in mind, the filmmaker and composer are given a far greater—
if not limitless—latitude in their respective artistic expressions.

Finally, discussions of several composers recur throughout the study. Any
critical study of the field will reveal that certain composers have made the
most noteworthy contributions to this neglected art.

The book has been written for an audience that includes musicians as well
as those with no musical background. Whenever the book briefly delves into
musical terminology, the reader with little musical background will not be
penalized for passing over such material. The musician, on the other hand,
may profit from these critical analyses of film-music excerpts. The book is
divided into the major areas of history, aesthetics, and technique. The historical section (Part I) will be of interest to students of film history, since some
of the material presented here appears in an organized form for the first time,
while other material appears in print for the first time. The section on aesthetics (Part II) will be of interest to students of film aesthetics because it adds
another dimension to their critical vision. The section on technique (Part III),
finally, is of general interest since it defines the technical parameters within
which the film composer creates his art.

Owing to the self-imposed limit of the scope of this book I have had to
leave out discussions of some of the work of numerous skilled and talented
composers working within the film medium. Their contributions have been
substantial and the group includes such fine talents as Ernest Gold, Roy Webb,
Franz Waxman, Bronislau Kaper, André Previn, Bernardo Segall, Lalo Schifrin,
John Williams, John Green, David Grusin, Maurice Jarre, Daniele Amfithea-
trof, Richard Rodney Bennett, John Barry, George Duning, Adolf Deutsch,
and Billy Goldenberg. The length of the foregoing list of composers should
give the reader some indication of the difficulties I encountered in choosing
those composers I felt should be included in this study.

Most of the music examples appearing in the text are from the original
manuscript form of the score. In cases where the manuscript was, for the
most part, illegible, the example was recopied in a legible hand. This accounts
for the several styles of music manuscript found in the music examples
throughout the book. In view of the fact that film scoring is a rather frenetic
though precise form of composing, I felt that leaving the examples in the
form in which they were used in the actual recording session, many with
scribbled comments by the composer, would be more valuable to the reader
than a slightly neater version.

In the years since the publication of the original version of this book I have pursued a career within the industry this book studies. In looking back at the material from this new perspective I am happy to report that it does, for the most part, hold up. Where it did not I have made the necessary changes. I have also added information and observations resulting from the more intimate contact with the subject that recent years have provided. Some of this material has found its way into existing chapters and some has become the focus of new chapters. Part IV, *Contemporary Techniques and Tools*, is completely new and is designed to inform the reader of current practices in the film music industry, especially the advent of digital audio as well as videotape technology and their application in the post-production process.

For someone coming out of an academic tradition the experience has been interesting, to say the least. Sometimes it has been terrifying. Most of all it has emphasized the potential and dangerous gap that can exist between theory and practice. While an entire book could be written on this topic (and probably needs to be) it is not a legitimate area to pursue in detail in this study. I would, however, like to address two specific aspects of this subject here because I feel so strongly about them and because they recur frequently throughout film studies. The first has to do with "artistic intent" and the second with the *auteur* theory of filmmaking.

If we accept the notion that art is an attempt by one person to communicate something to another then it would seem that the intent of the creative artist should take on considerable importance to the general audience, as well as the scholar. In the study of film the danger of misreading the artistic intent of the filmmaker is compounded by the enormous number of unpredictable variables that play a part in the making of a motion picture, including the ever-present accountants who can influence the creative aspects of a motion picture more than we ever dare to admit.

There is an interesting comparison between the financial restrictions imposed on the film composer which generate solutions that are later interpreted as "creative" decisions and the restrictions of orchestral size imposed on Mozart in his day. As pianist Charles Rosen points out, those restrictions in the performance practice of Mozart's symphonies had little to do with his true wishes. Rosen observes that ". . . the Viotti orchestra [Mozart] used in London for his last concerts there was a large one, and by this time the different orchestral colors are less contrasted and opposed than blended to form a new kind of mass sonority. The orchestra that Mozart preferred is surprisingly large, but he is quite clear about what he wanted: 40 violins, 10 violas, 6 celli, 10 double-basses (!) and double wind on each part. Even remembering that all the instruments of the time were a little softer than those of the present day, this is still a force almost twice that which any conductor dares to use now for a Mozart symphony. Of course Mozart did not often get an orchestra of such size, but there is no reason today to perpetuate those conditions of eighteenth-century performance which obtained only when there was not enough money to do the thing properly."*

As for "artistic intent" in filmmaking in general, a simple, true story should make my point. A British director told me of a picture he had recently directed which had been well received by the critics. However, in the critical analyses of the film a great deal of attention was directed to the "dark" quality of the picture. The director found this all quite amusing because, as he said, "we only had twenty-five days to shoot the entire picture and it was *bloody raining the entire time!*"

The auteur theory of filmmaking is a term credited to American film critic Andrew Sarris and springs from a concept put forth by François Truffaut in a 1954 essay which speaks of *"la politique des auteurs."* This "policy of authors," within the academic and film criticism communities, has taken on far more importance than it really deserves. Film directors of course love the idea, however far from the truth it might be, since it focuses attention almost entirely on them and excludes all of the other highly creative and essential individuals involved in the making of a film.

From an artistic standpoint my personal observation is that the most creatively influential people involved in making a film are the writer, cinematographer, and composer. I would, in many cases, include the art director and/or costumer in this category. Directors, on the other hand, *get things done.* In fact, this necessary quality in a good director would seem to run counter to the apparently insecure and indecisive personality of many creative individuals. Because of the high costs involved filmmaking abhors a vacuum created by indecision, and directors will make decisions and make them fast. I have often been involved in a situation during the post-production process of a film where an aesthetic question arises that genuinely requires and deserves some thought and discussion, and, almost invariably, the director will *immediately* offer a solution, however inept. This is not to say that directors don't have good ideas, they often do, but they sometimes confuse their ability to manage things efficiently with the creative process itself.

---

*Rosen, Charles. *The Classical Style.* New York: W. W. Norton & Company, 1972, p. 143.

The creative aspects of filmmaking are a corporate endeavor. No single individual could possibly possess the talent, training, and imagination to execute or judge every aspect of filmmaking. Those directors who think they do are of the worst kind and their work reflects it. Good directors recognize this and surround themselves with highly creative individuals whose talent and input are valued and utilized. This collection of tremendously creative individuals, all working toward a common goal, is one of the most exciting and rewarding aspects of filmmaking.

R.P.

Los Angeles California

Foreword to the First Edition

I have, for some time now, felt that those in control of the dissemination of symphonic music in the United States in the 1920's, 30's and 40's were guilty of a form of cultural murder. This was a time when American music was groping so intensely for a style and life of its own. It was the time of first maturation of the American composer. It is not enough to point to the contributions of Koussevitzsky and Stokowski through the Boston and Philadelphia orchestras, nor to the spasmodic contributions from New York. (The League of Composers was an inspirational beacon in the realm of chamber music.) Boston and Philadelphia were not to the United States what the musical capitals of Europe were to their respective countries. The impact of significant premiers was too often lost in the sponge of our enormity, in the lack of national communication, and in the lack of second performances. Aaron Copland, commenting in 1936 on the music of the 20's and 30's in perhaps the most authoritative book on this subject, *Copland on Music*, said of Bernard Rogers that: "Since none of his major works has been performed outside Rochester, where he makes his home, I cannot speak authoritatively about them."

How many potentially outstanding talents disappeared into the shadow of academic life because of lack of proper support, performance and recognition? How many young minds in this enormous country were never tapped, never stimulated by hearing the music of living composers, because conductors were unable either to feel and comprehend the music or to brave and overcome the prejudices and antipathetic attitudes of their own boards of directors and audiences? How many young promising talents and contributors to the core of American symphonic and chamber music were discouraged because they were convinced that they would never hear their own music performed? How many lay dormant outside the Northeastern perimeter we will never know. (Even now, too many young composers prefer electronic music, not for its own aesthetic, but because they doubt the possibility of having their instrumental—especially orchestral—music performed.)

I speak of this period (1920 to 1950) in particular because it was a period when American music was trying so desperately to come of age. While Europe was moving into and through new realms of compositional techniques—not only the particular approaches of Stravinsky, Hindemith and Bartók, but also the more universally pregnant serialism of Schoenberg, not to mention the explorations into electronics—America was still groping for its national image, a matter well determined in Europe before World War I.

But this discussion of style and image is only a part of the tragedy. What is even more crucial here is that potential composers outside the Northeastern stronghold were not only unaware of the American developments, but of all twentieth-century music! Thus, for them, the first music they heard by living composers was in films. I shall never forget the staggering impact made upon me in my mid-teens by Adolph Deutsch's modal score to *The Maltese Falcon*. Many potential composers who lived in the cultural vacuum that constituted the bulk of the United States heard through films not only their first symphonically oriented orchestra, but one that was used imaginatively, dramatically, and even experimentally—the sound of distant strings to evoke a memory, the collage of two musics to indicate two simultaneous situations—perhaps relating a psychological reaction to an ongoing experience.

Because of the necessity of tying the musical structure to the dictates of the visual image, much of the emphasis fell on orchestral color and variation. Thus the genius of many of our film composers went to creating sounds and ideas to enhance the dramatic, visual, and psychological intent of the film, rather than to musical structure and a pure musical aesthetic.

Many composers brought to films an eclectic personality. This pleased producers very much—the romanticism of Tschaikovsky, Rachmaninoff, Strauss and Wagner was most welcome. Later on, some adopted the styles of twentieth-century composers: Copland for the image of America, past and present, Schoenberg for eeriness and passionate violence, and Stravinsky (particularly the "Rite of Spring") for terror and brutality. But there has been another, more rare, kind of composer who was able to take an existing tradition or current approach, utilize it and carry it further in the manner of all great artists. I would like to draw attention to two who have particularly impressed me: David Raksin and Leonard Rosenman. Rosenman is one of those composers who started out as a composer of symphonic and chamber music, but rather than coming to Hollwood with nineteenth- and twentieth-century eclecticism, he came armed with an impressive skill and awareness of contemporary techniques. I am pleased that he has made a determined return to concert, particularly chamber, music, and that his structural inventiveness has not been hampered by the above-mentioned restrictions in writing film music. I might add that the first film which attracted me to his ability was *The Savage Eye,* a little-known film about Los Angeles. In this film, he was given carte blanche, the film being cut to the music. In essence it was a commission to write a piece of chamber music and, indeed, it has become known independently as "Chamber Music No. 1."

I call attention to Rosenman also because he has been lost to the concert hall and to the development of American music—to which he has much to offer. This may also be said of the highly gifted David Raksin, for, although his development largely took place in the studios, his music exemplifies the Gershwinian voyage from Broadway (the ballad, the dance tune) to abstract, or pure, symphonic music. I consider the American ballad—the "pop" tune or song—to be a very significant portion of what the world has taken to be America's particularly indigenous contribution to music, namely, jazz. The harmonic richness that stems from Beiderbecke and Gershwin finds a most free flowing expression in Raksin. An outstanding example is the opening portion preceding the main theme of the concert version of "Laura". This, to me, epitomizes to the highest degree the abstraction of folk elements—putting them into a universal and permanent genre.

The question I ask from my position as a composer vitally concerned with the personality and development of American music, is: What would these and similarly gifted composers have offered to the building of an American image and tradition if they had been stimulated to devote their energies to symphonic and chamber music?

What Mr. Prendergast has done so devotedly and with extraordinary care, insight and skill, is to take us deeply and meaningfully into the film medium's world of music. Film music is indeed a vital part of American culture and sometimes it is glorious, and sometimes, as Prendergast points out when appropriate, it is bastardized and servile. Some of the recent trends in music for television emphasize this latter situation. It is frustrating to realize that the business-minded impresarios too often wish to commercialize the product and not to consider, at all, the idea of bringing this art to the highest possible cultural level. After all, for better or worse, ours is a visual age. The visual media have the greatest impact on society, they have affected all the arts, they have affected the root of the arts, namely, the imagination.

The influence of the film medium itself cannot be avoided and one looks to it to assume its responsibility, as have literature, music, painting and sculpture. I should like to quote Ernst Krenek when asked by Will Ogden why, since he was such a "movie bug," he had never written a film score: "I have never been asked to—and that may be just as well, considering the way music has been treated there. But I feel that the film has become more and more the only medium for dealing seriously with the problems of our time." Mr. Prendergast has shown himself to be a gifted musician and analyst, as well as a painstaking and knowledgeable writer. *A Neglected Art: A Critical Study of Music in Films* is enormously impressive in its scope and scholarship and will rightfully become a standard source of reference.

William Kraft
Sherman Oaks, Ca.

Foreword to the Second Edition

That Mr. Prendergast is unusually well-equipped to discuss both the technology and aesthetics of film music is revealed once more in this second edition, particularly in the new section on synthesizers. And in this discussion he is disarmingly frank and perceptive. The "hands-on" experience he has had as one of Hollywood's leading music editors has allowed him to make comments and judgments that serve the history of film music.

One is forced to pause and consider the statement found in this section on synthesizers. "Just as opera was in the nineteenth century, film is the medium of our time and, as such, is constantly reflecting values and ideas from our popular culture." There is no doubt that the two are comparable as the most significant medium for mass communication at their particular time (except now for the incursion of television—which I suppose one can consider a form of film).

If one is to assume that "popular culture" refers to the general population, then, for the most part, the comparison should be made with the lighter operatic genre: the ballad opera in England, *singspiel* in Germany, *zarzuela* in Spain, *opéra comique* in France, and the operettas of Paris, Vienna, and England (Gilbert and Sullivan). Opera, as we generally think of it, did not cater to the general population but rather to a highly educated aristocratic audience. Therefore its subject matter was quite distinctive, dealing as it did with mythical, historical, literary, and biblical subjects, or with the foibles of aristocratic life (e.g., Verdi's *La traviata*). The greatest talents of the time were also involved: composers, performers, conductors, writers, scenic and costume designers, and often choreographers. In short, nineteenth-century grand opera was a totally artistic enterprise.

This is not to say that the film "industry" does not ever concern itself with such talents, but that it is, by far, the exception. Of course there are producers who, on rare occasions, concern themselves with quality and significance (the producers of *Reds, Dr. Zhivago, Apocalypse Now, Platoon, Full Metal Jacket, Lawrence of Arabia,* etc.). But for the most part Hollywood, which is notoriously famous for being money conscious, is additionally smitten by the doctrine of the 80s, "Greed is Good," and intends to make as much profit as possible. Thus we find synthesizers utilized, not for their dramatic and coloristic potential, but simply to cut costs. And string sections are replaced by a string quartet or quintet (if any strings at all) plus a synthesizer with the instructions *"Quasi* strings." Entire orchestras can be, and are, replaced. Marvelous instrumentalists cannot, as they once did, make incomes commensurate with their talent. And though electronics, in competent hands, are a welcome addition and dramatic complement to the palette of film music, they have also been used to cut costs, usually with a consequent cut in quality. We have even witnessed the creation of a segment of the current generation of electronic composers who are unable to notate music, let alone know what true composition and orchestration are about. In this situation, there can hardly be the inspiration to gifted young potential composers as mentioned in the foreword to the first edition.

Of course one can say it has always been thus in films—that there always was an imbalance between the artistic and the economic. But it seems to be a far more destructive imbalance now than before; destructive because it reflects the insidiousness of a society that is culturally deprived, poorly educated, particularly in the arts, and suspicious and even suppressive of the arts. We currently live in a society dominated at all levels by the corporate mentality. This has not always been so, and hopefully, it will not always be so. If this should change, then presumably values will also and one can only hope that such a change will reflect a greater sensitivity to humanitarian and aesthetic expression. That is the dream of all artists.

William Kraft
Alta Dena, CA.

Acknowledgements

I must, first of all, thank David Raksin for his constant encouragement and help in the development of this book. In fact, without his unselfish assistance in procuring important materials for this book, as well as his arranging for interviews with otherwise relatively inaccessible people in the film industry, my book would not be as thorough a study as it now is. Knowing of Mr. Raksin's concern over his position of having been so much help in a project which also discusses his own contributions to the art of film scoring, I must tell the reader that Mr. Raksin was always extremely forceful in his concern that I include *all* of his colleagues, past and present, whom I felt made significant contributions to this art. There is, of course, no doubt in my mind, or David's colleagues, that his work should be included in any study of this subject.

I would like to thank composers Leonard Rosenman, Jerry Goldsmith, Hugo Friedhofer, Scott Bradley, Alex North and Miklos Rozsa for taking time to discuss their work with me. Thanks also to filmmaker John Whitney and soundman James G. Stewart for interrupting their busy schedules to talk with me about their many contributions to the art of film.

A very special thanks to Dr. Kenneth Epple, a rare and generous man who brings a great deal of honor to his profession, and to Linda Smith, whose help and support have been invaluable.

Others I am grateful to for their help and support are Jack Jarrett, Claire Brook of W. W. Norton, Annah and Donald Prago, Jerry Artaud,

Mr. and Mrs. S. L. Crawford, Nancy Willis, Mr. and Mrs. Jack Sealy, as well as the Research Council of the University of North Carolina at Greensboro, whose financial assistance was invaluable. Thanks also to Dr. Byron Petrakis for his early editorial work (as well as many useful suggestions) in the preparation of the initial manuscript. The copywork of Robah Ogburn and the copyediting of Kathie Fried saved me many an hour of tedium, as did the editorial work of Robert Bull and Despina Papazoglou, both of New York University Press.

Ms. Jeanette Fitzpatrick of the index department at ASCAP was extremely helpful in finding copyright information. In the preparation of this expanded edition I am much indebted to Juli Goldfein of W. W. Norton for her indispensable editorial assistance. Her patience and enthusiasm, as well as her intelligent suggestions, are very much appreciated.

PART I

History

1

Music in the Silent Film

Since the days of the Greeks, music and drama have shared a close relationship. So it would seem natural that with the advent of the silent film, music would be used as an accompaniment to the screen action. But is the matter really that simple? Before moving into a general historical discussion of music and the silent cinema, it would be helpful to examine some of the reasons why music was chosen as an auditory counterpoint to the silent film.

There are several interesting theories on this point. The first, advanced by composer Hanns Eisler in his otherwise testy and relatively valueless book, *Composing for the Films,* rests on the assumption that silent films must have had a "ghostly effect" on its viewers. "Since their beginning, motion pictures have been accompanied by music. The pure cinema must have had a ghostly effect like that of the shadow play—shadows and ghosts have always been associated. The magic function of music . . . consisted in appeasing the evil spirits unconsciously dreaded. Music was introduced as a kind of antidote against the picture. The need was felt to spare the spectator the unpleasantness involved in seeing effigies of living, acting, and even speaking persons, who were at the same time silent. The fact that they are living and nonliving at the same time is what constitutes their ghostly character, and music was introduced not to supply them with the life they lacked—this became its aim only in the era of total ideological planning—but to exorcise fear or help the spectator absorb the shock.

3

"Motion-picture music corresponds to the whistling or singing child in the dark. The real reason for the fear is not even that these people whose silent effigies are moving in front of one seem to be ghosts. The captions do their best to come to the aid of these images. But confronted with gesticulating masks, people experience themselves as creatures of the very same kind, as being threatened by muteness. The origin of motion-picture music is inseparably connected with the decay of the spoken language, which has been demonstrated by Karl Kraus. It is hardly accidental that the early motion pictures did not resort to the seemingly most natural device of accompanying the pictures by dialogues of concealed actors,* as is done in the Punch and Judy shows, but always resorted to music, although in the old horror or slapstick pictures it had hardly any relation to the plots."

On the other hand, Kurt London, in his fine early study, *Film Music,* aligns himself with the simpler idea that music was introduced as a sound to neutralize the noise of the primitive projectors of the day. As London points out, inadequate acoustics rather than "any artistic urge" were responsible for motion-picture music. "Instinctively," London continues, "cinema proprietors had recourse to music, and it was the right way, using an agreeable sound to neutralize one less agreeable."

Eisler, however, feels that London's interesting thesis doesn't go far enough because "there remains the question, why should the sound of the projector have been so unpleasant?... It is basically the feeling that something may befall a man even if he be 'many.' This is precisely the consciousness of one's own mechanization."

Perhaps most interesting of all, in terms of film aesthetics, is London's observation: "The reason which is aesthetically and psychologically most essential to explain the need of music as an accompaniment of the silent film, is without doubt *the rhythm of the film as an art of movement.* We are not accustomed to apprehend movement as an artistic form without accompanying sounds, or at least audible rhythms. Every film that deserves the name must possess its individual rhythm which determines its form. (Form is here taken in the widest sense as a ruling concept.) It

---

*This was done by the Italian comedian Leopold Fregoli as early as 1898. Fregoli made a series of short comedy films, which he had projected at the end of his stage performances. Fregoli would then stand behind the screen and speak or sing in synchronization to the picture.

was the task of the musical accompaniment to give it auditory accentuation and profundity."

Of all the above theories concerning the use of music with silent film, this last one proposed by London seems closest to understanding music's unique relationship with the silent film.

While the answer probably owes something to all of the above observations, London's point that film music was not the result of "any artistic urge" should be qualified to read, "any *conscious* artistic urge." The implication one draws from the above comments is that film music had utilitarian rather than artistic beginnings. This utilitarian beginning for film music may partially explain why fine composers had to fight for a considerable length of time before they were allowed to write "artistic" scores for pictures after sound came in. To most producers and directors, film music was simply a necessary evil. Because of these utilitarian beginnings, there were few significant scores to silent films.

The first known use of music with the cinema was on December 28, 1895, when the Lumière family first tested the commercial value of some of its earliest films. The screening, with piano accompaniment, took place at the Grand Café on the Boulevard des Capucines in Paris. It is also believed that at the first public showing of the Lumière program in Britain, at the Polytechnic on Regent Street, a harmonium from the Polytechnic's chapel was used to accompany the showing. This performance took place on February 20, 1896, and, by April of that year, orchestras were accompanying films in several London theaters.

In the first years of commercial cinema the musical material used as accompaniment consisted of just about anything that was available at the moment and, more often than not, bore little dramatic relationship to what was happening on the screen. Musical selections ranged from light café music to some of the serious classics. In those early days musicians' professionalism left much to be desired since, in many theaters, the orchestra would play through a certain number of compositions and then simply get up and leave the film and the audience. As might be expected, producers of films were not always happy with this situation, but there was little they could do since the exhibitor determined what role the music should play in its relationship to the film.

As the cinema discovered its potentialities, it was inevitable that there arose a desire on the part of the more sensitive film producers to provide a specific score for a specific picture. This idea first came to fruition in 1908.

A company founded in Paris, known as Le Film d'Art, encouraged well-known actors to perform on film some of the more famous plays in the repertoire. The Comédie Française and the Académie Française lent support to the idea, and the group put together their initial production: *L'Assassinat du Duc de Guise*. The significant fact, however, was that famed French composer Camille Saint-Saëns was asked to compose a special score specifically for this film. Saint-Saëns readily accepted and later developed his music for the film into a concert piece, his Opus 128 for strings, piano, and harmonium. For various reasons, not the least of which was the considerable added expense to the picture's production costs, this idea of specially composed scores did not catch on to any great extent. Nevertheless, there arose an industry that answered the ever-growing need for music to accompany the cinema.

In 1909, one year after the Saint-Saëns score, the Edison film company began issuing "specific suggestions for music" with the films they produced. By 1913 theater orchestras and pianists were able to acquire music for specific moods or dramatic situations, all conveniently catalogued by the publisher. The most famous example of this concept was Giuseppe Becce's *Kinobibliothek* (or *Kinothek,* as it was called), which was first published in Berlin in 1919. *The Sam Fox Moving Picture Music Volumes* by J. S. Zamecnik appeared as early as 1913, but it was the Becce *Kinothek* that was to become the best known of the group. In the *Kinothek* were many pieces of descriptive music classified according to style and mood; many of the pieces were specially composed by Becce himself. This system of cataloguing tended toward pigeonholing, as seen in the example below, drawn from the *Handbook of Film Music* by Erdmann, Becce, and Brav.

DRAMATIC EXPRESSION (Main Concept)
1. Climax; (subordinate concept)
    (a) catastrophe; (Subdivisions)
    (b) Highly dramatic *agitato*
    (c) Solemn atmosphere; mysteriousness of nature.

2.   Tension—*Misterioso*
    (a) Night: sinister mood;
    (b) Night: threatening mood;
    (c) Uncanny *agitato*

(d) Magic: apparition;
(e) Impending doom: "something is going to happen."

3. Tension—*Agitato*
(a) Pursuit, flight, hurry;
(b) Flight;
(c) Heroic combat;
(d) Battle;
(e) Disturbance, unrest, terror;
(f) Disturbed masses, tumult;
(g) Disturbed nature: storm, fire.

Figure 1. A typical example of a piece from Becce's *Kinobibliothek*. This composition belongs to the very first printed *Kinobibliothek*.

4. Climax—*Appassionato*
   (a) Despair
   (b) Passionate lament;
   (c) Passionate excitement;
   (d) Jubilant;
   (e) Victorious;
   (f) Bacchantic.

As London points out, "other main concepts were: dramatic scenes; lyrical expression; lyrical incident; quite general incident, subdivided again into three subordinate headings, Nature (romantically descriptive), Nation and Society, Church and State."

In the United States it is generally acknowledged that one Max Winkler was the first to catalogue music for the silent film. Winkler was a clerk in the Carl Fischer store in New York City. During the year 1912 the demands on the Carl Fischer music store for music to accompany films became so great that Winkler began losing sleep over the matter. In an issue of *Films in Review,* Winkler recalls that "One day after I had gone home from work I could not fall asleep. The hundreds and thousands of titles, the mountains of music that Fischer's had stored and catalogued, kept going through my mind. There was music, surely to fit *any* given situation in *any* picture. If we could only think of a way to let all these orchestra leaders and pianists and organists know what we had! If we could use our knowledge and experience not when it was too late, but much earlier, before they ever had to sit down and play, we would be able to sell them music not by the ton but by the trainload.

"That thought suddenly electrified me. It was not a problem of getting the music. We had the music. . . . It was a problem of promoting, timing and organization. I pulled back the blanket, turned on the light and went over to my table, took a sheet of paper and began writing feverishly. Here is what I wrote:

MUSIC CUE SHEET
for
The Magic Valley
Selected and compiled by M. Winkler

Cue

1 Opening—play Minuet No. 2 in G by Beethoven for ninety seconds until title on screen "Follow me dear."

2 Play—"Dramatic Andante" by Vely for two minutes and ten seconds. Note: Play soft during scene where mother enters. Play Cue No. 2 until scene "hero leaving room."

3 Play—"Love Theme" by Lorenze—for one minute and twenty seconds. Note: Play soft and slow during conversations until title on screen "There they go."

4 Play—"Stampede" by Simon for fifty-five seconds. Note: Play fast and decrease or increase speed of gallop in accordance with action on the screen."

The Magic Valley was an imaginary film, but it made Winkler's point. Winkler wrote the New York office of the Universal Film Company and explained that if they would allow him to view their films *before* they were released he could make up similar cue sheets for all of their films. This sort of advance preparation would give the local theaters time to prepare adequate musical accompaniment for their films.

Paul Gulick, then publicity director of Universal Films, liked the idea and arranged for Winkler to try out his concept by having him come over in the evening and view some films. Winkler was then to make out cue sheets for the film.

Gulick was apparently impressed with the results, for Winkler was immediately engaged by the Universal Film Company to provide musical cues for all of their films. The response of the theater musicians, Winkler later recalled, "was overwhelming. Everybody was delighted."

Winkler later left Fischer's and formed a partnership with one of his inevitable early imitators, S. M. Berg.

As the demands on Winkler's music service became greater, the problem of supplying the theater musicians with enough material grew to crisis proportions. "In desperation we turned to crime," Winkler recalls. "We began to dismember the great masters. We began to murder the works of Beethoven, Mozart, Grieg, J. S. Bach, Verdi, Bizet, Tchaikovsky and Wagner—everything that wasn't protected by copyright from our pilfering."

Winkler recalled that "The immortal chorales of J. S. Bach became an 'Adagio Lamentoso for sad scenes.' Extracts from great symphonies and operas were hacked down to emerge again as 'Sinister Misterioso' by Beethoven, or 'Weird Moderato' by Tchaikovsky. Wagner's and Mendelssohn's wedding marches were used for marriages, fights between husbands and wives, and divorce scenes: we just had them played out of tune, a treatment known in the profession as 'souring up the aisle.' If they were to be used for happy endings we jazzed them up mercilessly. Finales from famous overtures, with the 'William Tell' and 'Orpheus' the favorites, became galops. Meyerbeer's 'Coronation March' was slowed down to a majestic pomposo to give proper background to the inhabitants of Sing Sing's deathhouse. The 'Blue Danube' was watered down to a minuet by a cruel change in tempo."

With the coming of sound Winkler's fortunes fell. He sold his entire stock of seventy tons of music to a paper mill for the meager sum of $210. Before he could collect, however, the paper mill went bankrupt.

Even though men like Winkler and Becce provided the theaters with music, there still remained the question of how all of this material was put to use by the music director of a cinema theater. As movies grew in popularity, so did the size of the orchestras to accompany them. The problem for the music director was that, while a pianist can watch the screen and improvise, an orchestra cannot; thus music had to be chosen to suit each film. This, of course, was more the case with the Becce *Kinothek* than with Winkler's cue sheets, since the *Kinothek* did not deal with specific films. This selection of music was by no means an easy task, and the difficulties were compounded by the small amount of time a conductor would have from the time of his first viewing of a film to the first performance of the music.

There was a general routine followed by the music director (or music illustrator, as he was then called). It began with his looking carefully at the film in order to gain impressions of its form and content. The film was then shown to him a second time, in sections, as he carefully calculated with a stopwatch single scenes that he intended to divide musically from one another. With that completed, he began selecting the music to be used. At this stage the music illustrator had to decide whether the score was to be a compilation of numbers, in the style of the old opera, or whether it was to be more in the style of Wagner's music dramas, using some sort of psychological arrangement of the leitmotiv. Generally the use of set numbers prevailed, with the occasional use of some main themes loosely related to the leitmotiv style.

The set numbers were, of course, placed at the climaxes of the film. This overall structure was filled out with other pieces or sections of pieces. Sometimes single sections were played side by side with no transitions at all, although short modulations were written when the contrast of styles appeared too crude.

These transitions from scene to scene were problematical for the music illustrator or conductor. Often, in order to solve the problem most easily, conductors resorted to writing their own. Film composer David Raksin's recollection of his father's method of conducting is instructive: "My father conducted music for silent movies—usually scores compiled from the various kinothek libraries; but when necessary he would compose music for part of a film himself."

Such original transitions written for a silent film might at first appear to be the least significant element in a silent film score. Actually, they were probably the portion with the greatest value, since, as London points out, these transitions and short bits of material were "created out of the feeling originally inspired by the film itself, whereas the compilations were at best only substitutes."

A particular score made up of various pieces would, of course, reflect the taste of the conductor or illustrator who created it. Some conductors avoided compilations altogether and accompanied the better films with bits from the works of a single composer. Thus it would not be unusual to hear a silent film score made up of all Debussy or all Tchaikovsky. Usually, though, time did not allow for this kind of luxury.

As Kurt London points out, the transition from piece to piece also created an aesthetic problem: "The silent film did not require a close interpretation of *all* its separate scenes; what it required was the opposite, the *musical simplification of the mosaic of film images into one long line.* The even flow of the music must therefore, apart from certain exceptions based on dramatic considerations, not be interrupted."

If not properly handled, transitions can be *very* interruptive in nature, however. It was a difficult and sometimes impossible task to achieve any kind of smoothness between stylistically different pieces. The problem was one of reconciliation of various types of compositions. While it is possible, using traditional musical practice, to write a modulation between two pieces of music of widely different character, such modulations are of little use when working with the rapid scene changes found in films. So the music illustrator's problem was one of avoiding jerky changes in the music without shattering the overall line of the film. The required combination was, according to London, "Variety in the film images and uniformity in the music."

Obviously, the solution to all of these problems is a score specifically composed for one picture. While this sounds simple enough on the surface and is easily done with a sound film, the silent film offered unique problems. One, mentioned before, was cost. Another was the fact that "general release" theaters did not have complete orchestras as did the bigger houses. Publishers could certainly not be expected to produce scores and orchestral parts for each of the myriad of instrumental combinations. It would have been unprofitable to publish such an assortment of music. Another problem with the specifically composed score was that some conductors would boycott it as an infringement on their artistic domain—*they* wished to do the selecting.

When a production company did make the decision to have an original score composed for its picture, it usually wanted it, as is still the case today, as quickly as possible. Like the music illustrator working in the theater, the composer first looked at the film, then measured the individual scenes with a stopwatch. After acquiring this information he began to compose. He used the climaxes of a film as his starting point and, from them, built the form and structure of the other musical sections.

Even with a score composed specifically for a picture, there remained the problem of keeping the music in some sort of synchronization with the film. Several systems were devised to accommodate this need, none of them wholly successful. One of the more successful was invented by Carl Robert Blum, a German, and was first displayed for the public in Berlin in 1926. Blum called his apparatus a "rhythmonome." Its workings are described by Kurt London: "Tapes registering the "phonorhythmical" signs run within the instrument in such a way that they pass a sight-index from left to right, that is, in the direction of reading. The sound can then be reproduced in the original rhythm, as the sight-index allows it to be read off in exact timing. The rhythmonome can thus be contrasted with a metronome, for, whereas the latter gives the metrical distribution (in equal beats), the former presents the ametrical (irregular) pulsations, that is *the living* rhythm.

"The instrument was placed on the conductor's desk and was coupled in synchronism with the film projector; the running speed could be constantly controlled by means of a "musical chronometer." The conductor only had to guide his orchestra in such a way that the music was timed to sound at every point exactly as the corresponding notes ran past the sight-index."

There were other attempts at solving the problem of synchronization between film and music but most were less than successful. One used a picture of a conductor, shown on a screen in front of the actual conductor; but most conductors were able to follow the other's baton with only moderate success. Still another invention had a ribbon at the bottom of the actual film showing, by way of an abbreviated score, the notes of the music that should, at the specific time they appeared, be the notes being played by the musicians. As might be expected, this system considerably bothered the spectators and was soon dropped.

Kurt London felt that any form of *exact* synchronization of music and picture was doomed to an aesthetic failure because "the plane dimensions of the picture on the one hand, and the plastic character of the ringing music on the other, did not coincide. . . . it was contrary to the inherent character of the silent film. . . . As long as the film remained silent, there was only one method of musical accompaniment for it: the comprehensive line that was compiled or composed, and not built up on absolute synchronization."

Despite these problems of synchronization, there were a number of fine scores composed for individual pictures. The score for D. W. Griffith's monumental film *The Birth of a Nation* is of little musical significance but is of considerable historical interest. It is a pastiche of original compositions, quotes from Liszt, Verdi, Beethoven, Wagner, Tchaikovsky, as well as a number of well-known traditional tunes from the United States such as "Dixie" and "The Star-Spangled Banner." Despite the score's lack of musical value, it did set standards of orchestration and cuing techniques that remained throughout the silent era.

The score for *The Birth of a Nation* was the joint work of D. W. Griffith and a composer/orchestra leader by the name of Joseph Carl Briel. Since

Griffith had studied composition in his home town of Louisville, Kentucky, and in New York, he was more than qualified for the task. The film had its premiere at the Liberty Theatre in New York City in March of 1915.

The undisputed master of the silent film score was the German composer Edmund Meisel. Meisel wrote the scores for Sergei Eisenstein's films *The Battleship Potemkin* and *October*. Although believed to be irrecoverably lost, Meisel's legendary score to *Potemkin* recently was discovered in the Eisenstein Archives in Leningrad, Russia, by the expert on Russian film, Jay Leyda. Another important figure in the restoration of the score was Arthur Kleiner, the former Music Director of the Museum of Modern Art film library. What Leyda discovered was a set of parts to Meisel's music for *Potemkin*. When Kleiner heard of the discovery, he immediately requested and received permission from Leyda to microfilm the parts. Kleiner then assembled the parts into an orchestral score and, with the aid of the KCET television in Los Angeles, synchronized the music to the picture. It should be mentioned here that the print used to join music and picture is more complete than most available versions—a result of the efforts of the Museum of Modern Art.

Meisel's score for *Potemkin* was not the only one, nor was it the first score for the picture. At the film's debut in Russia in 1925, it had an orchestral accompaniment believed to have been composed or compiled by Yuri Faier. In 1951 a score was provided for *Potemkin* by Nicolai Kryukov.

The film deals with the historic mutiny aboard the battleship *Potemkin* during the unsuccessful Russian revolution of 1905. The narrative is basically structured into five acts: depiction of the horrible shipboard conditions that were the impetus for the revolt, the revolt itself, the support by the people of Odessa, the bloody retribution dealt out by the Czar's cossacks (the famous "Odessa steps" sequence), and the final triumph of the mutineers. Eisenstein once said about the music that "The audience must be lashed into a fury and shaken violently by the volume of the sound. . . . This sound can't be strong enough and should be turned to the limit of the audience's physical and mental capacity." "Meisel," writer Alan Kriegsman points out, "took him at his word."

Kriegsman characterized the music rather accurately when he wrote: "In purely musical terms, Meisel's music is not especially memorable. Nor is there anything especially noteworthy about Meisel's compositional tactics. The instrumentation calls for a modestly scaled orchestral ensemble, fortified by a massive percussion section, including two timpani, military drum, bass drum, tam-tam, triangle, castanets, woodblocks, large rattle and sirens. Meisel relies to a great extent on percussive thunder with an abrasive edge. Four-square march patterns abound. . . . What gives Meisel's work its distinction is not the elements used, but the way in which he has forged them into a unified dramatic structure that not only runs parallel to, but actually redoubles the punch of Eisenstein's film imagery at every instant.

". . . Meisel strikes to the core of the drama with every note. He sets the stage with a tortured, angry fanfare, mirrors the grievances of the sailors with sullen, resentful murmurings that hint at repressed fury, and builds toward the bloody confrontations with passages of nearly unbearable suspense and turbulence. The music, like the film, is almost mathematical in its schematic unfolding of tension, but the effect is raw, intuitive and elemental.

"What Meisel so brilliantly understood was that the music for *Potemkin* could not remain a mere background or accessory. It had to become an ingredient of the film itself, one with the rhythms and textures and feelings of the picture. In consequence, the cumulative power of the graphic and tonal mixture is unique. For sheer visceral agitation, there is nothing in all film history to rival it, even today, and very little in any other realm of art that comes close."

When Meisel worked on a film score, he used a rather unusual system. He first analyzed the montages of some of the more famous silent films, examining their rhythm, emphasis, emotional climax, and mood. He then assigned a musical theme to each separate shot. Finally, he combined the separate themes using the rhythm, emphasis, and climaxes of the visual montages as his system of organization for the music. What Meisel was trying to prove was that there was a formal correlation between the montage of film and music: "He wished to prove . . . that the montage of a good film is based on the same rules and develops in the same way as music." In using this system, however, not all "good" films produced any worthwhile music but rather chaos. Other films produced a certain musical continuity; the finest of these is Eisenstein's *Potemkin.*

Potemkin has always been regarded as a revolutionary document, and so overwhelming was Meisel's score that the music was banned from the film's performances in Germany when it was first released there.

Meisel had the kind of director that few film composers ever have—one sensitive to the things music is capable of contributing to the overall effect of a film. In his book, *Film Form,* Eisenstein discusses his relationship with Meisel, commenting particularly on the unusual way the score for *Potemkin* was composed:

"It was written very much as we work today on a sound-track. Or rather, as we *should always* work, with the creative friendship and friendly creative collaboration between composer and director.

"With Meisel this took place in spite of the short time for composition that he was given, and the brevity of my visit to Berlin in 1926 for this purpose. He agreed at once to forgo the purely illustrative function common to musical accompaniments at that time (and not only that time!) and stress certain 'effects,' particularly in the 'music of Machines' in the last reel.

"This was my categorical demand: not only to reject customary melodiousness for this sequence of 'Meeting the Squadron,' relying entirely on a rhythmic beating of percussion, but also to give substance to this demand by establishing in the music as well as in the film at the decisive place a 'throwing over' into a 'new quality' in the *sound structure.*

"So it was *Potemkin* at this point that stylistically broke away from the limits of the 'silent film with musical illustrations' into a new sphere—into *sound-film,* where true models of this art-form live in a unity of fused musical and visual images, *composing the work with a united audio-visual image.* It is exactly owing to these elements, *anticipating the potentialities of an inner substance for composition in the sound-film,* that the sequence of 'Meeting the Squadron' (which along with the 'Odessa Steps' had such a 'crushing' effect abroad) deserves a leading place in the anthology of cinema.

"Here the 'silent' *Potemkin* teaches the sound-film a lesson, emphasizing again and again the position that for an organic work a single law of construction must penetrate it decisively in all its 'significances,' and in order to be not 'off-stage,' but governed, not only by the same images and themes, but as well by the same basic laws and principles of construction that govern the work as a whole."

Aside from Edmund Meisel, there were other famous composers at work on special scores during the silent-film era. Arthur Honegger composed scores for Abel Gance's *La Roue* and his forward-looking *Napoléon.* Darius Milhaud wrote a score for Marcel l'Herbier's *L'Inhumaine* and Dmitri Shostakovitch provided a special score for the Russian film *The New Babylon.*

While these specially composed scores were significant, they were also the exception, for most theaters continued to use compiled scores for their orchestras. For those smaller theaters that had neither the money nor the room for an orchestra, there were machines that could be purchased to take their place. These machines began appearing on the market around 1910 and carried such names as "One Man Motion Picture Orchestra," "Filmplayer," "Movieodion," or "Pipe-Organ Orchestra." In addition to music, these machines were capable of providing a battery of sound effects, and they ranged in size from what was essentially a player piano with small percussion setup to elaborate instruments nearly equalling a twenty-piece pit orchestra. Samuel A. Peeples, in an article in *Films in Review,* describes one of these apparitions: "The crowning achievement of the American Photo Player Company was their Fotoplayer Style 50, only one of which is presently known to survive in operating condition. Among the most splendid automatic musical instruments ever built, it was 21 feet long, 5 feet wide, and 5 feet 2 inches tall. It was capable of recreating the volume of a 20 piece pit orchestra, plus a full-scale theatre pipe-organ, with an incredible range of effects, such as the lowing of cattle, the drumming of hoofs in assorted gaits, several varieties of klaxons, street traffic noises, crackling flames, breaking wood and brush, rifle, pistol and machine gun shots, even the sound of a French 75MM cannon!"

One wonders about the quality of genius it must have taken to operate one of these devices.

Music played one other significant role in the era of silent films and that was one of inspiration on the sets of motion-picture companies. It was common to have staff musicians on hand to play for silent-film stars when they had a difficult scene to do. It is generally acknowledged that this type of thing was first done on the set of the 1913 D. W. Griffith film, *Judith of Bethulia,* although one of the stars of that film, Blanche Sweet, does not recall any music being used (this was possible, of course, because of the lack of any microphones to pick up the musicians' playing). Sometimes record players were used in the studio instead of live musicians, but both served the same function. The music was usually subdued, and the musicians were screened off from the players. The coming of sound ended all of this, in addition to presenting a whole new set of problems for the composer, not the least of which was getting some music, *any* music in some cases, in the first talkies.

2

Music in the Early Sound Film

And then, as Jack London would say, "the thing happened."
Came the miracle of the film that talked, and like the leaves on
Vallombrosa's brooks, the kinema orchestra disappeared, conductor, drummer and all. The leaves in the kinema music
library became so much waste paper, and the empty orchestra
pit became the den of a new and monstrous machine, an
electric complex of wobbling wails called a "Wurlitzer." This
phenomenon, hidden in darkness on the mezzanine floor,
upheaved at the interval in an incandescent tremolando,
equipped with a player apparently belayed to his seat. Having
assisted at the sale of chocolates and ice-cream, and gilded with
glistening gambas the promises of next week's "attraction," it
subsided again to its oozy bed; its glow faded and died, and its
sound was heard no more. Its operator was free to go, like
Gilbert's sentry in "The Gondoliers," in search of beer and
beauty. For the film shown on the screen now carried its own
music, contemptuously labelled by the displaced musicians as
"canned."

—Ernest Irving in *Music and Letters*

Filmmakers by no means unanimously regarded the arrival of sound in
the motion picture as a great step forward. The raw realism of the all-

19

talkie disturbed many filmmakers, because up to the introduction of sound, film had achieved all of its effects visually. The introduction of sound not only robbed the filmmaker of the dreamlike world of silent images but robbed him of nearly all camera movement as well. This lack of movement was due to the fact that the old, noisy cameras of the silent days were still in use. These cameras were so noisy that the camera and cameraman were put in rather small, soundproofed cubicles, weighing several tons, which were mounted on wheels and laboriously moved about in the studio by hand. With rare exception, such as Mamoulian's brilliant 1929 film *Applause,* camera movement was nonexistent and, for a while, film ceased to be an art of movement. Mamoulian's answer to camera immobility was simple: "I lifted the soundproofed camera off its feet and set it in motion on pneumatic tires." But Mamoulian was the exception: one needs only to see films such as *The Lights of New York* to realize how static the film was during the early days of sound. And whereas in silent days the director had the final say in all aesthetic matters, in the early days of sound the sound engineer ruled supreme on the set. No scene was shot without first consulting with him.

All of these developments were understandably upsetting to the directors of the day. In 1929 director René Clair wrote, "Words used like this destroy the workings of the imagination: the presentation of actuality must be conventionalized as it is in the theatre, and was in the silent film."

Directors were not alone in their criticism of the sound film. An article appearing in *The New York Times* on Sunday, June 4, 1933, related the studied displeasure of at least one musician as well. The occasion was the Florence Music Congress that was being held in Italy. Massimo Mila, "a young musicologist of Turin, deplored the advent of talking pictures at a time when music was beginning to take an integral and stylistic part in the pantomime of the 'silent' pictures, and suggested means of assigning it a more integral role."

But, for the most part, composers for the cinema were optimistic and hoped that music might be able to play a more integral and influential role in the making of a film. Clarence Raybould, who wrote the music scores to Rotha's *Contact* and *Where The Road Begins,* clearly understood the need for specially composed and synchronized music for each picture. Raybould felt that "It is clear that the only successful method of setting music to a film, especially where there is no spoken commentary, is for the music to be specially composed."

Instances of cutting the film to fit music previously composed for that film is so rare throughout film history that film composers long ago gave the idea up as a viable option to present to producers and directors. In 1933, however, only five years after the advent of sound, composers were still thinking in terms of the possibility of film cut to their music. Again Raybould clearly saw the problems involved in all of this. "Music," Raybould said, "by comparison with action such as expressed by the visual images of film, develops slowly. A mere pictorialisation in music of a succession of film 'shots' will not result in a satisfactory musical phrase or movement. On the other hand, a reversal of the procedure, attempting to illustrate visually a definite piece of music, will slow down and govern the shot-construction of the film."

Raybould's hopes, however, were tempered by what he was seeing in actuality. "The two jobs of construction [music and film] must be undertaken together, with a certain elasticity on either side. So far the elasticity has almost wholly been on the part of the musical composer." And so it was to remain.

But the signs of optimism were everywhere and, even as late as 1935, music critic M. D. Calvocoressi, writing in *Sight and Sound*, went so far as to suggest an Academy of Film "for film producers [which] should certainly include special music classes organised on a suitable basis." As if this were not enough to display Calvocoressi's blind optimism and ignorance in film matters, he later refers the reader to Jacques Brillouin's "relevant" remarks concerning the possibility of resorting, at times, to music alone. "Books [according to Brillouin] are divided into chapters, plays into acts and scenes. Nothing of the sort occurs in films, whose continuity (often achieved at the cost of overburdening the action with irrelevant particulars) seems a survival from the time when the cinema was in its nonage and the art of transitions, ellipses, and short cuts, was not yet part of its technique. When producers will have learned to divide films into suitable acts or chapters, music will come to its own during the intervals and prove all the more effective if elsewhere it is not used to excess for mere purposes of filling in."

Some composers directed their optimism in another direction. Writing in *The New York Times,* Dr. Ernst Toch grandly proclaimed that "The focus of film music to come is the original film opera. This cannot be done by adapting old operas for the screen, for the conception of stage-opera music is bound to be different from what film-opera must be. To adapt existing operas—with their arias, duets, ensembles, finales, dances, marches and the like—means to mutilate either screen action or the music itself. Music of film-opera has to create and develop its own forms out of typical screen action, combining its different laws of space, time and motion with constant music laws. The first film-opera, once written and produced, will evoke a host of others."

These were all grand ideas, to be sure, but based on the incorrect premise that films should first be artistic. The film industry was a commercial enterprise, not an artistic one; and the public wished, first of all, to be entertained.

In the very earliest days of sound film, music was used most effectively and most frequently in the musical films that proliferated at that time. *Rio Rita, The Street Singer, The Rogue Song,* and *The Vagabond Lover* were some of those early musicals. The public soon tired of this never-ending stream of musicals and such pictures began to fail at the box office. When the studios decided to drop the production of musicals they also decided they were no longer in need of musicians. Writing in the book *We Make the Movies,* composer Max Steiner recalled that in September 1930 "the studio would not require our services any longer and intended to dismiss everyone not under contract. In most instances the studios even tried to buy up existing contracts." Steiner remembered that at that time, "Musical activity in Hollywood was almost at a standstill."

The production of these early musicals created problems and frustrations for the composer. As remarkable as it seems, the early sound films were made without benefit of re-recording, or dubbing.* Max Steiner, who came to Hollywood from Broadway in 1929, remembers some of the difficulties film composers faced during the infancy of sound. "In the old days one of the great problems was standard (actual) recording, as dubbing or re-recording was unknown at that time. It was necessary at all times to have the entire orchestra and vocalists on the set day and night. This was a huge expense...."

It is hard to imagine a film being produced in a way that would require the entire production staff—sound-effects men, orchestra, and actors—on

---

* The term dubbing really has two meanings for people in the film industry. Film composers speak of recording their music for a film as "dubbing" a film. To many others working in film "dubbing" means the process of blending the numerous dialogue, sound-effects, and music tracks into a single, balanced track.

the set for every take involving their talents. The process was, understandably, time-consuming and costly. Steiner remembers that "it was impossible to work fast. Many rehearsals and many recordings (takes) were necessary before a satisfactory result could be obtained. I have known instances where one short number, of two or three minutes' duration, would take two days to record."

As to the expense involved in this kind of production technique, Steiner remembers that "during the filming of a certain picture . . . it took us two days to find a suitable spot for the double bass, as the acoustical conditions on the stage were such that every time the bass player touched his instrument the soundtrack would *overshoot* (distort or blur). This experience with the entire company—actors, singers and musicians—on the set, cost the company seventy-five thousand dollars." It should go without saying that during this period musicians were required to play very softly.

Even though a large number of musicians had been laid off in September of 1930, by the spring of 1931 producers and directors began to realize the need for music in their dramatic films. Directors began to add a little music here and there to support love scenes or silent sequences. The feeling among producers and directors at this time was that the music should have some reason for being in the film. Again, Steiner recalls the rather pedestrian concept of film music then held by producers and directors. "But they [producers and directors] felt it was necessary to explain the music pictorially. For example, if they wanted music for a street scene, an organ grinder was shown. It was easy to use music in nightclub, ballroom or theatre scenes, as here the orchestras played a necessary part in the picture.

"Many strange devices were used to introduce the music. For instance, a love scene might take place in the woods and in order to justify the music thought necessary to accompany it, a wandering violinist would be brought in for no reason at all. Or, again, a shepherd would be seen herding his sheep and playing his flute, to the accompaniment of a fifty-piece orchestra."

Since there was no re-recording in those very early days, if a director decided to do some editing of a scene containing music the score was usually ruined. It was impossible to cut the sound track without destroying the continuity of the music.

There were two primary approaches to the use of music in films during the early days of sound. One was to utilize music essentially as it had been utilized in the silent film: having constant music in the background throughout the film. The other was simply to use no music at all. Some films, as Steiner points out, used music only where it seemed in consonance with the new "raw realism" of the talkies, which meant only when there were actual musicians playing on the screen. These rather artistically naïve notions about the use of music in films are better understood when one considers what a technological miracle synchronized sound must have seemed to audiences of the day. To hear music coming from a film was nothing new—it had always been there—but to hear a door slam or two people carrying on a conversation were aural pyrotechnics with which music clearly interfered. Some films, such as *Little Caesar,* used music very sparingly, but the dialogue and sound effects were used so well that they ushered in an entirely new era of film. On the other hand, the 100 percent talkies which used no music at all were unimaginative, like their 3-D counterparts in the early 1950s. Owing their existence merely to a technical gimmick, they soon fell victim to lack of public interest.

The effect, then, of the arrival of sound in film was that the art of film had to be rediscovered. The filmmaker had to learn a new discipline, as did the film composer.

Attempts at the imaginative use of music in films were not long in coming, and one of the best attempts made in the very early days of sound is found in Josef von Sternberg's film *The Blue Angel.* This 1930 film featured Emil Jannings and Marlene Dietrich and was scored by Friedrich Hollaender. The film's score demonstrates a disciplined use of "source" music, or music emanating from a clearly visible musical source on the screen. The musical score itself is made up of the main theme songs, including "Falling in Love Again and "Blonde Woman," which are sung by Marlene Dietrich, as well as various arrangements of a German chorale. "Background" music is nonexistent throughout, with the exception of the music accompanying the main titles that open the film. The music of this main title is simply an arrangement of "Falling in Love Again."

From the main titles the film moves to the first instance of "source" music: while eating his breakfast, the professor, played by Jannings, whistles a few notes of the chorale melody to a bird in a cage. The chimes over the university play this same tune while striking the hour. During the action in the Blue Angel café, the stage band and, of course, Marlene Dietrich's singing, provide the "source" music. There are several other scenes where the "source" music is handled cleverly. In the Blue Angel café the stage band accentuates the action realistically even to the extent of their music starting and stopping with the opening and closing of doors as characters approach the stage area. In a classroom scene, children's singing voices are started and stopped when a window is opened and closed.

For a short period of time during the early years of the sound film there existed what Kurt London characterizes as a "theme song craze." While von Sternberg's *The Blue Angel* would probably fall under this category, it is certainly one of the more sensitive examples of this genre. The impetus for the use of theme songs was economic, just as it is today. Theme songs were not found exclusively in sound film; there are numerous examples of silent films that had their own songs. If the song added little in the way of artistry to the film, it did contribute, if it became popular, to advertising the film, as well as to enriching the production company.

There are, however, inherent aesthetic problems with films that use a theme-song approach to music. Generally, at some point in the film, the song itself must be stated in its entirety. This was usually accomplished by having someone sing the song, as Marlene Dietrich does in *The Blue Angel*. The problem was that the insertion of the song usually broke the dramatic tension at some of the more important points of the film because, as London points out, "it held up the action. And the film must never linger without reason: requiring, by its very nature, incessant motion." While the audiences of the day soon tired of endless numbers of theme-song films, the craze has returned periodically through the years and is even today a potent force in the writing of music for films.*

---

* A present-day example of this nonsensical use of music in films can be found in the film *Butch Cassidy and the Sundance Kid,* scored by Burt Bacharach. There is a scene in the film consisting of a montage of bicycle-riding shots. The music over this scene, the song "Raindrops Keep Falling On My Head," entirely demonstrates London's premise that a theme song "holds up the action." The scene has no dramatic purpose in the picture other than to afford an opportunity for the song to be rendered in its entirety. Gerald Mast has claimed about contemporary film; "If there is to be music it must be . . . deliberately artificial (a

In the early 1930s there were some interesting experiments attempted in "sound montage." Sound montage is, essentially, constructing films according to the rules of music. The investigation was carried out by the German Film Research Institute in Berlin. Edmund Meisel, the composer of the music for both *Potemkin* and *October,* was actively involved in the earlier experiments of the Institute.

While the experiments were started before the advent of sound, the researchers admitted that the idea of sound montage could only be totally successful if the music could be perfectly synchronized so that the time of the cutting and time of music would correspond exactly. The sound film made this possible.

By the time the Film Research Institute had acquired sound cameras, composer Meisel had died, so the experimenters had to search for suitable music. They finally settled on an African Negro recording with a rhythm that seemed strong enough for a visual rhythmic montage. It should be pointed out that the montages they wished to create were to have no relationship to the *shape* of the music. Ernest J. Borneman, writing in *Sight and Sound,* pointed out that the shape would include "time, rhythm, counterpoint, the melodic curve, vigour and faintness, crescendo and decrescendo, accord and discord, harmony and discord."

One area of experimentation of particular interest involved the filmic expression of time and rhythm. The researchers began with synchronized cutting from one shot to the next in time and rhythm with the music. They later tried a rhythmical variation in the intensity of light in shots of longer duration. The object of the latter was, according to Borneman, to "prevent the spectator from becoming tired by the excessive short cutting which the quick rhythm of the music logically demanded."

Another idea used to express time and rhythm with film was the moving of the camera itself. They used panning, traveling, and flying camera shots to show things not only from unusual angles but, Borneman

---

song on the soundtrack that exists specifically to be noticed and plays either in harmony or in counterpoint with the sequence's visuals). In *Butch Cassidy and the Sundance Kid* (1969), the story stops for an idyllic ride on a bicycle accompanied by a pleasant Burt Bacharach rock tune." This proposition that the song was placed in the film as a "deliberately artificial" device is sheer nonsense. The song was placed in the film in the hopes that it would "make the charts" and make that much more money for the film.

claims, "to interpret their inner sense and value by musical movement. Time and rhythm, for example, could now be expressed by horizontal and vertical to-and-fro movements; crescendo and decrescendo by approaching and retreating the camera; the melodic curve by corresponding curve-movement of the camera. Slow-motion and ultra-rapid-motion were used to represent musical time variations; fade-in and fade-out for musical increase and decrease; one-turn one-picture for syncopation; prisms for accords; composite shots and double exposures for various sorts of harmonies and discords."

The group was even able to express complicated musical occurrences as well as instrumental alterations by pure filmic camera means. "Refrains, for instance, might be expressed by the frequent repetition of a certain series of shots, or ever-recurring themes might be represented by the underlining of certain images. Instrumental tricks like mutes might be clearly interpreted by gauzes, mirror distortions and distorting lenses."

The conclusions drawn by this group were alarming and would undoubtedly draw a sustained argument from most film composers. Borneman surmises that "One of the most important results of this series of experiments is the surprising discovery that the musical accompaniment of films is not so stimulating as we are inclined to believe."

In rethinking the values of music to film in the silent days and music to film in the early days of sound, composers, producers, and directors needed to consider the inherent aesthetic differences between silent and sound pictures. While this consideration of differences necessarily covers all aspects of the art of film, we shall deal only with those involving music.

Again we turn to London for some interesting ideas on this subject. London points out that in the sound film, "there are never more than relatively short lengths of film running 'silent' and having no other sound than music, whereas the whole of a silent film must inevitably be illustrated." London goes on to say that the music in a sound film has a variety of functions, including the connecting of dialogue sections without friction in order to "establish associations of ideas and carry on developments of thought; and, over and above all this, it has to intensify the incidence of climax and prepare for further dramatic action."

While these comments on the function of music in the early sound film and music's relationship to the silent film are true to some extent, the reader should bear in mind that there have been developments in the aesthetics of film music since the time of London's observations in 1935.

One can detect in the previous remarks by London an implied resistance to the concept of "background" music. Indeed, later on in his book, London becomes very critical of the notion. Before examining his thoughts on this, however, it is worth pointing out that this is one area in which London was only partially correct in his criticism. Most of his observations made in his book, *Film Music*, are correct, if only because they are still true today. London's fear of the misuse of background music was ill-placed, however. Since the time of his book some of the most artistic and masterful moments ever to have come out of film music have been that same background music he so feared.

London's primary objection to background music in films was based on the notion, prevalent among filmmakers at that time, that music for a film must emanate from some musical source on the screen—the "source" music just discussed. This attitude is reflected in London's complaint that background music is used "where there could be no possible justification for it, either in the form of an orchestra playing behind the action of the film or of a radio instrument appearing in the picture." London seems strangely upset that as we watch a film "we do not quite know whether to listen to the melody or the commentator." This is certainly an artistically naïve notion and leads one to wonder if London, when listening to a vocal concert, had trouble deciding whether to listen to the words or the music. Much more convincing is his observation that if music "is employed to strain after effects which the film itself cannot induce, then it degrades the film and itself." But even this axiom has its faults, for it is generally agreed that good film music, including background music, tells the viewer something the film is incapable of telling. The validity of London's point is seen in the case of a producer or director hoping to improve a fundamentally weak scene through the addition of music. This particular practice has never ceased in the film industry, and every composer is forced to deal with it.

London closes his argument against background music with a call to an end to this "barbarous habit." "Background music," he concludes, "is nothing else but a return to the primitive film." From his 1935 perspective, of course, London could not foresee the sensitive and artistic use of music behind dialogue scenes.

There was one unfortunate side effect created by the rush to sound in films which caused an economic disaster for musicians working in movie houses. With the sound and music permanently affixed to the film, there was simply no need for musicians to be employed in the individual theaters exhibiting films. As a result, thousands of musicians were thrown out of work. This sudden economic shock to so many musicians is still being felt today and is manifested in the antagonism of musicians toward any form of recorded music. This antagonism and fear quickly found its way onto the Hollywood recording stage, as seen in a 1937 *New York Times* report: "The musicians' union says that half of the 'B's' and nearly all of the quickies are made without benefit of an orchestra. Track is taken from the library and added to the picture. In some instances, they say, major lots order orchestras to record popular and standard music after they have completed their assignments on 'A' films, and these recordings are filed away against the day when they will be needed."

As the realization of the need for music in films grew, the film studios developed their own music departments. During most of this early period of sound, no one person composed an entire score for a picture. Instead, the scoring of a picture was a group effort on the part of several individuals. In his highly succinct foreword to Clifford McCarty's book, *Film Composers in America,* critic Lawrence Morton points out that these scores of the early 1930s "were created not by individual composers but by a music staff working under the supervision of a music director. They collaborated in a practical way by using common thematic material and employing one or another of the currently fashionable styles—the neo-Gershwin, for instance, the western folk, or the Wagner-Strauss symphonic." Morton also says that this kind of collaboration proved very successful "from the standpoint of music-department operation and theatrical effectiveness, whatever the strictly musical results may have been."

It should be also pointed out that the composers of these "paste-pot-and-scissors" scores, as Morton characterizes them, seldom received screen credit for their work. Instead, it was the music director of the studio who received screen credit for the music. There were exceptions to this, as in *Stagecoach* and *Union Pacific,* where the multiple authorship was given on the screen. There were also many instances where no screen credit at all was given to the people handling the music.

As strange as this sort of method of film composing seems, there is a precedent for this kind of compilation of dramatic music. In the eighteenth century there existed a form of opera known as *pasticcio* opera. The word *pasticcio* literally means "pie," although a modern translation might read "patchwork." There were two distinct types of pasticcio operas. One type can be illustrated by an opera entitled *Muzio Scevola* (London, 1721) which contained a first act composed by F. Mattei, a second by Giovanni Bononcini, and a third by Handel. This first type of pasticcio opera is most like the method of film composition under discussion. There was, however, a second type of pasticcio opera that also bears some resemblance to the musical practices of some composers in the film industry. This type involved composers of operas freely substituting new arias for old in revivals of their work or in performances of their opera by a different cast. "A composer of Rome, for example, who had orders to revive a Venetian opera to suit the taste of the Roman singers and public, would have no compunction about replacing some of the original composer's arias with some of his own." In fact, it was unusual for an opera to receive exactly the same performance in terms of content in two different cities.

The English, too, got into the act by creating what is known as the "ballad" opera. The creation of this form was a reaction on the part of the English to the Italian *opera seria* so prevalent in England at that time. The most famous example of the ballad opera is John Gay's *The Beggar's Opera* (1728).

But unlike his eighteenth-century counterparts, whose styles of composition were all very much alike, the film composer of the twentieth century had to be able to compose in a number of styles as well as be able to create a homogeneous score with his colleagues.

Film composer David Raksin recalls how this type of pasticcio film score was put together in a short period of time. In 1938 Raksin went to work for Twentieth Century-Fox Studios "starting as an arranger and orchestrator, and very shortly after that . . . composing there as well. In those days all but the top features at '20th' were rushed through the post-production process (after completion of principal photography) at such a rate that Lou Silvers (he was Musical Director on the WB 'talkie,' *The Jazz Singer)* had developed a kind of (post-) production line to cope with the insane pressure imposed by the people in charge of seeing that schedules made no concessions to the limits of human endurance. It worked this way: On the day when the new film was turned over to the Department for scoring, the staff gathered in our projection room. Present would be Silvers, his assistant, Rudy Schrager, the composers—David Buttolph, Cyril Mockridge and myself, two or three orchestrators, the head of Music Cutting and a couple of his assistants.

"By lunch we had 'broken the film down' into sequences adjudged to call for music, determined what kinds of thematic material would be required and who would write it. After lunch, while the music cutters prepared the timing-sheets that would enable us to synchronize our music with the film, Buttolph, Mockridge and I went off to our studios to compose whatever specific material had been assigned to us. We would shortly meet again, with several versions of each theme, to decide which ones in each category would best serve our purposes, which were usually quite clear—though never defined; these themes were photostated and each of us got a set of all the material for that film. By that time the timing-sheets were ready, so we divided the work into three parts, and each man headed for home to compose his third (not to be confused with Beethoven's).

"Sometimes there was time to orchestrate one's own sequences, but usually the rush was so great that by the next morning we were already feeding sketches to the orchestrators, and by noon they were delivering pages of score to the copyists. On the morning of the fourth day the recording would begin; the Studio had a fine orchestra under contract, and available on very short notice. The scores were from thirty to forty-five minutes in length, often including "chases" at very fast tempi—which means a lot of notes to cover long, open spaces, and slows down the work; even with the skill and professionalism of all concerned it was quite likely that while we were recording one sequence the next was still being copied.

"On the fifth day a couple of days of re-recording (putting all of the dialogue, music and sound effects tracks together for the preview or final print) would commence. After that there might be a brief respite and then the process started again. . . . It was wild, and we all enjoyed it."

The practice of utilizing music written for one film and then using it again for subsequent films has been around since the early days of sound. A quote from Goldner and Turner's *The Making of King Kong* describes the exodus of Max Steiner's score to the classic 1933 film *King Kong:* "All this music [to *King Kong*] proved extremely durable and was used by Steiner's successors at RKO—Roy Webb, Nathaniel Shilkret and Constantine Bakaleinikoff—for dozens of subsequent features and innumerable editions of RKO-*Pathe News.* Among the soundtracks containing sizable chunks of the Kong music are *The Last Days of Pompeii, The Last of the Mohicans, Muss 'Em Up, We're Only Human, Back to Bataan, and Michael Strogoff.* Steiner, himself, reprised portions of this material in several of his much later works for Warner Brothers. 'A Boat in the Fog' builds suspense as admirably for Bette Davis in *A Stolen Life* as it did for the passengers on the 'S.S. Venture' fourteen years earlier."

This early period of sound was necessarily devoted to the sound film's attempt to discover its potentialities. The musical results of this search are disappointing, as there were few significant scores written during this period. Those scores that are significant belong to the category of the documentary and avant-garde film.

A fine example of a documentary film from this period is the Joris Ivens documentary, *New Earth,* which deals with the Zuider Zee reclamation project in the Netherlands. The score by Hanns Eisler is based on what is, by today's film music standards, a rather unprofound principle: machinery in the film is represented by natural sounds and men by music. *New Earth* is notable because of its success in putting Eisler's highly individualistic compositional style into a documentary that must have appeared, on first viewing, to offer little musical scope.

The animated film *L'Idée,* is an avant-garde film of the times with an imaginative score by the French composer Arthur Honegger. In his score for this essentially political film, Honegger uses an electronic instrument called the Ondes Martenot. First introduced in 1928, the Ondes Martenot is an electronic instrument combining the principle of the Theremin (another electronic instrument) with a keyboard. It has devices that can achieve vibrato as well as glissando effects and also has provisions for the introduction or removal of filter circuits affecting the upper partials. The instrument was, of course, a forerunner of our present-day music synthesizers. One of the most notable aspects of Honegger's music for this 1934 film is the high degree of synchronization, for synchronization of music to action was certainly not prevalent at that early date.

Other significant avant-garde and documentary films of this era were *Le Sang d'un Poète* (Jean Cocteau, 1931; score by Georges Auric), *Zéro de Conduite* (Jean Vigo, 1933; score by Maurice Jaubert), *Rising Tide* and *Contact* (Paul Rotha, 1933; score by Clarence Raybould).

With the advent of sound the film composer, like the actor, now had to contend with a microphone. Early microphones had several drawbacks as far as the composer was concerned. Violins, horns, and timpani all recorded poorly in those early days of sound. Composers, more than anyone else involved in film production, experienced the frustrations of inadequate microphones. In 1933, composer Clarence Raybould decried the fact that "the musician is at the mercy of a well-meaning body of sound engineers who cannot yet reproduce the tone of a single violin adequately, let alone a mass of strings; whose idea of the characteristic tone of an oboe seems to be founded on toothcomb and tissue paper; and who, when criticised, think themselves unjustly abused because the banjo, the plucked string and the saxophone come off fairly well in recording."

While most film composers ignored these reproduction problems in their orchestrations of film scores, one enterprising gentleman, a sound-engineer turned composer named Eric Sarnette, went so far as to invent "microphone instruments." He was aided in this venture by Adolph Sax, Jr. Essentially alterations of existing instruments, Sarnette's instruments carried such unlikely names as the saxtrombone and the saxhorn. Not satisfied with the development of new "microphone" instruments, however, Sarnette advocated restructuring the orchestra when writing for the microphone. His film scores usually contain clarinets, alto clarinets, contrabass clarinets, bugles, trumpets, and bass trumpets as well as saxhorns and saxtrombones. Sarnette's aversion for strings appears to have gone beyond the merely acoustic, since he advocated their removal even from the conventional symphony orchestra and attributed their influence to a "feminist" movement in music.

While most film composers simply ignored the problem of the microphone and orchestrated their music as they saw fit, other important composers attempted to deal with the problem. One such composer was Englishman Arthur Benjamin, who made a serious attempt at accommodating his orchestrations to the microphone. In such films as *The Man Who Knew Too Much,** The Clairvoyant,* and *The Turn of the Tide,* Benjamin reduced the strings to the level of mere filling-in parts, seldom giving the strings any melody. Other devices of orchestration used by Benjamin were the avoidance of the timpani and the use of the tuba or piano to render the *pizzicato* of the double basses. Benjamin seldom used an orchestra of more than twenty players.

Besides Benjamin, there were a goodly number of other internationally known composers beginning to write for the screen. In England during this period could be found such notables as Arthur Bliss, whose score for *Things to Come* is regarded as a substantial achievement. William Walton

----

* Benjamin's cantata for this film, "Storm Clouds," was used in the 1956 remake of *The Man Who Knew Too Much.* The remainder of the brilliant score for the 1956 version was by Bernard Herrmann.

made his first attempt with the 1935 film, *Escape Me Never,* although the results were less than satisfactory for Walton since the music was cut up in accordance with the producer's requirements. In France, Darius Milhaud wrote a score for the 1929 film *Petite Lili,* an experimental film screened at a festival in Baden-Baden. During this same festival the renowned German composer Paul Hindemith provided his only score for films with his music for another experimental film, *Vormittagsspuk.* In Italy, Giuseppe Becce, whose *Kinobibliothek* was so useful to theaters in the silent days, could then be found writing for sound films. His credits during this period include *Son of the White Mountain, Ecstasy, The Rebel,* and *The Blue Light.* Although Becce is of little significance as a composer for the sound film, his musical output was enormous and he undoubtedly wrote more for films than any other composer up to that time. In Russia, Dmitri Shostakovitch composed the music for the 1930 film *Alone.*

In 1933 another Russian composer, Sergei Prokofiev, was approached and asked to do his first film score. Leningrad director A. Feinzimmer asked the composer to provide a score for the film *Lieutenant Kije,* based on the Yuri Tynyanov story of the same name. Prokofiev completed the score quickly and, late in 1933, his music for the film was recorded in the Leningrad Belgoskino Studios. The orchestra was conducted by another up-and-coming Russian film composer, I. O. Dunayevsky.* The film was soon forgotten, but Prokofiev's delightful score for this satirical film has lived on in a suite of the music put together by him in 1934.

In short, the symphonist had arrived on the film-music scene; we turn next to his influence and its results.

---

* Dunayevsky later became one of Prokofiev's political accusers in the early 1950s.

3

Film Music Comes of Age: 1935-1950

Gerald Mast has pointed out that in 1939 Americans went to the movies; "in 1970 they go to a movie." In 1938 there were approximately 80 million Americans (65 percent of the population) attending movies every week. In contrast, only 10 percent of the present American population attends movies. In the 1930s and 1940s the American studios were producing over 500 feature films per year. It was a lucrative circle: the large attendance necessitated a large number of films to be shown in theaters, which in turn necessitated busy studios that could produce such a large volume of material in order to keep the theaters full.

These years had their financial worries, to be sure. But although the stock-market crash of 1929 worried many in Hollywood, the film industry was strangely unaffected. Americans were finding money for movies somewhere. While 1933 saw some economic sag in the industry, it proved to be temporary.

The need for a large number of films guaranteed the survival of the studio system in Hollywood. When the studios converted to sound they merely added new departments to an already complex organizational structure. New departments of sound mixing and dubbing as well as music joined the already established order. There was a certain degree of impersonality as far as the film itself was concerned, since it traveled from department to department until it reached completion. While this structure in some ways restricted creativity, the era proved to be

Hollywood's most financially lucrative period, and also produced some of the greatest film scores ever created.

Because of the somewhat impersonal treatment of the film product, the studio system produced a certain amount of tension between film art and film business. It is difficult to produce art through mass production. Although this tension was probably less evident in the area of music, it certainly existed, and still does.

Many factors about the music departments of film studios during the 1930s and '40s support this impression that film music was, like other aspects of a film, an industrial product.

First, the music departments of studios were a plant. There was usually a music building on the studio lot containing executive offices, cubicles for composers to work in, a music library, and a sound stage where the scores were recorded. This, of course, represented a sizable capital investment to the studios.

Second, the music departments consisted of a compartmentalized labor force: executives and their secretaries; bookkeepers, librarians; rehearsal pianists; composers, arrangers, and orchestrators; copyists, proofreaders, and orchestral musicians. All of the department's work was totally compartmentalized, and the entire operation was run according to agreements with the Musicians' Union as to wages, hours, and working conditions.

Third, the autonomy of the music department was restricted by the necessity for close cooperation with producers, directors, sound engineers, the studio's legal department, and the comptroller. The department head had to be a good executive, to understand budgets and time schedules, hire capable workmen, and maintain an effective relationship with other departments. Over and above these responsibilities, he sometimes functioned as a composer and conductor, as in the case of Alfred Newman, who headed up the Twentieth Century-Fox music department.

That this sort of structure was necessary becomes obvious when one considers the size of the audience: between 80 and 90 million people a week went to see movies. The amount of music that reached film audiences during this era far exceeded that of "art" music. At no time before or since has music had such a wide and varied audience. It should be pointed out, however, that this audience was a captive one; and probably only a small percentage of those audiences were even aware of the music they were hearing.

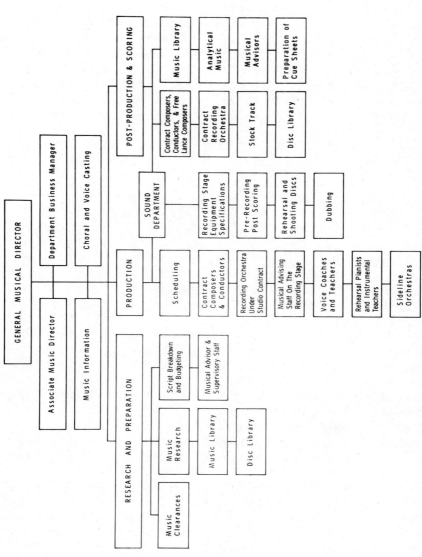

Figure 1. Organizational chart for a music department in a typical Hollywood studio of the 1930s and '40s.

Because of the size and diversity of the film audience, as well as the speed with which scores had to be produced, film music in this era developed a large number of habits, formulas, and clichés. These included the brass-blasting Main Title, which often contained a special fanfare, or "flare," for the producer's credit, the love theme, and the glamorizing of heroines by the use of "beautiful" string motifs. Another practice was the underscoring of natural cataclysms such as earthquakes and forest fires even though the music was more often than not drowned out by the roars of nature herself.

It is hard to imagine music being written under these conditions that could qualify under the vague term "art." However, several factors favored music over some other cinematic elements during this period and were responsible for the production of some music of genuine "artistic" worth. First, every film score, like a work of art from any other medium, is unique. It was, and still is, custom built and tailor made for the picture. Even if unimaginative and unoriginal, it is still the only one of its kind. Its course and form are, for the most part, dictated by the particular events of a particular screen narrative.

Second, an examination of the best scores created during this period will establish the fact that they carry the imprint of their composers just as surely as the best films have always borne the marks of their producers and directors.

Third, there was never an assembly-line technique in the *creation* of a film score, but only in its reproduction as images on the edge of a roll of film. From the composer's point of view, the artistic life of his score is finished as soon as it has been recorded. Whatever happens to that score thereafter has nothing to do with the creation of a work of art but only with its distribution.

One unfortunate characteristic of the music-department system of the Hollywood studio era was that many other departments—photography, set designing, costuming, direction—were more independent and were thus able to exert more influence.

A key principle in the Hollywood studio's way of thinking was that an idea that worked before would probably work again. Unfortunately, Hollywood traditionally has not known when an idea has run the length of its usefulness until the box office demonstrates the fact. Mast, in *A Short History of the Movies,* points out that films from these years of studio prominence "were not special, individual conceptions but tended to bunch together as types, in cycles." This could also apply, to some extent, to their musical accompaniments as well. The symphonic orchestral texture became the standard medium for the composer working in films.

The composer of this period, like the director, was forced to be eclectic. A director might jump from a jungle adventure to a backstage musical, to some sort of historical drama, and then to a gangster film. Jumping with him would be the studio composer, changing his compositional style to meet each new picture's coloristic demands. The composer was also, like his directorial counterpart, forced to work under severe time restrictions. This was not necessarily a detriment to his craft for, as Vaughan Williams has pointed out, "film composing is a splendid discipline, and I recommend a course of it to all composition teachers whose pupils are apt to be dawdling in their ideas, or whose every bar is sacred and must not be cut or altered."

It was during this period that composers solidified the forms and styles to be used by film composers for quite some time to come. Max Steiner, Erich Wolfgang Korngold, and Alfred Newman were more responsible for setting this style than any other composers. The question arises: Why did these composers choose the style they did, namely, the mid- to late-nineteenth-century symphonic idiom as exemplified in the stage works of Wagner, Puccini, Verdi, and Strauss? One answer that has been offered is that audiences would "understand" that idiom more readily than another. This answer, however, merely reflects a fundamental misunderstanding of the relationship of music and the dramatic arts. When confronted with the kind of dramatic problems films presented to them, Steiner, Korngold, and Newman merely looked (whether consciously or unconsciously is unimportant) to those composers who had, for the most part, solved almost identical problems in their operas. These three progenitors of film music simply looked to Wagner, Puccini, Verdi, and Strauss for the answers to some of their problems in dramatic film scoring. The answer seems overly simple but it is a logical one if the relationship of music and drama in opera is understood. Unfortunately, however, much of the limited amount of writing on film music tends to separate film scores and opera scores in a way that suggests fundamental differences between the two. The assertion in these writings is that in opera the music is of primary importance and in films the music is nearly always a secondary factor to the total dramatic framework. This attitude reflects a fundamental misunderstanding of opera more than it does a misunderstanding of the dramatic function of film music. The functional similarities between music in opera and music in films are fundamental and indicate a direct link between the two.

In his book, *A History of Western Music,* Donald Jay Grout points out that, "For Wagner, the function of music was to serve the ends of dramatic expression." This statement could just as easily be applied to the function of music in a film. We can also find music speaking to the psychological factor of the drama in opera. In Wagner's *Ring des Nibelungen,* "The action of the drama is considered to have an inner and an outer aspect; the former is the province of instrumental music, that is, of the orchestra, while the sung words make clear the particular events or situations that are the outer manifestations of the action." If we equate the dialogue in a film to the "sung words" of opera, we can see there is little difference between opera and film. Indeed, the recitative of opera, like dialogue in a film, serves to move the plot forward. Opera, like film, tends to emphasize the separation of the drama and the music at times. In opera this separation is almost literal: the orchestra is hidden in the pit; in the sound film the orchestra is "hidden" on the sound track. In opera the stage is the most visible element and, like the screen in a film, it draws most of our attention. In opera when the stage becomes musical (as when an aria begins) then the two forces of drama and music come together to form a unified force. This same sort of thing happens in films at those points where the music is allowed to speak in a forceful and contributive way. In opera, like film, when the action on stage is the most important element, the orchestra dissociates itself from the action and becomes a commentary upon it.

When one considers the epic proportions of Wagner's *Ring des Nibelungen,* it is easy to understand why the formal device of the leitmotiv fell naturally into use in the composition of scores for some of Hollywood's epic films. A brief quotation describing Wagner's use of the device will demonstrate the leitmotiv's similar function in films. Grout suggests that the leitmotiv "is a musical theme or motive associated with a particular person, thing, or idea in the drama. The association is established by sounding the leitmotif (usually in the orchestra) at the first appearance or mention of the object or reference, and by its repetition at each subsequent appearance or mention. Thus the leitmotif is a sort of musical label—but it is more than that: it accumulates significance as it recurs in new contexts; it may serve to recall the thought of its object in situations where the object itself is not present; it may be varied, developed, or transformed in accord with the development of the plot; similarity of motifs may suggest an underlying connection between the objects to which they refer; motifs may be contrapuntally combined; and, finally, repetition of motifs is an effective means of musical unity, as is repetitions of themes in a symphony." This same observation could be redirected at some of the better leitmotiv scores for films and be just as valid as it is for Wagner's *Ring des Nibelungen.*

From this discussion, however, arises a serious question: Why did film composers not attempt to devise new solutions to these fundamental dramatic problems? Why did they choose, instead, to look back to the solutions offered by Wagner, Puccini, Verdi, and Strauss? It is generally agreed that in the past innovations in the arts have resulted in a burst of creativity. It is also acknowledged fact that film is more than an innovation; film is the only new *art form* to have been created in the last two thousand years. So why have film composers for the most part been content to use the old solutions, however valid, for dealing with the dramatic problems film presents? The answer is quite simple. Film is an extremely commercial form of art and, as such, must always pay its own way. While directors of films have had the chance to experiment and make serious but instructive errors, composers, because they are usually the last contributors to the corporate art of film, have had little opportunity to experiment with their art form and, through experimentation, thus devise new solutions to the old problems. The film composer has always been at the mercy of economics. A composer can write an opera with nothing more than pen, paper, and his own creative imagination. A film composer, on the other hand, cannot write a film score without a film, whose production is a costly endeavor.

Composer David Raksin made just this point in a letter to Dr. Harold Spivacke of the Music Division of the Library of Congress: "The point is that although we were expected to produce work of professional quality, and did, there were still some on-the-job training aspects of all of [my] early work. The stakes were so great, in almost all respects (money, prestige, 'the product,' etc.) that no first rank studio could afford to have anyone around who wasn't top notch. So the apprenticeship aspect was manifest in a limited encouragement to experiment (a studio with deadlines to meet can't tolerate too many ineptly calculated risks), and in the opportunity of hearing one's music played within a few hours of its composition, by virtuoso orchestras. Still, we were working in the kind of pressure-cooker that separates the men from the boys, at an age when boys are just beginning to wonder whether they are entirely separated from the earlier stage."

One of the first films of this era with a significant score was John Ford's *The Informer,* scored by Max Steiner. It is worth noting that Ford and Steiner worked together in a rather unusual way: they conferred on the use of music in *The Informer* before the film was shot. The film deals with the character Gypo Nolan (Victor McLaglen), a former member of the IRA, who betrays a friend to the British. Gerald Mast, in *A Short History of the Movies,* points out that "the film's power is its achievement in making Gypo's tortured mind manifest, in showing the man's hurts, hopes, fears, and conflicts." This psychological manifestation is accomplished through the highly subjective use of the camera. Gypo's mind is mirrored with dissolves, blurred focuses, and physical projections of the man's terrified mind. The music, too, aids in this psychological manifestation.

Steiner's music for this film is in some ways dated but it reflects the best Hollywood had to offer musically up to that time. Certain elements about the score, such as the high degree of synchronization of music to action, disturb some today. Steiner commented in *The New York Times* that "every character should have a theme. In *The Informer* we used a theme to identify Victor McLaglen. A blind man could have sat in a theater and known when Gypo was on the screen. Music aids audiences in keeping characters straight in their minds." This comment merely reflects studio thinking, on musical matters at least, at that time. Steiner was not expected to be too subtle with his music any more than the director was when he bathed the film in fog as a sort of heavy-handed allusion to Gypo's befogged mind. But even with its dated quality the music to this film has a good deal of impact for those willing to listen to it in a historical perspective.

Steiner's method of writing music for a film, described by him in *We Make the Movies,* is instructive because it is typical of this period. Steiner writes: "While the cue sheets are being made, I begin work on themes for the different characters and scenes, but without regard to the required timing. During this period I also digest what I have seen, and try to plan the music for this picture. There may be a scene that is played a shade too slowly which I might be able to quicken with a little animated music; or, to a scene that is too fast, I may be able to give it a little more feeling by using slower music.

"After my themes are set and my timing is complete, I begin to work, I run the picture reel by reel again, to refresh my memory. Then I put my stopwatch on the piano, and try to compose the music that is necessary for the picture within the limits allowed by this timing. . . . Once all my themes are set I am apt to discard them and compose others, because, frequently, after I have worked on a picture for a little while, my feeling towards it changes."

An interesting aspect of the music to *The Informer* is the way in which the music makes its entrances and exits. It almost always enters or exits on some sort of physical action, such as a door opening or slamming shut. This is especially true of the more highly charged scenes in the picture. This sort of thing is not generally noticed by an audience but it gives the music, especially in cases of the music's entrance, an unconscious "reason" for being there.

Another interesting element, and one that is characteristic of Steiner's film music in general, is the high degree of synchronizatoin of music to action. Indeed, it was Steiner who invented the click track, a highly accurate method of synchronizing music to picture. The following music cue is given here to demonstrate this point. The music that was written for this cue is found in Figure 2.

Music Cue From *The Informer*

Cue:		Minutes	Seconds	Feet	Frames
	The captain throws money on the table.		0	0	
1.	Gypo grabs money and exits .		20	30	
2.	Door slams.		26	39	
3.	Cut to blind man		33	49	5
4.	Gypo grabs blind man's throat		41	61	6
5.	Gypo leaves him.		58	87	
6.	The blind man's step is heard.	1	5.5	97	7

A comparison of the above timings with their equivalents in the music example will demonstrate Steiner's method of matching music and picture. Note, for instance, at 26 seconds, when the door slams, the use of

Figure 2. Music cue from *The Informer,* music by Max Steiner.

a diminished seventh chord. Also note the sudden, but required, shift in mood at 33 seconds where the blind man first appears and the *sforzando* chord at 41 seconds when Gypo grabs the blind man by the throat.

This kind of musical reflection of action offends some who claim it is insulting to the audience's intelligence. It should be remembered, however, that theater audiences in 1935 were not so nearly as sophisticated as today's moviegoers although, musically, they are little different.

This sort of close synchronization of music and action seems to work better in films not containing a heavy dramatic plot. One of the finer examples of the synchronous music-picture concept can be found in the film *The Adventures of Don Juan* (1949) starring Errol Flynn. The score, by Steiner, is as glorious a romp as the film; it is the type of film where Steiner seems at his best.

Lawrence Morton, writing in *The Hollywood Quarterly,* best described Steiner's unique talent when he said that Steiner is "one of the best film composers. . . . Never can it be said that he earned his reputation by bad performances; nor has he come to be regarded as one of the founding fathers of film music without having made large contributions to its technique and its literature. Of atmospheric and dramatic music of the plainer sorts he is a real master; and he has a formidable repertory of devices to fit almost any movie situation. Hollywood produces a hundred pictures every year that would profit from his music."

On September 29, 1935, *The New York Times* reported that the film industry "has been casual in grasping the importance of music and its relation to the cinema. Now film music is a vital element in screen fare; it provides an accentuated background for every mood and piece of action."

As music became a more important element in American films, the European trend of inviting composers of high reputation to score films began to manifest itself in Hollywood. On November 8, 1936, *The New York Times* said that "Hollywood has in several instances called on outstanding American composers to provide music for its output. The trend toward inviting men of serious purpose has been developing steadily. . . ."

Indeed, no less an avant-garde composer than George Antheil, who was then working in Hollywood, proclaimed in 1936 that "Music in the motion picture business is on the upgrade. It may interest musicians to know that I have been remonstrated with because I did not write as discordantly as had been expected. 'We engaged you to do "modernistic" music—so go ahead and do it.' Out here in Hollywood they still call any kind of music 'modernistic' but one can no longer doubt that Hollywood is developing a real taste for it."

Part of the impetus for this trend was the employment, by the Paramount Studios, of a Russian musician by the name of Boris Morros, as Music Director-in-Chief of Production. Morros set the tone for the Paramount Music Department when he said "only modern composers should write the scores of the modern motion picture of today." Morros's first action, upon coming to Paramount, was to discharge over half of the existing music staff. He then began contacting the most prominent composers of the day. George Antheil reports in his December 1936 column, "On the Hollywood Front," of gossip on the Paramount lot to the effect that Boris Morros "is negotiating with the Soviet Government for the loan of Dmitri Shostakovitch; Paramount, in return, will trade them several of our best sound technicians—men sorely needed in present-day Russia to judge by the hideous quality of their sound recording."

The excited speculation continued as more and more prominent names began to appear. In February 1937 Antheil reported that "last week the Hollywood newspapers announced in their calm way that an Austrian composer had been engaged by Paramount to score their newest and most expensive production, *Souls at Sea*. The man, it seems, is Arnold Schoenberg, who has been, for some time, a resident of Southern California . . . they also thought fit to add that a Russian composer had been engaged for Paramount by the name of Igor Stravinsky. . . . Schoenberg, according to Morros, has accepted the commission and will soon start work on *Souls at Sea;* but he will have, as an understudy, one of the Studio staff composers, Ralph Rainger, who will simultaneously compose a second score in case of emergency! As for Igor Stravinsky it is understood that he has accepted Morros' invitation to come here but that a picture will not be assigned to him until he arrives in Hollywood. (Neither Schoenberg nor Stravinsky, it must be added here, have either denied nor confirmed this rumor.)"

Speculation was high, however, as seen in the April 11, 1937, edition of *The New York Times,* which reported that "Igor Stravinsky is considering a Hollywood offer, the West Coast having invited him to modernize a Hans Christian Anderson fairy tale (musically, of course), probably that Disney feature length cartoon, 'Snow White and Rose Red.' "

But Hollywood's infatuation with prominent composers was short lived.

In fact it never really materialized, for in December of 1937, George Antheil wrote: "Hollywood, after a grand splurge with new composers and new ideas, has settled back into its old grind of producing easy and sure-fire scores. Even Boris Morros, who is certainly one of the most intelligent music directors out here, and who started out marvelously, has retracted to some extent; perhaps pressure was put on him from the top." Antheil went on to swipe at his colleagues, motivated perhaps more by bitterness than by fact: "Meanwhile many excellent composers have come out to Hollywood and returned East again. Scarcely any of them have gotten jobs. While on the other hand, the routine Hollywood composers who have been here many years, have grown alarmed at the influx of new men, and have used their influence to sew up every future score available. In other words Hollywood music is, at the present writing, a closed corporation."

Antheil's hopes were not dimmed, however, for he said in his column of April 1938: "I still believe Hollywood producers and directors really want a new music. There is only one trouble—there are not enough intelligent and forward looking music directors in Hollywood."

But the final ax was to fall in 1939 when Boris Morros resigned from Paramount with a somewhat diminished reputation. According to Antheil, Morros "developed the overwhelming desire to see himself in newspaper print entwined with the greatest musical names of the age. This weakness led him (often without sufficient basis in fact) to announce publicly the acquisition by Paramount of persons like Stravinsky and Schoenberg." Antheil goes on to say that Morros is resigning "more in sorrow than in anger."

Morros's contractual arrangements with Schoenberg and Stravinsky never bore fruit. Schoenberg claimed that "his understanding with Paramount was a very elastic one and concerned one of his pupils, Ralph Rainger, more than himself." Stravinsky came out to Hollywood but no suitable picture could be found for him to score. It was later reported in *The New York Times* by Bruno Ussher that Schoenberg said, "I would be willing to write music for a film . . . if I were asked. I would want $100,000 for the score. They must give me a year to write it and let me compose what I want. And, of course, I would have to say something about the story." Little wonder why Schoenberg never composed a score for a film.

Boris Morros left Paramount, and his position was filled by Lou Lipstone.

While Schoenberg never scored a film he did have considerable contact with composers and musicians working in the film industry. Indeed, it was reported in *The New York Times* on March 21, 1937 that screen composer Alfred Newman "was responsible for getting [Schoenberg's] four almost unplayable quartets recorded for posterity at Mr. Goldwyn's expense in the Goldwyn Studios—the commercial companies having refused to make recordings of such strange cacophonies—however masterful."

One composer working in films who studied with Schoenberg, David Raksin, later recalled his initial contact with him: "Oscar Levant had told me that Schoenberg wanted to meet Charlie, so I brought them together [see Figure 3]. Although there was plenty of mutual respect, the two great men did not find much common ground for conversation, so that occasion was somewhat formal. The 'Old Man' was very gracious to me and I asked if he would accept me as a pupil. He replied that he would want to see some of my music before committing himself. I was not able to muster the courage to initiate further contact with him until several years later when Oscar said to me, 'The Old Man is wondering what happened to you.' I then took some of my music out to Schoenberg's house in Brentwood and he accepted me, saying something like, 'You are talented but I think it is time that you learned something about music—and we were into our first lesson. In order to show me what he would expect in the way of 'competence' he brought out the score of the first symphonic piece of a former student: the *Passacaglia,* Op. 1 by Anton Webern!"

Even though Hollywood would seldom utilize the talents of America's greatest concert composers, it was still creating the best film music in the world, since little of significance was being written abroad. There were, however, some notable exceptions.

In 1938 the famed Russian composer Sergei Prokofiev visited a number of film studios in Hollywood during a visit to the United States. It was a fortuitous experience, for when he returned to Russia in the same year he was asked by director Sergei Eisenstein to compose the music for his film *Alexander Nevsky.* Prokofiev's reaction was positive: "I was an old admirer of Eisenstein's films, and was delighted to accept his offer." The relationship proved to be fruitful. Prokofiev later elaborated on his delight by commenting "in addition to being a brilliant director, Eisenstein was a keen musician."

Since *Alexander Nevsky* deals with the twelfth-century invasion of Russia by the Teutonic Crusaders, it is understandable that Prokofiev was at first tempted by the idea of using music of that period. He studied

Figure 3. Left to right: Charlie Chaplin, Mrs. Arnold Schoenberg, Arnold Schoen-berg, and film composer David Raksin. Photograph taken in 1935 at the Chaplin Stu-dios. Many of the Hollywood film composers studied with Schoenberg while he was living in Los Angeles. The photograph was taken during the period when Raksin was assisting Chaplin with the music to *Modern Times*. Photo by Max Autrey.

twelfth- and thirteenth-century Catholic chants but he soon realized that the music had lost its meaning and, hence, its dramatic impact for film audiences. His decision to write the music in a somewhat pseudo-style or, more correctly, "to write the music not as it had sounded at the time of the 'Battle on the Ice' but in a way in which we could imagine it today."

Eisenstein and Prokofiev had an exceptionally cordial artistic relationship, and in his book, *The Film Sense,* director Eisenstein is extremely complimentary about Prokofiev's "film sense": "He is a perfect composer for the screen." Eisenstein felt that Prokofiev's music was "amazingly plastic. . . . [It] never remains merely an illustration but reveals the movement and the dynamic structure in which are embodied the emotion and meaning of an event. Whether it was the March from *The Love of Three Oranges,* the duel between Mercutio and Tybalt in *Romeo and Juliet,* or the galloping of Teutonic knights in *Alexander Nevsky,* Prokofiev had grasped before anything else the structural secret that conveys the broad meaning of a subject."

In rather overblown cinema rhetoric, Eisenstein then goes on to say that Prokofiev, "having grasped this structural secret . . . clothes it in the tonal 'camera-angles' of instrumentation, compelling the whole inflexible structure to blossom into the emotional fullness of his orchestration. The moving graphic outlines of his musical images which thus arise are thrown onto our consciousness just as, through a blinding beam of a projector, moving images are thrown onto the white plane of the screen."

During the filming of *Alexander Nevsky,* Prokofiev had artistic luxuries seldom afforded his American counterparts in the film industry: director Eisenstein would sometimes cut shots to previously recorded music, for example. There were, however, sequences done in the conventional manner wherein the music was composed to a final cutting of film. There were many times when Eisenstein would watch composer Prokofiev in the screening room begin to tap his fingers during the showing of a sequence. Eisenstein learned that "Prokofiev was marking the structure of the film where the length and tempi were combined with the action of the characters."

When Eisenstein was unable to relate what he wanted in terms of a precise effect that he wanted to be "seen" in the music, he resorted to a rather unique procedure. "I ordered some prop instruments made, and a shot of these being played visually (without sound) was shown to Prokofiev. Almost immediately he handed me an exact 'musical equivalent' for the visual image of pipers and drummers that I had shown him."

There were, as might be expected, times when the collaborators did not agree. Victor Seroff relates one such instance: "When Prokofiev's score was finally recorded on the soundtrack, Eisenstein asked him to write an overture. Prokofiev refused. 'The film begins,' he said, 'with a tragic episode—'Russia under the Mongolian yoke'—'but an overture should be historically victorious.' And he said that he could not see the transition from such an overture to the tragic music. He added, however, that he was willing to write any amount of music if the film required it, but from a purely artistic point of view he could not write an overture. But Eisenstein insisted. Well then, Prokofiev said, he would compose the overture on one condition: Eisenstein should start the film with a less tragic episode. Eisenstein did not see how he could change the plan of the film; the overture was never written."

Having acquired some knowledge of sound recording during his Hollywood visit, Prokofiev proceeded to take an active role in the recording of the score. This cannot be regarded as unusual since most film composers conduct the studio orchestras through their cues. Prokofiev, on the other hand, insisted on having someone else conduct in order that he might be in the engineer's booth. This would enable him to hear the music as it would sound through the loudspeakers.

Having studied all of the technical possibilities of the Moskfilm studio, Prokofiev proceeded to even make use of the distortion created by the microphones of the day. "For instance, a powerful stream of sound directed at the microphone during the recording session affects the record to such a degree that during the performance it produces an unpleasant crackling sound. And since the sound of Teutonic trumpets and horns were no doubt unpleasant to the Russian ear," Prokofiev said, "in order not to miss the dramatic effect, I have insisted that these fanfares be played directly into the microphones."

Prokofiev also experimented with a crude form of multiple-microphone recording techniques. Prokofiev expressed the idea that "in our orchestras we have very powerful instruments, such as a trombone, and in comparison the more feeble sound of a bassoon. If we place the bassoon right near the microphone and the trombone some twenty meters away from it, then we will have a powerful bassoon and in the background a barely audible trombone. This practice can offer a completely 'upside-down' means of orchestration, which would have been impossible in compositions for a symphonic orchestra."

Seroff also points out that "Prokofiev also suggested placing the horns and trumpets in one studio and the chorus in another. From each studio there was a direct line that led into the box in which the sound recording was being made and in which, with a simple movement of a switch, the volume of each group's sound could be augmented or diminished, depending on the requirement of the dramatic action."

During the course of recording the score Prokofiev would sometimes place the orchestra in four groups: one for each microphone. This was another, less unique, attempt at achieving what would today be called multiple-microphone technique.

Prokofiev (like many other film composers) often criticized the mixer and, at times, even insisted on taking the mixer's place at the mixing console. During such a recording session Prokofiev disregarded the various meters on the recording devices but was guided only by his ear. After the session Prokofiev announced that he was satisfied and that the musicians were free to go. He then left the studio. But the poor mixer remained and asked Eisenstein to let him redo the sequence Prokofiev had just completed. "A few days later, when Prokofiev's own recording was played, Prokofiev exclaimed, 'This is not worth a damn.' And he liked the recording made by the 'mixer.' " Prokofiev then turned to the mixer and said, 'Well, it serves me good and right—one should never *mix* in other people's business. Still,' he added, 'you have swallowed one eighth note in the transition from one group to another.' "

The film, *Alexander Nevsky,* was first shown to Soviet audiences on December 1, 1938. Prokofiev's next film would also be a collaboration with Eisenstein: *Ivan the Terrible.* But it was to be his last film, for Eisenstein died soon thereafter. In 1949 Boris Volsky, who had worked as a mixer during the filming of *Ivan the Terrible,* approached Prokofiev about the possibility of his doing another picture. Prokofiev demurred. "Since the death of Sergei Eisenstein," Prokofiev said, "I consider my motion-picture activities terminated." *

---

* There is a delightful contemporary use of Prokofiev's film music in the 1975 Woody Allen film, *Love and Death.* In this film, however, Woody Allen has used excerpts from *Alexander Nevsky* and *Lieutenant Kije* to create a wonderful comic effect, especially for those viewers who know the films from which Allen extracted his score.

One important characteristic of films during the studio era was that the sound film was a talking film. This produced certain stylistic consequences in the films themselves. The position of the camera, as well as its angle, showed the speaker and other characters' reactions to him well enough, but it illuminated little else. Any type of extreme shots such as high or low angles, extreme close shots and tilts were uncommon even in some of the more visually imaginative films. The editing of a film was as functional as the camera work. It was felt that any kind of quick cutting distracted the audience from the words of the speaker. The use of montage was cut back considerably from its use during the silent era. Montage was now reserved for more obvious showcase effects such as the passage of time. Film lighting also became functional rather than expressive as it had been in the silent days. Film lighting was generally clear and bright so as not to distract the audience from the speaker. The designers and cameramen used lighting to make the stars even more beautiful than they already were. Thus, it is hardly surprising that the extraordinary dark film *Jane Eyre* received so much criticism about its dark quality when it was released.

In effect American film had become an externalized, narrative medium, and what the characters did—and said—became the most important aspect of the film. Human psychology became formulaic and was strictly functional, existing sorely to serve the narrative incidents of the picture.

This turn to functionalism on the part of the studios may, in part, explain the growing awareness among film composers of the psychological value of music in a picture. If all of the other elements were directed at the narrative aspect of the picture, then music might take on, single-handedly, the psychological aspects. While music as a medium was well suited to the task, there are, nevertheless, hundreds of scores from this period that are as externalized as all the other elements of the film.

With the art of film in such a state it is little wonder, then, that Orson Welles's brilliant film *Citizen Kane* shocked the audiences of 1941.

Citizen Kane is consistently regarded as one of the greatest films ever made. There is little doubt that it deserves that accolade. The individuals involved in all aspects of the picture were people of exceptional creative ability. The film's director and star, Orson Welles, though inconsistent in his career, is still regarded as one of the great geniuses of film. The film's composer, Bernard Herrmann, is regarded as one of the greatest composers of music for films.

Citizen Kane was Bernard Herrmann's first film score but it was by no means his first experience in setting music to drama. Bernard Herrmann was born in New York in 1911 of a nonmusical family. After completing high school he studied composition at New York University, then went on to further study at the Juilliard School of Music. In 1933 he was hired by CBS Radio to compose and conduct musical backgrounds for their documentary and dramatic programs. It was at CBS that Herrmann began his association with Orson Welles.

In scoring *Citizen Kane,* Herrmann had the luxury of being present during the entire production. He often made sketches during the shootings of the sequences. The scoring of the film was not without its problems, however. In view of Herrmann's tumultuous personality, the following recollection by the man who dubbed *Citizen Kane,* James G. Stewart, is amazing for its courage, albeit naïve courage. It is worth pointing out that by the time *Citizen Kane* was made, Stewart had already been working as a soundman in Hollywood for twelve years and was (and still is) a man of no mean experience. Stewart recalls: "The music for *Citizen Kane* was recorded over a period of time. The picture was not ready for dubbing all at one time, which is normally the case. After one of the early music sessions the music came up to the dubbing stage for the sequence to be dubbed. Without either Welles or Herrmann being present I played the sequence a couple of times with the film. I didn't like the music very much and I think my complaint was mainly about the mechanics of it. It didn't seem to work with the scene. Then Bernard Herrmann came along. I knew nothing about him except that he had come out of the radio field where he'd had considerable success; this was his first picture so far as I knew. I mentioned to him that I didn't think it was quite right—the usual things that you say when you're dissatisfied with something—and he simply stormed all over me: I was an idiot, I didn't understand his music, I didn't understand what he was doing with the scene, and so on. He was in a rage. He left the stage and returned a little later with Welles. I had met Welles and talked with him a few times but I didn't know him at all well. We ran the sequence and Bernard Herrmann made his remark about my incompetence and the fact that I shouldn't even be on the show. Welles' comment was, 'Well, I don't like the cue either, so I think we'll have to do something about it.' The music was redone although I don't recall the cue's subsequent history."

Mr. Stewart's contribution to *Citizen Kane* certainly went beyond the realm of music critic, however. While it has been pointed out that Welles brought from his radio experience to film an acute awareness of sound, the observation has never been made, unfortunately, that it was the sound engineer (in this case, James Stewart) who turned Welles's artistic awareness of sound into electronic reality.

Sound can, when handled imaginatively, take on some of the functions of music. One need only see Hitchcock's film, *The Birds*, to realize this. In *Citizen Kane* sound and music would sometimes work in consonance to create the desired effect, as Mr. Stewart points out: "Welles' thinking was that sound could be used without reference to what was going on on the screen, something I call non-objective sound. This was, of course, the result of his experience in radio where sound was not related to a visual image. In non-objective sound you see and hear the realistic sound but in addition you may be listening to some other sounds which are totally non-objective and unreal. One of the very best modern examples of this is in *The Exorcist*, where sounds which the people on the screen are in no way reacting to are still there in the theatre. In my opinion much of the tension and much of the drama in *The Exorcist* scenes are carried in the sound track.

"But Welles simply freed sound. In that day and age (1941) if you did something unrealistic in the middle of a scene most producers would say, 'What's that? . . . What's that going on there?' Welles didn't believe in this. He believed that anything you could do to heighten the drama of a scene was worth doing and also of course the use of sound with the emphasis on its more dramatic content rather than on its factual content was part of his concept. The opera rehearsal scene in *Citizen Kane* that ends up with the stagehand up on the parallel holding his nose as he listens to the offstage vocalizing is an example of this. In that particular scene you got the sense of travel and height by hearing more and more reverberation as the voice became more and more reverberant while still staying very audible and very live—to produce the effect that you were going higher and higher into the scene loft.

"In addition, Welles was willing to spend infinite time, usually my time, getting something exactly the way he wanted it to be. This had to do with dialogue, music and effects. Welles brought radio techniques to the motion picture screen where they had been used very little in the past, and he also brought a freedom in the use of sound which opened up possibilities not only in his own pictures but in so many later pictures. One of the difficulties, and it's still true today, is that almost a burlesque of his techniques is now used. Filmmakers seem to feel that the broader the concept of sound they use the more they will be recognized as being of the New Wave. I don't believe in this. I feel that when you go too far it's like everything else—too much of a good thing doesn't work."

While much has been written about the score to *Citizen Kane,* Herrmann's own observations on the score have not received sufficient exposure. The lengthy quotation from *Film Music Notes* is given in its entirety because it illuminates his approach to this most influential film.

"The film was so unusual, technically, that it afforded me many unique opportunities for musical experiment. It abounded in montages, which were long enough to permit me to compose complete musical numbers, rather than mere cues to fit them. Mr. Welles was extremely cooperative in this respect, and in many cases, cut his film to suit these complete numbers, rather than doing what is ordinarily done—cut the music to suit the film. In the scenes of Kane's newspaper activities, I was able to write a kind of miniature ballet suite, the various photographic montages being presented in the form of complete little dance numbers of the 1890s, including galops, polkas, hornpipes, schottisches, etc. Later on in the breakfast scene between Kane and his first wife, the montage showing the passage of years and the waning affection was expressed in the form of a theme and variations. The very style of the montage practically dictated this form.

"The emotional impact of these musical numbers was much greater than that of background music which has no real beginning or ending. The audience receives, in addition to the effects created for the eye, the actual physical and mental impetus of a musical composition as well. I attempted to treat the familiar old forms in a modern way, so as to be consistent with the general musical style of the picture. The occasional 'radio scoring' I felt was rather new. The movies overlook opportunities for musical cues which only last a few seconds, the reason being that the eye covers the transition. In radio drama, every scene must be bridged by some sort of sound device, so that even five seconds of music becomes a vital instrument in telling the ear that the scene is shifting. An example of this is found in the transition between Kane, the young newspaper owner, and Kane, as the middle-aged man giving up his papers.

"Although I am not a great believer in the technique of the 'leit-motiv' for motion picture music, the nature of this film demanded some 'leit-motivs' in linking together the various time juxtapositions. The most important motif—that of Kane's power—is given out in the very first two bars heard. The second motif which should give away the secret of 'Rosebud' is also heard early in the film. These two motivs are the most important in the entire picture and they occur throughout the film in many phases and in many orchestrations. The motif of power becomes a vigorous piece of ragtime. It is transformed into a hornpipe polka. It becomes the very last part of the finale, used to portray the best part of his nature. Only one other motif of importance is derived from the tune, 'Oh, Mr. Kane,' a theme used in a satiric sense. Many sections were written for odd instrumental combinations which avoided the conventional orchestra sound. I had sufficient time to orchestrate all of the music and to conduct it and think about it. Twelve weeks were devoted to the score as against the usual six weeks or even less given to other pictures of this length and importance."

In the same year that *Citizen Kane* was released a complaint was filed in the United States District Court for the Southern District of New York that was to have a far-reaching impact on film composers.

The complaint was filed by the United States government, although it had been initiated by 164 theater owners against the American Society of Composers, Authors and Publishers (ASCAP).

Most film composers belong to ASCAP and, up until 1948, ASCAP was receiving from theater owners an estimated $1,500,000 per year for the right to show ASCAP-licensed films. Under the licensing contract the producers of the films paid ASCAP for the right to employ copyrighted music in their films, and then the theater owners paid an extra fee to show the pictures containing the music. Approximately 80 percent of the music used in motion pictures at that time was copyrighted by ASCAP members. The theaters paid a set annual fee, determined by ASCAP according to the type of theater and its number of seats. For instance, a 499-seat neighborhood house paid, on the basis of 10 cents per seat, $49.99 per year. The Radio City Music Hall, with 6,200 seats, paid $1,500 per year on the basis of 25 cents per seat. In August of 1947 ASCAP attempted to raise substantially the license fee for exhibitors.

In an Amended Final Judgment of Civil Action No. 13-95, entered on March 14, 1950,* presiding Judge Vincent L. Leibell ruled that ASCAP

---

* This ruling was amended again on January 7, 1960, Judge Sylvester J. Ryan presiding.

had violated the antitrust laws. While the judgment also involved other aspects of ASCAP's operation, Judge Leibell ruled that ASCAP was "restrained from ... granting to, enforcing against, collecting monies from, or negotiating with any motion picture performance rights." The judgment went to say that "Defendant ASCAP is hereby ordered and directed to issue, upon request, licenses for rights of public performance of compositions in the ASCAP repertory as follows:... To any person engaged in producing motion pictures ... so long as ASCAP shall not have divested itself of such rights, a single license of motion picture performance rights covering the United States, its territories and possessions, without requiring further licenses."

The resulting financial impact on film composers was relatively severe.

While such a unique film as *Citizen Kane* cannot easily be categorized, it is worth repeating what has been pointed out earlier in this chapter, that films of the studio era tended to bunch in cycles. One such cycle was the detective melodrama. In this type of film the detective is invariably a "tough guy" type who eventually yields to the irresistible charms of a woman. The classic film of this genre is the Twentieth Century-Fox production of *Laura,* directed by Otto Preminger and starring Gene Tierney, Dana Andrews, Clifton Webb, Judith Anderson, and Vincent Price in the main roles. The music is by David Raksin. It is from this film that the popular, and now classic, song "Laura" was extracted. The song is one of the greatest classics among the popular songs to come out of the United States. It was a highly sophisticated song for the 1940s, and Raksin recalls, "the first time I played 'Laura' in public, at a party, I completely lost my audience." Even after the initial success of the film and the corresponding popularity of the title song, many people in the music industry refused to believe that a song with such a relatively complex harmonic and melodic idiom could be successful in the world of popular music where simplicity of style was, and still is, for the most part, the byword. Raksin recalls that "there were a lot of people in that day (1944) who refused to sing it, to play it, or anything else. For instance, Bing Crosby never sang it, although every other top-ranking singer did. Bing said, 'It can't be sung.'

"Another odd incident involved the 'Lucky Strike Hit Parade.' The man who owned Lucky Strike cigarettes was George Washington Hill, and when he learned that 'Laura' had gotten on the Hit Parade he was unbelieving, absolutely unbelieving. When he finally heard that it had made number one, he was convinced that his own survey was crooked."

The tremendous success of the song "Laura" as an entity apart from the film was something of a phenomenon in 1944 Hollywood and, aside from the contribution of his own lyric gift, Raksin is aware of various intangibles that went into the success of the score to *Laura*. Raksin feels that "The story of 'Laura' is like that of everything else which is a prototype of some kind. It's as though a lot of elements that are floating around in the air and ready to be grabbed off by somebody, suddenly coalesced in one gesture, and that gesture at that time happened to be 'Laura.' To say *that* is a lot more puffed up than even an egocentric guy like myself can live with, but I'm trying to be 'historic' and objective about it. It suddenly happened, and everybody went wild. If I had written 'Laura' last year (1973), in the present pop music climate, it would have been a failure."

The overwhelming success of "Laura" as a song exerted a tremendous influence on film scoring immediately thereafter with varying results, for Raksin as well as for other film composers. Raksin recalls: "In the noble Hollywood tradition, in which imitation is more than the sincerest form of flattery—it's a way of life—those who weren't trying to write 'another Laura'" were demanding that others write it for their pictures. In the middle of all of the excitement and acclaim, on a grander scale than anything that happened to film composers in those dear, innocent days, there was something absurd about it all. It isn't that I wasn't enjoying the long-awaited instant fame (just add blood, and stir), but along with the appreciation from one's peers—which is the best kind—there was a kind of philistine adulation that bothered me a lot. It was fine to be admired, but not so good to be admired for the wrong reasons. People made such a fuss about the 'originality' of that melody! I was thrilled about what was happening, thrilled to have composed a song that had 'reached' so many people, and I too felt that there was something different, or special about the song. But to a musician it did not seem proper when uninformed people talked about a piece that started on a *supertonic seventh* and made its way partly through a *cycle of fifths* as though its composer had invented that harmonic procedure.

"It isn't unusual for composers and authors and others in the entertainment arts who have assimilated some of the discoveries of the great and inspiring pioneers in their fields to transform such ideas (more or less unconsciously) into popular art. An example of this would be the

Figure 4. A photostat of David Raksin's original sketch for his now-classic melody, "Laura."

influence of Picasso and his great contemporaries upon the young cartoon animators of UPA (United Productions of America) like John Hubley and *his* generation. I do not believe that it demeans *Laura* to consider it as that kind of phenomenon; in fact, it is embarrassing to a musician who loves music to hear undiscriminating praise. I had always loved the great American songwriters, the men who composed *Look for the Silver Lining* (Jerome Kern), *The Man I Love* (George Gershwin), *My Funny Valentine* (Richard Rodgers), *Last Night When We Were Young* (Harold Arlen), *Tea for Two* (Vincent Youmans), *Dancing in the Dark* (Arthur Schwartz), *April in Paris* (Vernon Duke), *I've Got You Under My Skin* (Cole Porter), and there is no describing what it was like to be welcomed to their company. When the editors of *This Week* asked Cole Porter which of all the songs written by others he would have wanted most to have composed, and he answered 'Laura,' that was just about the ultimate accolade. But when producers would say 'Write me another *Laura,*' as likely as not for some violent and brutal epic, *that* turned my stomach. And it must have been even worse for those of my colleagues who heard the same emetic phrase."

The music for the film *Laura* is basically monothematic, that is, the material for the entire score is drawn, essentially, from one melody. There are small subsidiary themes that Raksin uses throughout the film, but the great majority of the music is derived from the main theme.

It should be pointed out that monothematic film scores can be dull and repetitive—for obvious reasons. It is difficult for a composer to draw anywhere from forty to sixty minutes of music from one melody and still keep the score musically viable and interesting.

There are several reasons for the aesthetic success of the monothematic score to *Laura.* First is the haunting quality of the melody. In Raksin's words: "When I talk about 'Laura'—the melody and its composer—(which is not very often), it is as though I am remembering somebody else, someone I understand very intimately although he lived more than a quarter of a century ago. I feel certain that the reason people responded as they do to that melody, in the picture and on its own, is that it is 'about' love, specifically about that yearning particular to unrequited love, upon which I was, at the time I composed the melody, one of the world's great authorities."

A second, and perhaps more important, reason is the dramatic purpose for which the theme is used, namely to evoke the quality of the (presumably) murdered girl that drew others to her. In the course of the first five reels, where she is seen only in flashbacks, it is this quality that makes the hard-boiled detective fall in love with her. The theme is not used in the traditional "Love Theme" manner, in scenes between Laura and the detective. Film composer Elmer Bernstein's comment on the evocative aspect of "Laura" is worth repeating here because it expresses very succinctly the effective thematic use of Raksin's score: "The single theme . . . can identify a character, as in David Raksin's eternal 'Laura'. A technique that can be—and nowadays usually is—a boring cliché had its classic expression in *Laura*. The film portrayed a man falling in love with a ghost: The mystique was supplied by the insistence of the haunting melody. He could not escape it. It was everywhere. It was there when he was in Laura's apartment. It was there when he turned on the record player. It was never absent from his thoughts. We may not remember what Laura was like, but we never forgot that she *was* the music and in that music she has of course come into our lives to stay. In that instance, the music and its insistence was the most compelling feature of the film."

Still a third reason for the score's success is the fact that the melody is never heard in its entirety at any time during the film. Raksin recalls: "When I got around to timing the theme for its first appearance in the film, which would be in the Main Title—the opening credits—I found that from the end of the 20th Century-Fox fanfare to the beginning of the story, the opening narrative sequence, there were fifty-one seconds. At the tempo that seemed to me suitable for the initial statement of the melody at that point, this meant that I could play approximately thirty measures. There was no way that I could, within the available footage, get as far as the end of the tune, and the fact is that I didn't *want* to come to a full closing resolution. To do so is, to me, to risk interrupting the forward flow of the film's purpose, to say—in a way that is not likely to be lost on your audience—that the thought or the action have reached a point of stasis, which is all right if that is what is actually happening: but far more often it is the job of the music to keep the energy going, through transitions or changes of time or place, and the like. Also, in the case at hand, there was the matter of moving smoothly into the opening scene, in which, over scenes of an elegant New York City apartment, the voice of one of the characters in the film speaks a brief narrative that sets the scene. (Since the narrative is told in retrospect, from a point in time at which the narrator is dead, it has never been quite clear to me how he managed that; which can also be read as a tribute to our sleight of hand, although I am not ready to suggest that without the theme the deception might have failed.)

"To get back to the music of the Main Title, I decided that a suitable place to make the transition to the narration sequence would be the chord on measure 29 of the theme, which is an A 9th with augumented 5th; I would have the upper sections of the orchestra land on that chord first, and then the bass parts would enter on the A-natural. The next music cue would begin with the same note, as the titles faded out and the actual picture began, and the upper chord would be mechanically faded out with the titles, so that the two low A-naturals could be cross-faded, and we would be into the story. Having done this, I realized that it was one of those simple stratagems that (if it was right in the first place) would be apropos as a device consistently used throughout the score to keep the tune from coming to rest before I really meant it to do so. It may also have been that I composed more than one sequence in which I used the same device, more or less unconsciously, before I hit on the idea of making a subliminal point of it, and I'm not even sure that I intended that it should *never* be played to its conclusion in the film; but I'd be willing to bet that in my innocent movie-composer mind recognition of the connection between the ephemeral girl and the interrupted melody was inevitable. The fact that this device of *resolutus-interruptus* is consistent even unto the end may be attributable to the nature of the final scene, in which I think the music is saying farewell to Laura (with the dying murderer), and in which there is a direct reference to an Impressionist orchestra piece. Or it may be that I wanted to qualify under Emerson's dictum: 'A foolish consistency is the hobgoblin of small minds!' "

The decision to make *Laura* a monothematic score was Raksin's, although he received some enlightening encouragement on the matter from Alfred Newman who was at that time head of the music department at Twentieth Century-Fox.

Raksin recalls: "After I had been working on the score for about a week, I was in reel two. We had our offices at Twentieth Century-Fox in a building called the Lasky Building, and it was there that I ran into Al Newman, who was talking to his secretary and he said to me, 'How's it going?' I said, 'It's going all right, Al.' And he replied, "Well, the words say it's going all right, but it doesn't *sound* to me like it's going all right.' I said, 'Well, actually, it is, except I'm upset about the sequence I just did.'

So he put down the letter he was dictating and said, 'Would you like me to look at it?' That was exactly what I was angling for, because he had an unerring ear. So we went into his office and played the sequence I had just done. Newman said, 'Well, it looks fine to me. What's the matter with it?' I said, 'I don't know what's the matter with it, but somehow it isn't of a piece with the rest of the stuff I've written thus far.' He replied, 'Well, I can tell you, since you ask. Where's that beautiful tune?' So I said, 'Oh come on, Al, I'm into reel two and I've used nothing but that damn tune. It's coming out of my ears.' Newman said, 'It is not coming out of the audiences' ears.' I realized that what he was saying was that writing takes time, and I'd spent a week with that tune and I was getting sick of it. Newman told me to go back and try it again. So I went back to my office and I sat down and redid the sequence, and I realized that the simple point which had eluded me (as simple points often seem to) was that the audience is *not* bored with the tune if it's the 'right' tune."

One sequence in the film, the "apartment" sequence, demonstrates Raksin's fine dramatic sense. The sequence is discussed here for its aesthetic interest as well as for the unusual addition, for its time, of a "piano track." This piano track is a piano sound mechanically and electronically altered. Raksin's use of such a device is historically interesting, from the standpoint of film music, in that such alterations of conventional instrumental sounds were not very common in 1944—in or out of film music. It is even more surprising that it would be done on a film sound track, considering the musical tastes of the controlling studio powers.

Raksin's decision to use something unusual for this particular sequence was a combination of aesthetic need and serendipity. Raksin later recalled: "I knew I was going to have to use the theme in an evocative way. In this scene the detective goes into Laura's apartment. The audience has to realize that he has fallen in love with her. The detective is the epitome of the pragmatic man, and it torments him. You see him walking around Laura's apartment. He looks through her letters; he has her diary; he goes through a closet and finds a negligee. It is that sort of thing. He's really upset, and I realized I had to do something different in this sequence so that the theme, which had already been heard quite a lot, would now appear in a different way.

"I heard that a fellow in the Sound Department who was chief of one of the re-recording crews, Harry Leonard, had been faced with a problem

Figure 5. An excerpt from the "apartment" sequence of *Laura*, music by David Raksin. Note the "piano tracks" at the top of each staff.

in a picture called *Keys of the Kingdom*. Gregory Peck was in it, and he
played the part of a priest. In the part he had to age to the point where he
was over eighty, and he also had to develop a quaver in his voice. There
was no way he could do the quaver and still act the way he wanted to.
Harry Leonard hit upon the idea of taking a playback machine and
replacing the center bearing. The center bearing is made, I believe, out of
brass and is very finely milled as near to perfection in the round as is
possible. Harry, however, produced one which was *not* round, which had
a little bump in one place. He made some which had more than one
bump; but the idea was that when the film went through, this bump in the
center bearing would produce a speed variation and, hence, there would
be a quaver in the recorded voice of Gregory Peck. Well, I heard about
this and I said, 'My God, I bet I can use that!' So I went searching for
these bearings and I finally found that they had a box of them and that
they were of varying speeds; they had made various tests with them. I
experimented with them until I found a certain frequency. As I recall
there were about three speed variations per second and also a variation of
something like a quarter-tone above and below the mean. I then told Al
Newman, who was my boss, that I had an experiment I wanted to do and
I asked him if I could borrow the orchestra. Since he was in one of his
better moods he said, 'Why not?' So I made an orchestration of the theme
Laura in which there were just strings and a solo trombone. I recorded the
section to clicks in order to make sure we had a perfect tempo.

"To digress for a moment, many years before that I had used a stunt of
which I was, in a sense, the inventor. People had found that by cutting off
the impact of a piano chord they could get a certain kind of odd sound.
The problem with that was, however, that you would still get a noise when
the sound came in, and if you tried to ease the sound in by using the dials
in the mixing controls you would have too short a chord. I was doing the
score to a picture called *The Undying Monster,* and I needed some low
chords of a certain kind, and I hit upon a simple expedient: after first
placing the microphones the way the sound engineer and I wanted them, I
would sit at the piano and I would start counting. On *three* the sound
engineer would 'close' the microphone completely, on *four* I would strike
the chord on the piano, and on *five* he would start bringing up the level,
and continue bringing up the level until he got system noise. From that
we could make an actual sound loop and duplicate it. We could turn one
the other way around and equalize them so we got the chord we needed.

It was the interplay of the *partials* without the *ictus*. I decided to use this same device for the apartment sequence of *Laura*. I then wrote out chords consistent with the harmony of the passage.

"Then I went and got the best concert Steinway on the recording stage, and had Urban Theilmann, the studio's pianist, play the chords, while we recorded them in the aforementioned manner. I then put the recordings on two playback dummies that had the Len-a-tone center bearings, and alternated the two tracks. I simply sat there and cued the music mixer, Murray Spivack, as to which track to use. We mixed them so that they were slightly overlapped and you would hear a slight wrench, a little one, as one chord went out and the other one overlapped it. The chords were superimposed over the basic orchestra track, and they came out with this wavering tone, which infuriated the Sound Department. They said, 'We've been trying to take the "wow" out of sound pictures for years, and here you are putting it back.' So I promised them I would go around the country with a pointer explaining that it wasn't their fault. But it produced a completely different sound. Today it is easily done but, at that time, nobody had ever done it before."

In the review of *Laura* in *Film Music Notes* the reviewer could not quite figure out what that strange sound was in this sequence. In the reviewer's words, "a very unusual atmosphere is created and projected when Mark [the detective] keeps his vigil in Laura's apartment, the vibraphone or possibly some electrical instrument contributing a weirdly human and menacing quality."

When asked how the original tune for *Laura* came about, Raksin recalled: "I am not going to recount the entire story, which would bring a blush to readers of *True Confessions,* but what happened was roughly the following: Otto Preminger wanted to use as the theme a beautiful Duke Ellington song called "Sophisticated Lady" (not "Summertime," as is occasionally said). I saw my chance to compose a score of my own in my first major assignment at 20th-Fox vanishing, *and* I genuinely believed that the tune was wrong for the picture. Preminger defended his choice, saying, 'This is a very sophisticated girl.' When I pretended not to understand how he meant that, he said, 'My dear boy, this girl is a whore!' I replied, 'By whose standards, Mr. Preminger—by whose standards?' He turned to Al Newman and asked, with asperity, '*Where* did you get this fellow?' Newman, who was much amused, said, 'Maybe you ought to listen to him, Otto.' Preminger, who—despite his fearsome reputation, was always wonderfully generous to me (*after* he understood that I was really a composer), said in his brusque way, 'Well, today is Friday; you come in with something on Monday or we use 'Sophisticated Lady!' Well, Monday I arrived with 'Laura.' "

A second major cycle of films that became popular in the early and mid-1940s was the psychological thriller. This type of film usually revolved around a character with some sort of psychological defect, usually amnesia, and the film used this psychological element to help build suspense. Usually the film's treatment of the psychological problems was superficial, but the trend was prominent enough to elicit articles on the subject of psychology in films from psychologists and psychiatrists.*

One of the better films of this cycle was the Hitchcock thriller *Spellbound,* with a score by Miklos Rozsa.

Miklos Rozsa was born in 1907 in Budapest, Hungary. By the age of seven he was performing music in public while being schooled in general subjects. In 1926 he entered the Leipzig Conservatory where he studied under Hermann Graebner, Max Reger's successor, who thought highly of Rozsa's work.

Rozsa's initial endeavors in composition were for the concert hall, and he has continued to write concert music to the present day. His first contact with film music was through his acquaintance with Arthur Honegger. Rozsa recalls: "I was in Paris and Honegger and I had a night out together. I was making very little money at the time and I asked Honegger what he did for a living. He said, 'I write film music.' I said, 'Do you write fox-trots?' and he replied, 'No, I don't write fox-trots.' I answered, 'Isn't film music fox-trots?' Of course I had no idea of what was involved. Honegger said, in answer to my question about fox-trots, 'Oh no, not at all. I just finished doing the music for an Abel Gance film."

Rozsa was intrigued by the idea of writing film music and the following morning he was at the cinema at ten A.M. The theater didn't open until noon. Rozsa later recalled that "after hearing the music I called Honegger up and told him I could do the same thing."

---

* See Franklin Fearing, "Psychology and the Film," *Hollywood Quarterly,* Vol. 2, no. 2 (January 1947), pp. 118-121; Franklin Fearing, "The Screen Discovers Psychiatry," *Hollywood Quarterly,* Vol. 1, no. 2 (January 1946), pp. 154-158, and Lawrence S. Kubie, "Psychiatry and the Films," *Hollywood Quarterly,* Vol. 2, no. 2 (January 1947), pp. 113-117.

Rozsa soon after moved to London where he came in contact with a fellow Hungarian, Sir Alexander Korda, whose staff of London Film Productions Rozsa then joined. At the time Rozsa joined the group its musical director, Muir Mathieson, was already utilizing the talents of such fine English composers as Arthur Bliss and Arthur Benjamin. Rozsa's first film for this group was *Knight without Armour*. His most famous score from this period is for *The Jungle Book*.

One of Rozsa's early significant contributions to film music was his score to *Spellbound*. The film itself, like others in this cycle, was little more than a melodramatic excursion into the world of pop psychiatry, but Rozsa's score imbues it with an eerie, distorted quality not heard before that time. He achieved his most effective moments with the now-famous electronic instrument, the Theremin. It was played by holding a hand over it and moving the hand back and forth and up and down to control the sound oscillations. Rozsa had tried to use a similar instrument, the Ondes Martenot, in his music for *The Thief of Bagdad*. Historical events swept the possibility aside, however. Rozsa recalls: "I had been trying to get the Theremin into pictures since 1939. I had wanted to use it in *The Thief of Bagdad* but I was unable to because the man who was going to play it, Martenot, was unavailable. The Second World War had broken out and, since he had agreed to play it, I wrote him asking if he was going to be able to come over to London and record it. He wrote back, from the Maginot Line, that he was very sorry he couldn't come but he was defending his country."

Hitchcock's attitude toward his film *Spellbound* is interesting in light of his celebrated reputation for being very concerned about music in his pictures. Rozsa points out that "I had nothing to do with Mr. Hitchcock. When I did *Spellbound* I had one meeting with Mr. Hitchcock and Mr. Selznick [the producer] in Mr. Selznick's office. After that, Hitchcock was gone. Hitchcock had seen *Double Indemnity* and he had liked my music." Rozsa goes on to say "They then said that they had a psychological picture and that they wanted something unusual. I then told Selznick I wanted to use the Theremin. He didn't know what it was so he said to compose the music for a scene and then he would listen to it to see if he liked it. Well, the fact is they liked it but then they wanted to use it everywhere in the picture."

At that time, the Theremin was a highly effective device for expressing the warped psychological state of the film's main character. Rozsa very

soon thereafter used the Theremin in the film *The Lost Weekend,* to
denote Ray Milland's craving for alcohol. Rozsa used the instrument
effectively but, as with most successful things in Hollywood, imitators
began using the instrument indiscriminately, with the result that the
Theremin soon lost whatever effectiveness it had.

A third, very popular, cycle of films throughout the 1940s was the film
having as its main character a famous composer of the past. In *The Song
of Love* the great love affair of Clara and Robert Schumann is idealized,
while *A Song to Remember,* perhaps the first film in which great classical
music was used as a thoroughly integrated element of the screen story,
romantically portrays the life of Frédéric Chopin. In this same vein were
such other films dealing with musicians as the 1948 film *Humoresque,*
starring John Garfield in the role of a concert violinist. The dubbing in
this film is particularly good; the synchronization between Isaac Stern's
recording and John Garfield's visuals is near perfect. Another film of this
type was *Deception,* with a score by Erich Wolfgang Korngold that
includes a cello concerto.

The basic problem with these films from a musical standpoint is that
they used what was essentially concert music. In order to bring some of
the famous concert works in line with the dramatic needs of the story,
great works of musical art had to be severely cut.

One positive side effect of these films was that they provided many in
the audience with their first exposure to music of this type. Lawrence
Morton reported in 1945 in the *Hollywood Quarterly* that after *A Song to
Remember* was released, record and sheet-music sales of Chopin's music
skyrocketed. "A telephone poll of ten record shops revealed that there has
been a run on the special two-disk set of Iturbi's performances of pieces
featured in the film. One shop sold its allotment of 40 sets in two hours of
a Saturday morning. Another, in Beverly Hills, sold 160 sets altogether, or
320 records—a normal two-year supply of Chopin. A West Los Angeles
shop reported as many requests as there had been for the Andrews Sisters'
'Rum and Coca-Cola.' Practically every Chopin record in stock has been
cleared from local shelves, including those by some of yesteryear's virtuosi
whose royalty accounts have been inactive for many seasons."

But the music for this type of film, however great on its own merits, was
really the antithesis of good film music, for it was certainly not conceived
with the dramatic requirements of the picture in mind.

In July of 1945, a group of film composers organized the Screen
Composers' Association (SCA) in order that they might better present

their grievances to two groups. One of the complaints held by the screen composers was against producers and involved the right of the composer to own his own music and is discussed at a later point in this book. The second problem the composers had (and still have, although to a somewhat lesser degree) was with the American Society of Composers, Authors and Publishers (ASCAP). It was pointed out earlier in this chapter that in 1950 ASCAP lost, as a result of a suit filed and won by theater owners, its revenues from theater owners in the amount of $1,500,000 per year. Before the loss of these revenues, however, the screen composers felt, and it would appear rightly so, that their income from ASCAP for their film scores in no way reflected the amount of money ASCAP was collecting from theaters who were running ASCAP licensed film scores. As Leonard Zissu, Counsel for the SCA, pointed out in an article for the *Hollywood Quarterly* in April of 1946, "the hope for the composer's rights proves, upon examination of the workings of the Society [ASCAP], to be slight indeed. The film composer whose rights are thus absorbed, theoretically for his own benefit, receives scant return from ASCAP for those rights. It is a fact that ASCAP's present method of making domestic distribution of money to composer members, including film composers, effectively ignores the use of performance of music in motion pictures. ASCAP's composer allocations are systematically based upon a classification system whereby all composer members in the same class receive the same fixed sum. Composer members are given a classification by a committee, theoretically on the basis of 'the number, nature, character and prestige of works composed, written or published by such member, the length of time in which the works of the member have been a part of the catalogue of the Society, and popularity and vogue of such works.' So far as may be ascertained, this committee does not appear to attach any weighty significance to the fact that composers' works are used in films. The ASCAP policy in respect to performances seems, with minor exceptions, to attach importance only to such performances as are carried over the four major American radio networks. Nowhere does ASCAP give recognition to the fact that a film performance equally reaches millions of people and involves creative effort by outstanding composers. Reaching so vast an audience, therefore, can the film medium be justifiably ignored in the commercial 'give and take' with respect to the basis upon which the revenues from performing rights are to be distributed to composers? Would an allocation system be supportable which, when permitting consideration to be given to performance uses, effectively ignores such renditions in films? The answer seems obvious."

The "scant return" of monies to film composers can best be shown by comparing ASCAP's payment for a year to one of its screen-composer members and the British Performing Rights Society payments to one of its screen-composer members. The following table is from the Screen Composers' Association Bulletin of June-July 1946.

ASCAP COMPOSER

Year: 1943

Composer: Class "3" Member of ASCAP

Number of pictures listed	32
Number of scores composed during year	5
Number of theaters licensed by British Performing Rights Society (BPRS)	5,000
Net Royalty from BPRS (After deduction of British income tax of 50%, the ASCAP publisher's share of 50%, and ASCAP handling charges, approximately 5%)	$1,129.70
Average royalty per picture.	$35.30
Biggest royalty earner	$137.26
Number of theaters licensed by ASCAP in the United States .	15,000
TOTAL ROYALTY RECEIVED FROM ASCAP	$120.00

BRITISH PERFORMING RIGHTS SOCIETY ROYALTY COMPOSER

Year: 1945

Number of pictures listed	25
Number of scores composed during the year.	4
Number of theaters licensed by BPRS	5,000
Net royalty, British Isles and British Overseas.	$3,191.00
Swiss fees.	$126.00
Australasian (payable in 1946).	——
Swedish (payable in 1946).	——
Canadian	——
TOTAL	$3,317.00

Less Income Tax of 50% on British Isles fees. $1,106.00
Net royalty from BPRS $2,211.00
Average royalty per picture (after taxes). $88.44
Biggest royalty earner $855.00

Note that while the ASCAP composer wrote five scores during the year, the actual number of picture titles listed on the statement is thirty-two. This means that pictures composed prior to 1943 were still playing the theaters, in effect giving the composer a "catalog" of works.

Note also that one picture exhibited, the biggest royalty earner, paid royalties amounting to $137.26 after all tax deductions and handling charges, while the composer received a total of only $120.00 from ASCAP for his *entire* catalog for a comparable period. This discrepancy is further emphasized by the fact that the British royalty was earned in 5,000 (approximately) theaters licensed by the British Society while, in America, ASCAP licensed over 15,000 theaters.

The 1950 ruling against ASCAP by Judge Leibell, of course, completely wiped out theaters as a source of revenue to both ASCAP and its film-composer members. While ASCAP's payments to screen composers have improved somewhat over the years, they still only represent about 30 percent of the monies film composers' work puts into the organization. Most of the money collected by ASCAP from the film industry is either from ASCAP-licensed music owned by the film studios in the form of recordings or music that the film studios use in more than one film, as well as the substantial amount of work being done by film composers in the field of television. Music for television is often used for more than one program and ASCAP pays the composer for each use. ASCAP, however, is still regarded as being far behind in its distribution system as compared to its European counterparts.

It was pointed out earlier that the Wagnerian device of the leitmotiv fell naturally into use in the composition of scores for Hollywood films. Perhaps the best example of the use of this device in films is Hugo Friedhofer's score for the 1946 film *The Best Years of Our Lives.* This film was one of the first significant postwar films to come out of Hollywood and Friedhofer won a well-deserved Academy Award for his score.

As Canadian composer Louis Applebaum has pointed out, Friedhofer chose to work on the "developmental juxtaposition and superimposition of leitmotifs more or less in the Wagnerian tradition. The material itself is definitely not Wagnerian in character, but the manner of its handling derives from the Wagner of the Niebelinger [sic] Ring." So compact is Friedhofer's score for this film, it is possible to list most of the important thematic material in a few brief examples.

The most important theme in the score is the one on which the Main Title is based. In the score Friedhofer has dubbed this the "Best Years Theme." This important material can be seen in Figure 6.

Figure 6. Excerpt from *The Best Years of Our Lives,* music by Hugo Friedhofer.

Applebaum has said about this material that "Its simplicity, based as it is on the triad, its straightforward, warm harmonization, ably reflects the general theme of the film, principally as it concerns the Harold Russell characterizations of Homer." Note the bracketing of the two important motifs within this theme that are utilized throughout the score. The first section (A) states the triadic motif while the second (B) is a chordal, almost hymnal phrase. The most important aspect of both ideas is that both are easily recognizable and, because of their simplicity, capable of developmental treatment.

The second theme is called "Boone City." This music can be found in Figure 7. Note that this theme, like the first, contains two ideas: A is a five-note motif with the characteristic leap of the major seventh, which serves to set it apart. B is a syncopated, moving, broken-triad motif.

Figure 7. Excerpt from *The Best Years of Our Lives.*

A third theme is, like the B motif from the first theme, more chordal in structure, as Figure 8 demonstrates.

Figure 8. Excerpt from *The Best Years of Our Lives.*

This particular theme is associated with the neighborly relationship between the families of Homer and that of his girl friend next door. The most interesting aspect of this material is its harmonization, which is strongly suggestive of much of Aaron Copland's writing, a fact Friedhofer freely admits to.

The remaining ideas are, necessarily, different in character from the preceding ones. Figure 9 represents the material written for Homer's girl, Wilma, and is a simple, delicate, folksy, almost plaintive melody, much like the girl herself.

Figure 9. Excerpt from *The Best Years of Our Lives.*

In Figure 10, another theme, much in the style of Gershwin, underlines the rather tenuous relationship between Fred and Peggy:

Figure 10. Excerpt from *The Best Years of Our Lives.*

A theme called "Peggy" follows in Figure 11.

Figure 11. Excerpt from *The Best Years of Our Lives*, music by Hugo Friedhofer.

Despite Friedhofer's economy of material, there are two or three dramatic sequences in the film that receive special treatment, with no reference to any of the principal motifs; for instance, the highly dramatic moment in the tool shed when Homer, driven to frustration and embarrassment over his mechanical hands, smashes the window in the tool shed. It is the curiosity of children that drives him to this violent action and Friedhofer makes use of a children's play song, interestingly orchestrated and harmonized, for the music behind this scene (Figure 12).

Figure 12. Excerpt from *The Best Years of Our Lives*.

Another example along these same lines is the musical material accompanying the moment of Fred's nightmare—a recollection of his terrifying war experiences. Note the full utilization of a minimum of musical material, a recurring Freidhofer trait, in this case mostly the interval of the fourth. This material is shown in Figure 13.

Figure 13. Excerpt from *The Best Years of Our Lives*.

Frederick Sternfeld's rather extensive analysis in the *Musical Quarterly* of a scene from this film demonstrates some of the metamorphoses of Friedhofer's initial material. The sequence is the one in which Fred Derry finds a vast graveyard of dismantled bombers. He climbs into one of the deserted B-17 Flying Fortresses and imagines himself back in the air on a dangerous mission. Sternfeld observes: "When the bomber scene begins Captain Fred Derry is ostensibly not on the screen. As his father reads the Distinguished Flying Cross award the music enters with the ascending second-motif from the earlier scene and continues with a treatment of theme (B) of the Prelude:

Figure 14. Excerpt from *The Best Years of Our Lives*.

"It is given out softly until it reaches, as in the Prelude, the heroic chords. Now the entire passage is played again, continuing as a counterpoint to the actual words of the award. But as citation and dialogue come to an end the sound-mixer increases the volume of the music which now expresses in full-fledged sovereignty, better than words, 'the heroism, devotion to duty, professional skill, and coolness under fire displayed by Captain Derry.' As the camera shifts to the line of junked planes the ascending second-motif looms more important, the interval finally (after eight repetitions) being extended to a fourth:

Figure 15. Excerpt from *The Best Years of Our Lives,* music by Hugo Friedhofer.

"Now we see the interior of the dismantled bomber, as the ex-captain enters and the music gives us, for the third time in this scene, the half melancholy, half martial treatment of [Figure 6 (A)] with its heroic conclusion. The obsession of reliving the deadly missions takes hold of the bombardier as we approach the climax, and while trick camera angles of the camera suggest an imaginary take-off, the progressive diminution of the ascending second-motif symbolizes the warming-up of the engine and, more than that, the accelerated heartbeat of a frightened individual. Here, the trumpet statement of [Figure 6 (A)] against the final diminution of the ascending second reveals, if not the psychological origin of this scene, at least its potential substitute, the signal for taps. The tension increases as an inverted pedal on E-flat, sustained for ten measures, accompanies a close-up of the perspiring hero and leads to the quarter-note descent used earlier in the nightmare scene, being in rhythm and pitch (E-flat) a replica of the climax in the earlier scene. The quadruple statement of this simple yet ominous five-note figure that has not been heard for almost two hours has a dreadful suddenness; yet it is nevertheless prepared."

This score reflects the qualities that critic Lawrence Morton found in Friedhofer's music. Morton observed that "Friedhofer seems to get inside a film, so to speak, to take part in its events, and then retire into his study where, after tranquil recollection, he puts down on paper what it felt like to be a participant. His approach to films is contemplative and poetic."

Figure 16. Excerpt from *The Best Years of Our Lives.*

Despite the interesting and varied uses to which music was put in the films of the 1940s, the decade also saw the beginning of one of the saddest political eras in United States history. The implications for the American film industry were enormous. It was in 1947 that the House Un-American Activities Committee began its "investigation" of Hollywood films. The committee's activities established a climate of fear and suspicion throughout American society, hitting the film industry particularly hard. An especially negative effect was the blacklisting of some of America's finest cinematic talent.

The charge that American films contained "Communist propaganda" was preposterous—so much so that it occasioned frequent laughter. One friendly witness claimed there was a "Communist" line inserted in a Ginger Rogers picture. The line was "Share and share alike, that's democracy." John Howard Lawson, in *Film: The Creative Process,* recalls a memorable moment when Jack Warner was asked about Warner Bros.' films. Warner "parried with another question: 'Do you want me to answer that as a motion picture producer or as an American?'"

Lawson rightly points out that "The most irreparable damage done by the blacklist is in its effect on the content of pictures. The climate of fear has discouraged experimentation, stifled initiative, and dulled moral sensibilities."

There were, however, a few films during this time that attempted to deal with social problems on more than a superficial level. Most of them were not acclaimed by the public. One such film, *Force of Evil,* was not well received in the United States, although in Europe it is still regarded as a minor classic. This film, starring John Garfield and directed by Abraham Polonsky, has an extraordinarily compact score by David Raksin. "It is a neat little bundle containing a minimum of themes with a maximum of development. This thriftiness was made possible by versatile thematic material that lent itself gracefully to a great variety of treatment." One might contrast this highly compact score to Raksin's music for the film *Forever Amber,* where he was both generous with invention and resourceful in the treatment of his themes.

For purposes of illustration the final 2½-minute sequence of the film is quoted (Figure 17). This particular sequence is selected to demonstrate how the music device of recapitulation can be employed in a film score. This device cannot be used in every film, but *Force of Evil* illustrates how such a device can be used effectively. The final scenes of *Force of Evil* sum up and evaluate the events that are just coming to an end; they suggest a solution to the social problem that has been the central theme of the film.

It is apparent that there are two kinds of strongly contrasting material. At one extreme is the atonal idiom of the opening saxophone solo. The atonality is not twelve-tone but it is highly chromatic. Lawrence Morton has described the theme as "heavily charged with emotion, mounting almost to hysteria in the high F-sharp. Its tension is released in the drop of the minor third below and then dissipated in the strange flutterings of the woodwind figures that follow." As the theme is being played in this final sequence (which is under narration), Joe (John Garfield) and Doris (Beatrice Pearson) are seen running in the street, then along a great stone wall and down a huge flight of stairs. It should be strongly noted that the music used at this spot is not "running" music, i.e., the music is not "mickey-mousing" * the action. At this point the composer has scored the emotional, not the physical character of the scene; he plays *against* the visual. By being *asynchronous* with the picture, the music directs itself to what is implicit in the scene.** This particular saxophone theme occurs several times earlier in the film, and the implication of the theme during those earlier sequences is variously introspective, mysterious, and tragic. However, as the theme appears here, its most characteristic qualities are caught by the saxophone.

---

* A pejorative term obviously derived from music written for animated cartoons where nearly every movement on the screen is "caught" by the music.

** This is in keeping with William Pechter's observation in *Film Quarterly,* in 1966, that "the astonishing thing about *Force of Evil* . . . is the way in which the

In contrast to the atonal saxophone solo there is the pedal-point (measures 11-19) and the following broad string melody, both of which are broadly expressive and diatonic. The dominant pedal-point of measures 11-19 builds to a sense of tension until the downbeat of bar 20. At this point (bar 20) Garfield has arrived at a spot under the George Washington Bridge. The shot in the film here, showing Garfield standing under one of the arches, creates a cathedrallike effect. It is here that Raksin begins his long, diatonic string melody. The music reflects the picture on the screen, as Morton points out, "The special quality of the tune itself comes from the breadth of its arch and its wide leaps, both securely anchored in almost immobile accompaniment chords." This theme is played as Joe searches for his brother's body. Again, this is not searching-under-the-bridge music. The music plays rather to the calmness of spirit that has come to Joe with the resolution of his conflict with society. It is also interesting to note that this diatonic theme is used earlier in the film in the scenes between Joe and Doris. Joe's relationship with Doris is the only relatively serene one he has known; therefore, the theme is used three times before in scenes involving the two of them.

Another interesting musical aspect of the sequence described here has to do with the thematic tightness of the score. With a few exceptions of "source" music heard over the radio in a gang-war episode, the material quoted in this example is practically the whole of Raksin's material for the score. As Morton points out, "The welding together of these materials is accomplished by the juxtaposition of their fragments, by repetition, by their transformation in the time dimension, and by the usual developmental procedures." As an example of this notice the ascending thirds, with their cross relations, in bars 6 and 8; and then their transformation into the tenths in the bass of bars 29-30. Also compare the arched phrases of bars 16-17, with the melodic line of bar 21.

The material in this example has four kinds of thematic significance typical of the score as a whole: First is the sixteenth-note figure in bar 11. These sixteenth-notes provide the rhythmic pattern for the final polytonal

---

image works with the word. Nothing is duplicated, or supererogatory. Even in so simple an instance as that of the heroine's face in close-up, as the first person narrative runs "Doris wanted me to make love to her," is the relationship of word to image complementary rather than redundant. The soundtrack is the image slantwise; refracted through an individual consciousness, and, to that extent, interpreted."

Figure 17. Excerpt from *Force of Evil,* music by David Raksin.

chords in bar 46. It is interesting to note that Raksin uses this same rhythmic pattern in another score for the film *The Redeemer* (discussed in chapter four). Second is the ascending sixteenth-note figure in bars 29-30. This motif was created as a somewhat Gershwinesque tune, which, as things turned out, was not needed, so only this fragment survives in the film. Third is the piled-up fourths of bars 32-34, which were previously heard in the second police raid. These fourths represent part of the chromatic-atonal material that abounds in this score. Fourth is the long crescendo phrase beginning in bar 37. This is a shortened version of material heard twice in earlier dramatic scenes. The effectiveness of this material comes from the contrast created by the leanness of the two-part writing and the richness of the orchestration.

Critic Lawrence Morton succinctly summed up the score to *Force of Evil:* "The most characteristic feature of this score is that it has avoided any expression of the conventionally beautiful. The only lyrical idea of the score is in the one extended melody, and even here there is no sweetness of sentiment. Everything else is quite dissonant, and even brutality is not absent. This kind of expressiveness was of course requited by the film. And for this reason there must have been a strong temptation to 'soften the blow' with music of a more conventional kind, as Hollywood so often does. It is much to the credit of Raksin, producer Roberts and writer-director Polonsky that they did not surrender to this temptation by having a 'pretty score.' Indeed, this music is not pretty; but it does fit the picture and refuses to vitiate the story's harshness, its drama, and its artistic purpose. It is also good music."

To say that the atonal quality of this score influenced similar scores of later years (such as Leonard Rosenman's serial score to *The Cobweb,* for instance) is probably to overstate. Generally the only kind of influence Hollywood is susceptible to is commercial success, which *Force of Evil* did not have. If anything, the film's lack of commercial success mitigated against this kind of score as well as this kind of film. Indeed, Polonsky, after being blacklisted, made only one other film.*

Up to this point we have been concerned with prototypes of the uses of music in film during Hollywood's most musically productive era. An important phenomenon of the Hollywood studio films of this era was the necessity for the orchestrator, whose misunderstood function has given

---

* *Tell Them Willie Boy Is Here.*

rise to one of the most pervasive myths ever to come out of the Hollywood music scene. The myth is simply that Bernard Herrmann is the only major film composer in Hollywood who does his own orchestrations. Despite two fine articles by critic Lawrence Morton on the subject in the early 1950s, the myth still persists. Even as late as 1973 the myth crops up as purported fact in Tony Thomas's book, *Music for the Movies*. This assertion has found its way into the film-music aficionado's lore and seems to owe its existence to two things: (1) An ignorance of the real relationship between the composer and the orchestrator in Hollywood, and (2) a blind faith in the word of Bernard Herrmann on this subject who is in no small part responsible for the propagation of the myth.

There are numerous composers in Hollywood whose sketches are so complete and so detailed that the orchetrator really becomes, in effect, an intelligent copyist. Nor is this practice of orchestrating from highly detailed sketches restricted to the film-music world. Prokofiev, with the ironic exception of his score to the film *Alexander Nevsky,* had all of his scores orchestrated from detailed sketches. As Victor Seroff points out, "Prokofiev devised a system that permitted him not to lose time on the long trips across the country.

"Because the vibration of the train made it impossible to write the orchestral score, he did all his preparatory work by marking in his piano score which of the instruments was to play this or that melody or passage, including the indications for accents and dynamics, so that when he left the train and found himself for a short time on 'firm ground' all he had to do was to copy automatically his indications into the orchestral score.

"At first it seemed impossible to write into the piano score the names of the instruments, particularly when the chords occupied all the staffs, but with practice he succeeded. He was pleased with having perfected this method, for it allowed him to turn over the piano score to a capable musician who could then easily transcribe it into the orchestral score."

But this invoking of a concert-music composer's methods of orchestrating really is academic if one understands how this process worked in Hollywood during the 1930s, '40s, and '50s.

Lawrence Morton has pointed out that "the final judgement as to the correctness, style, and practicability of an orchestrator's work can only be made by the composer. Criticism may thereafter voice the opinion that it doesn't like the composition of the orchestration, but only the composer can say if it matches his conception of what he wants to hear. And it would seem to me that if the orchestration is proper to the music, it should make no difference who did it."

The question is most easily resolved by describing exactly what an orchestrator does. As mentioned earlier, many composers' sketches are so complete as to make the orchestrator nothing more than a glorified copyist. One Hollywood orchestrator, when asked to describe his job, replied, "I take the music off the white paper and put it on the yellow." Morton claims that "In such instances the orchestrator's discretion may be exercised only in such matters as assigning a phrase to the third clarinet instead of the second, spelling off the trombones in a lengthy passage requiring frequent change of position, making a practical division of labor between two percussion players, or deciding whether the harp part would be better notated in flats or sharps."

This is not to say that all composers who have worked in Hollywood have made up such detailed sketches. No one can tell who they are, though, since the list of credits does not tell. Neither does the absence of an orchestrator credit mean that the composer involved has orchestrated his own music. Aaron Copland, for example, always used orchestrators when he worked in Hollywood. The reason it is not evident in his music, according to Morton, is that his sketches are so complete "that no other musical personality has an opportunity to intrude itself upon his music."

Other composers who have worked in Hollywood who also are known for their complete sketches include Adolph Deutsch, Hugo Friedhofer, David Raksin, Alex North, Leonard Rosenman, and Jerry Goldsmith, to name only a few.

Figure 18 is probably more illuminating than anything else. It should be clear, after examining the excerpt from David Raksin's music to *Carrie*, that Mr. Raksin does not need an orchestrator. It was the studio that needed one, for the studios were forever in a hurry. "It is part of the industrial scheme that while Mr. Van Cleave orchestrates, Mr. Raksin goes on to compose the next scene," observes Morton.

What the myth seems to reduce to is that Mr. Herrmann is the only composer to have worked in Hollywood who notated his music *onto the score paper* rather than making out detailed sketches and then allowing someone else to make the transfer.

But even *this* is not true for, as Lawrence Morton points out, "Less well-known composers who work for small, independent producers do actually orchestrate their own music. The reasons here are economic:

Figure 18. Excerpt from *Carrie* by David Raksin. From this example musicians can
see precisely what details were left to the discretion of the orchestrator, Nathan Van
Cleave, who also orchestrated *The Heiress* for Aaron Copland. He worked out the
divisi and double-stops of the violas and cellos, and the voicing of the horn-trombone
chords. However, the whole conception of the orchestral color is the composer's.

small budgets do not allow for orchestrators. In many cases the music is composed and orchestrated for the single orchestration fee, which has been established by the Musicians' Union. But since there is no wage scale for composition, many composers are obliged to 'throw it in' for the price of orchestration in order to get the job done. That is, they are paid very well for their drudgery, but not at all for their creativity."

There are, of course, cases wherein the composer is either totally unable (which is more true of the pop-music oriented Hollywood of today than in previous eras) or is unwilling to orchestrate his own music. In these cases the responsibility of the orchestrator is great and often times amounts to composition. The orchestrator may have to change harmonies, supply inner voices, invent accompaniment patterns, insert counterpoint, or disguise completely the probable keyboard origin of the music.* The composer then is more than likely little more than a hack, a dilettante who had not bothered to learn his craft so that he might express his vision, however limited.

Another practice of the pre-World War II Hollywood film industry that had implications for film music was the heavy reliance of Hollywood studio films on the talents of the screen writer. After the war, lacking a large, permanent staff of writers, studios began turning to the adapted play for their material. The studios and independent producers began buying established, already written properties, which they then had to translate into film form. This practice proceeded through the late 1940s and all the way through the 1950s with such films as *The Caine Mutiny, Marjorie Morningstar, Exodus, From Here to Eternity, Not as a Stranger, Tea and Sympathy,* and *Sweet Bird of Youth.* The list includes several hundred titles, but one, *The Heiress,* with an outstanding score by Aaron Copland, is especially relevant to our discussion.

In 1949 Aaron Copland was asked by Paramount Pictures to score William Wyler's screen version of the Henry James novel *Washington Square,* entitled *The Heiress.* The score for this picture was to win Copland a well-deserved Academy Award for the best dramatic score of the year.

Aaron Copland's international recognition as a composer of "art" music should in no way affect a critical judgment of his music for films.

---

* In cases such as this the orchestrator is really closer to being an arranger—an important distinction.

There are numerous examples of "serious" composers attempting to write for the screen and failing rather decisively where the dramatic requirements of the film are concerned. Too often the judgment of a film critic or reviewer is dazed by someone of the caliber of Copland. Critics approach films such as this with the notion that the score will necessarily be successful since so much of Copland's other music is outstanding. With Copland this has proven to be the case, but it has not always been true of other composers whose reputation lies outside of the film world.

When Copland first approached film as a compositional medium, he immediately realized film's unique demands on a composer. The demands were, according to Frederick Sternfeld, that "A dramatic composer must realize the limits of complexity that he may reach without losing his listener. The ballets of Copland's *Rodeo* and *Appalachian Spring,* intended to exercise a wider appeal than the Violin Sonata and the Third Symphony, are written in a deliberately simplified style."

When Copland came to score *The Heiress* he brought with him a good deal of experience in composing for films. He had already scored three features (*Of Mice and Men,* 1939; *Our Town,* 1940; and *The Red Pony,* 1949) as well as several documentaries.

In their adaptation of Henry James's novel, first for the stage and then for the screen, writers Ruth and Augustus Goetz reduced a story of narrative prose to fit the dimensions of time involved in a dramatic presentation. There was the additional burden of translating an essentially psychological plot with little external motion into cinematic language. This is never an easy task because unlike this film's parent, the stage play, the motion picture relies less on dialogue than on its photography and sound-dialogue-music track. In order to depict the rise and fall of the heiress, Wyler rejected the highly rhythmic montage as a cinematic device but relied heavily on pans, dolly shots, and close-ups. This is understandable when one considers that the plot is predominantly concerned with the development of character and proceeds in a deliberate but leisurely manner. At emotional high points in the film Wyler relies on the simple, though strong, means of close-up, dissolve, music. These same devices are used in Laurence Olivier's monologues in *Henry V.*

Several scenes in *The Heiress* rely heavily on the music for their dramatic effect. One, which runs over two minutes, is when Catherine has just realized that her fiancé has forsaken her. She moans to her aunt that someone must love her, that her fiancé Morris must love her for all those who did not. At this point the music takes over where the dialogue leaves off. The music for this scene is derived from some material that appeared earlier in the film. This earlier material is given in Figure 19.

Figure 19. Excerpt from *The Heiress,* music by Aaron Copland.

Figure 20 is the music that begins this scene, and the first five measures are a variation on the material found in Figure 19. During these first five measures the screen shows the aunt and the girl sitting motionless, contemplative. The basso ostinato (C-sharp in the bass) during these first five measures has the same static quality as the visual. But then in measure 6 Copland uses a device dramatic composers have used often for this very type of psychological situation: the bass line is reminiscent of a passacaglia and the music rises to a fortissimo climax (measures 6-12 of Figure 20), at which point the heroine breaks down completely and sobs. A passacaglia bass has a certain psychological impact of inevitability on the listener; here it's as if it represents Catherine's realization of the inevitability of her loneliness. There is ample precedent for this kind of dramatic use of the passacaglia: one need only look to Purcell's "Dido's Lament" from his opera *Dido and Aeneas,* or to the "Crucifixus" of the Bach *B-Minor Mass.* In Figure 20 the passacaglialike bass has the additional function of adding the necessary dissonance in measures 6-12. Indeed, if the music is played without the bass line it sounds almost heroic as well as being extremely diatonic, a quality that would be inappropriate to this scene. However, when the bass is added the music suddenly takes on a quality of excruciating psychic pain, finally exploding into sobs. The scene concludes with the two women sitting next to each other and the music dying away. It is a masterful scene, demonstrating the overwhelming power music can have in expressing psychological states that photography and dialogue are incapable of portraying.

The music in another scene of the film is significant, for it demonstrates music's ability to direct the consciousness of the listener/viewer in a specific direction. This scene, like the last one, has no dialogue. Catherine

Figure 20. Excerpt from *The Heiress*.

is waiting in excited anticipation for the arrival, by carriage, of her fiancé.
A carriage noise is heard outside: she proudly says good-bye to her aunt
and magnanimously announces, "I will write you, Aunt." The girl then
hurries out of the house and into the street where she expects to find her
fiancé waiting with the carriage. As the music and sound effects
crescendo, the carriage nears the house—only to pass it by. Catherine,
defeated, reenters the house, and the scene, together with the music,
concludes.

At a preview showing of the film, this scene had no music and the audience laughed. Wyler asked Copland to compose some music to direct the audience's awareness to the tragic significance of the scene. The results are stunning. In order to catch Catherine's excited anticipation before the carriage comes, Copland wrote an interplay of runs in the flutes, clarinets, and bass clarinet. This music can be found in Figure 21. This triplet idea is then carried into the carriage scene. The music over the triplet bass line, played by the muted horns, muted trumpets, and trombones, seems to convey the tragedy of the situation before Catherine faces it.

In yet another scene from *The Heiress* we find music functioning as good dramatic music should: adding another dimension to that which is already there. In this scene Catherine's father calls in both Catherine and the maid to tell them he is ill. After the maid is dismissed, an argument ensues between the father and his daughter. It should be added, in order to clarify the significance of this scene, that the father threatened to change his will upon hearing of Catherine's impending marriage to Morris. It was this which drove Morris away. This argument comes to a climax when the father assures Catherine that he has done her a considerable favor by breaking up her engagement to a worthless trifler. Catherine then angrily disagrees:

Catherine: You have cheated me. You thought any handsome, clever man would be as bored with me as you were . . .

Doctor: Morris did not love you . . .

Catherine: I know that now, thanks to you.

Doctor: Better to know it now than twenty years hence.

Catherine: Why? I lived with *you* for twenty years before I found out that *you* did not love me. I don't know that Morris would have hurt me or starved me for affection more than *you* did. Since *you* couldn't love me, you should have let someone else try.

The function of the music here is to express the doctor's anguish over his daughter's hatred. The music for this sequence is seen in Figure 22. As the scene progresses Copland accents the dialogue skillfully with musical punctuation. Catherine's father pleads: "You will meet some honest, decent man some day. You have many fine qualities . . ." "And thirty thousand a year!" interrupts Catherine after the G-sharp in measure 5 of Figure 22. The father continues to argue, "You know him to be a

Figure 21. Excerpt from *The Heiress*, music by Aaron Copland.

scoundrel." Immediately after the G-sharp in measure 9 of Figure 22
Catherine snaps back, "I love him, does that humiliate you?"

Figure 22. Excerpt from *The Heiress,* music by Aaron Copland.

Such recitativelike treatment of dialogue is not uncommon in films but
it demonstrates how adept Copland is in writing for the screen.

Unfortunately, the Main Title music to *The Heiress* is not Copland's
but is, rather, the song "Plaisir d'Amour." The effect is less than
satisfactory, but when the Main Title ends and one begins to hear the
music written by Copland, the contrast between the two is all too obvious.
When the film opened in New York, Copland wrote a letter to the press
disclaiming responsibility for the title music. Lawrence Morton reported
that "I have heard privately a recording of the title music that Copland
composed for [*The Heiress*]. It is not pretty, perhaps, as its substitute, but
it is certainly much more relevant to the film that Wyler produced."

What Copland brought to the screen orchestrally was a refreshing new
sound. This was because Copland seldom used the full orchestral tutti as a
dramatic device. A contemporary review of his score to *The Heiress*
catches the essence of Copland's orchestral style in this film: "Copland

has stressed the importance of small ensembles and a certain softness of texture that is extremely significant and quite pleasing to note, especially to the professional musician. The usual Hollywood sequences and over-blown mid-nineteenth century climaxes (as an attempt to underline the emotional aspects of the film) are happily avoided."

The recurrent criticism of Hollywood film music of this period as being extravagant or overorchestrated has a certain amount of truth, and was recognized by professionals in the business. There was a feeling among musicians that the studio orchestra was overbrassed; some suggested that the musician's union insist that the studios engage enough string players to maintain a symphonic orchestral balance. The studios were, of course, reluctant to do this, for the string sections would have had to be increased by twenty or thirty players at a guaranteed minimum wage of $7,500 each per year. John Green, then head of the MGM music department, told an audience in 1951 that "Hollywood must get over the notion that a microphone can make four fiddles sound like a full section. For certain scores [I] insist on having enough string players to make the music sound as it ought to."

But to present a blanket criticism of film music of this period as being uneconomical in its instrumental resources is to gloss over the larger issue of how and when to be economical. There are a variety of considerations a composer must take into account, not the least of which is the size of his budget. He almost must consider whether or not he has any earthquakes, chases, battles, or horse races to score, or whether the film is a pastoral-scenic or an historical epic. Economy is admirable if there is a reason for it inherent in the film, but "the history of music gives no evidence that large sounds are inherently more vulgar than small ones. The crucial point . . . is that economy is a matter of style rather than of numbers of performers. It is style that makes a Mozart quartet sound more economical than one of Schubert's, such as the great G-major. And even Mahler's *Song of the Earth* is proof enough that some composers need very large orchestras to be economical with."

The assertive comment by one English writer in the *Hollywood Quarterly* that certain composers "can do more with one bass clarinet or a string quartet than most Hollywood composers can do with an orchestra of ninety" is wholly misleading. To begin with, the Hollywood orchestras of the era seldom exceeded fifty players; thirty-five was about the average. The other misleading aspect of this statement has to do with the implication of the word "more." More what? Lawrence Morton is correct when he insists that "One thing that can't be done with a string quartet is to equal the full sonority of an orchestral *tutti,* a noble and honorable sound that very few composers (even the most fastidious) and very few audiences (even the most snobbish) are quite willing to do without in dramatic music."

Numerous film scores from this period use relatively small ensembles, but the small ensembles are there because the composer thought it necessary in terms of the picture. David Raksin's score to *Man With a Cloak,* for instance, used an orchestra consisting of 2 flutes, 1 oboe, 2 clarinets, 1 bass clarinet, 1 bassoon; 1 horn, 1 trumpet, 1 trombone; 1 percussion, and a solo viola d'amore. For several of the climactic scenes in the film the orchestra was augmented by a second bassoon, second and third horns, tuba, harp, piano, 6 cellos, and 1 bass. Small resources indeed for a "Hollywood" production.

"In the meantime, it will be no victory for music when Hamlet's funeral march is scored for a wind quintet or when Ben Hur drives his chariot around the Coliseum to the accompaniment of a clarinet cadenza."

Another recurring, though less perceptive, criticism of the films of this era is that they contain more music than do their more contemporary counterparts. This fact of a quantitative difference in music continually evokes the question from contemporary audiences: "What is all that music doing there?" Since this question, irrelevant as it really is, is asked frequently and by people who should really know better, we shall make a brief attempt at answering it. First of all, the question of what the music is doing on the soundtrack can be roughly equated to asking why, in Shakespeare's plays, the characters lapse into poetry now and then. We now begin to see the irrelevance of the question, for an artistic medium will absorb whatever elements will enhance it. By questioning the existence of music in films a person is merely saying that he would prefer a less enhanced art form. There is really nothing more "realistic" about films than any other art form. In fact there are certain mechanical elements about film which, taken by themselves, would seem to mitigate against its ever being considered a "realistic" art form. When one views an hour's worth of film, for instance, he has, because of certain mechanical factors, sat in darkness for 27 minutes of that hour. But this is really all beside the point, for the important question is not "What is all of that music doing there?" but, rather, "Why is the music playing that particular material?" Indeed, the first question only arises, as it does in any other art form, when the music in a film is not used to an effective end.

In this chapter we have been discussing music in the American film-studio system of the mid-1930s to the late 1940s, a period which has proven to be the most creatively rich in terms of the imaginative uses of music in films. In the next chapter, dealing with films from the 1950s to the present, we will examine some of the new parameters of the use of music in film.

4

From 1950 to the Present

In 1946 the American film business grossed $1,700,000,000. This was the peak year in the history of film in America. By 1962 the receipts had dropped to $900 million, which is just a little over half of the 1946 gross. As box-office revenues fell, moreover, production costs went up. What forces were responsible for this enormous drop in Hollywood's earnings over a scant fifteen-year period?

There are two reasons for this tremendous decline in Hollywood's revenues and both were to have a catastrophic effect on the quality of music in films. First, the United States courts had begun an assault on the corporate chains that bound the picture-making studio to the theaters exhibiting their pictures. The courts ruled that this sort of arrangement violated the antitrust laws. Block booking was found to be unfair to the individual competitive exhibitor since the studio-owned chains of theaters gave the studios monopolistic control of the film market in the distribution of their own films. Although the government's suit was originally filed in July 1938, the case did not finally come to a close until 1949, World War II having been in part responsible for the delay.

The second reason for Hollywood's loss of revenues is attributable to a electronic toy, perfected in the mid-1930s, which combined picture and sound. At first Hollywood laughed at the invention of television. But by the late 1940s and early 1950s, it was forced to deal with television in no uncertain terms.

As the courts consistently ruled against the studios, the studios were forced to sell their theater interests. This did away with the studios' outlet for their product whether that product had been good or bad. What this meant was that now each film would have to be good enough to sell itself. In the meantime more and more Americans bought televisions—and stayed home to watch them. At this point Hollywood declared an all-out war on the new invention. No Hollywood film could appear on television, nor could a film star appear on television. American audiences countered by staying home and watching British movies on television, as well as the new stars that television itself developed.

The biggest studios were hardest hit by all of this. In 1949 MGM declared wage cutbacks along with tremendous layoffs. What were once assets—property and people—had now become liabilities. The studios had to pay people's salaries despite the fact they had no movies for them to produce.

By 1952 Hollywood realized that it would be unable to stem television's rising popularity. If films and television were to coexist, Hollywood thought, then movies must give American audiences what TV did not. The most obvious and striking difference between TV and films was the size of the screen. While TV was in its technological infancy, films had the benefit of over fifty years of technological research in color, properties of lenses as well as special effects. TV, on the other hand, had not yet developed color or videotape. Hollywood's two primary weapons in its counterattack on TV were to be size and technical gimmickry.

One of the first attacks launched by the film industry on the American TV-watcher was 3-D, a three-dimensional stereoscopic effect achieved by shooting the action with two lenses simultaneously. The audiences viewing the movies were required to wear plastic polaroid glasses to blend the two images into a single three-dimensional one. Even though the effect had been around for years in the form of a stereoscope, Americans rushed out to the theaters to see the new novelty used in a feature-length film. Hollywood responded by rushing into production such 3-D films as *Bwana Devil, House of Wax, Creature from the Black Lagoon, The French Line, Kiss Me Kate,* and *Fort Ti.* Gerald Mast observed, in *A Short History of the Movies,* that "Audiences eagerly left their television sets to experience the gimmick that attacked them with knives, arrows, stampedes of animals, avalanches, and Jane Russell's bust; the thrill of 3-D was that the necessarily confined, flat, projected picture convincingly threatened to leap out of its frame at the audience."

The 3-D craze lasted little more than a year, for the novelty soon wore off and Americans went back to their TV sets.

Cinerama was another attempt on the part of Hollywood to draw American TV viewers back to the theaters. But it, too, was a mere technical gimmick with the story existing solely for the presentation of effects. Not until Stanley Kubrick's 1968 film, *2001* was the gimmickry subordinated to the subject matter of the film.

A third movie gimmick was the introduction of the wide screen. The novelty, called CinemaScope, has been more durable than some of the other novelties to come out in the early 1950s.

The only attempt at gimmickry that involved the music in films was the introduction of stereo sound in the 1952 film *Julius Caesar.* Unlike his directorial counterparts who were floundering in their attempts to raise 3-D and the wide screen above the level of a gimmick, composer Miklos Rozsa immediately recognized the artistic and dramatic possibilities open to the composer through the addition of stereo sound to the film.

Rozsa exploited these possibilities in a scene in *Julius Caesar,* the death of Brutus. At the same time that Brutus is dying, the armies of Antony and Octavius are advancing. The music, Rozsa points out, "starts after Cassius dies and continues from here to the end of the picture. The themes of Cassius and Brutus appear again in a subdued, low and depressed manner."

Throughout these scenes Rozsa "wanted to give the impression that the victorious armies of Antony and Octavius are continuously advancing and coming nearer and nearer and nearer. This scene, however, is the culmination of the tragedy, when its noblest character, Brutus . . . faces his inescapable death." To articulate this contrast musically, Rozsa wrote two entirely different scores that were contrapuntally worked out but in content are completely independent. Figure 1 represents Antony's nearing army, and the music is a march based on Caesar's theme. The material is scored for brass, woodwind, and percussion instruments. Figure 2, which plays to the scene actually on the screen, speaks to the tragedy of Brutus. This music is scored for strings alone. Thus, there is a contrast of orchestral color between the two pieces of material which only reinforces their emotional, rhythmic, and thematic differences.

Figure 1. Excerpt from *Julius Caesar,* music by Miklos Rozsa.

Figure 2. Excerpt from *Julius Caesar.*

With the new stereophonic techniques Rozsa was able to emphasize the differences between these two pieces of thematic material still further while also adding to the dramatic impact of the scene. As the direction of the approaching army is from the right corner of the screen, "we put the march track on this loudspeaker and the string track on the two others, screen center and left corner. Thus there is complete separation of the two scores, and geographically the listener immediately feels that the army is marching from the right corner of the screen."

As Brutus dies the march becomes increasingly louder, and as Strato runs out of the scene the march music completely overpowers Brutus's string music and dominates the whole scene.

Stereo sound was used rather extensively in CinemaScope productions during the 1950s but has since fallen into oblivion. A few recent films have used stereo sound for the music track but these films have amounted to little more than filmed rock concerts. Examples of this genre include the Rolling Stones' film *Gimme Shelter* as well as *Woodstock* and *Ladies and Gentlemen, the Rolling Stones.*

With the demise of the American film-studio structure, the dictatorial head of production, and the huge quantitative demands of a large annual output, the independent producer came into his own. The new film producer concentrated on putting together and selling a single product at a time. The independent producer, even within the studios, selected the property, the stars, the director, as well as raising the money for the production and supervising the selling of the finished film. Mast observes that "the producer usually owned no lot, no long-term contract with stars, no staff of writers and technicians. He assembled a company for a particular film, disbanded it when the film was finished, and assembled another company for his next film."

As might be expected, the producer, forced to make each film pay its own way, searched for stable and predictable production values.

What, then, was the effect of all of this on the quality of American film music? For a while after the demise of the studio structure the quality and style of film music changed little from the studio days. Then, in 1952, Fred Zinnemann directed a picture called *High Noon.* It has since come to be known as Hollywood's first "adult" western. The title song of this fine film, "Do Not Forsake Me Oh My Darlin'," sung by the late Tex Ritter, became a popular hit in its own right and unknowingly rang the death knell for intelligent use of music in films. The composer of the song,

Dimitri Tiomkin, a Russian concert pianist turned film composer, repeated his success two years later with the title music to *The High and the Mighty.*

The impact of the success of Tiomkin's song to *High Noon* on a financially strapped film industry was immediate. Producers saw in the success of "Do Not Forsake Me Oh My Darlin' " a means of making additional money from their films. While there had been, in years past, songs from films which became popular in their own right, Hollywood had given little thought to the earning potential of the music that accompanied its films. The loss of its theaters and the subsequent loss in revenues, coupled with the advent of the long-playing record in the early 1950s, changed all of that. And where film studios once sold the recording and publishing rights to the music in their films to other firms, studios now began their own record companies and publishing houses in order not to miss out on any of the profits. The aesthetic effect on film music was immediate and devastating. Every producer, in order to help assure the financial success of his film, now wanted a film score with a song or instrumental number of a type that would "make the charts." No longer did producers care if the music written for their films was the best possible music for that specific picture; they now wanted music that would sell *away* from the picture. The artistic problems for the composer were obvious. He was now asked to impose a strictly musical form and style, the pop song, onto a film whether it was appropriate to the film or not.

In *High Noon,* however, this structure works. Tiomkin's score is not monothematic and has many musical elements that were not new. The music in the film is, for the most part, understated, although the music used to accompany the scenes involving the character of Helen Ramirez is a little heavy-handed in its Spanish flavor. The song itself is used little throughout the film. When it is, moreover, it is used only over visuals so that it never competes with dialogue.

The film met with a good deal of critical acclaim. *High Noon* moved the Western from a mere action yarn into the realm of psychology and moral decision. Howard Burton, writing in the *Hollywood Quarterly,* pointed out that "when Will Kane [Gary Cooper] faces death in the person of Frank Miller, and when his fellow townsmen desert him, the film *High Noon* is remarkably parallel to the morality play *Everyman.* In both vehicles the heroes are left alone in their greatest need."

Tiomkin's score substantially aids the film's psychological aspects. In one scene, just before the gunfight, Gary Cooper is seen walking down the town's deserted street. As Cooper walks the length of the street the camera slowly pulls up in a long crane shot, emphasizing the hero's lonely plight. The music rises with the camera into the higher ranges of the strings and, together with the camera angle, creates a barren, bleak and lonely atmosphere.

The dialogue in the film is frequently treated operatically by Tiomkin. One such instance is when the town judge, packing to get out of town, quotes to the marshal the mighty oath of revenge sworn years ago by the film's villain, Miller. The judge's words become a text set to the great, towering strokes of the orchestra.

But the most dazzling sequence musically and visually is the one beginning with the marshal's setting down on paper his last will and testament. The dreaded hour of noon is only minutes away, and the camera cuts from a shot of the marshal's will to the clock in his office. The pendulum of the clock swings rhythmically and the music begins, taking its tempo from the clock's swinging pendulum. There then ensues a montage sequence that builds to an excruciating climax. The tempo of the music never changes, and it is obvious that the film was cut to the music. This one sequence should demonstrate beyond all doubt that cutting film to the music *can* be brilliantly effective where appropriate. With the music at a high emotional pitch, the sequence ends with a shot of the chair in the courtroom in which Frank Miller received his sentence. The sequence is abruptly ended as the whistle of the noon train drowns the music out on the sound track. This sequence is one of the finest, most unnoticed moments in film music.

An equally influential score, written in 1951, was Alex North's music for the film *A Streetcar Named Desire*. While the music did not gain any great popularity away from the film (it was not suitable for pop market exploitation), it did open the door for the use of jazz in films. Indeed, the score is the first substantial use of stylized jazz in a film for anything other than source music. It would not be until 1955, with Elmer Bernstein's score to *Man with the Golden Arm*, that stylized jazz "made the charts" and exerted any amount of pernicious influence on the type of scores being written for pictures.

Alex North's score to *A Streetcar Named Desire* was his first film score for director Elia Kazan. North had previously provided incidental music for Kazan's New York stage production of Arthur Miller's play *Death of a*

Salesman. North's score to the film *A Streetcar Named Desire* proved quite influential within the industry, and also stands as a fine score in itself. North's feelings about this score reflect as sensitive and intelligent an approach to film scoring as one is likely to encounter in the film industry. North, writing in *Film Music Notes,* says "I find it practically impossible to score anything which does not move me emotionally and I attempted to convey the internal, rather than external aspects of the film. By this I mean the music was related to the characters at all times and not the action. Instead of 'themes' for the specific characters, there were mental statements, so to speak, for Stanley vs. Blanche, Mitch vs. Blanche, and Stanley vs. Stella.... I think you will find some of the scoring running counter to the scene because of the attempt to reflect the inner feeling of the personalities rather than the situation. It may be interesting to note that in the first five reels there is more stylized jazz than in the remaining reels because these take place mostly at night when the 'Four Deuces' dive is in operation. (One sees flickering lights throughout.) I tried to make the transitions from the source music (popular tunes) to the underscoring as imperceptible as possible so that one was not completely aware of the transition. I don't say this was entirely successful, but it was worth trying. I also believe strongly in tension and relaxation (as applied to absolute music) in functional music. Because of this you may find strident string chords over an innocent melody which is definitely going some place, to punctuate an emotional response; or brass figures interspersing a melodic line to convey the ambivalent nature of human behavior."

Figure 3 is the music used under the Main Title and gives the reader a very good idea of the character of much of the music in the film. Figure 4 exemplifies the asynchronous qualities of the score which North speaks of above. This music accompanies the fantastic street cries of "Flores para los muertos" and vividly depicts the breakdown of Blanche's mind. Over an ostinato that slides from the tonic to the subdominant and back, chromatic scales descend while strings and woodwinds climb higher and higher, with the whole working to a climax of frenzy.

It was not until the early 1950s that Hollywood film scores solidly moved into a twentieth-century musical idiom. The two composers most responsible for this movement were Alex North and Leonard Rosenman. It can be said of their respective compositional styles that North represents a style along the lines of Bartók and Stravinsky, while

Figure 3. Excerpt from *A Streetcar Named Desire*, music by Alex North.

Figure 4. Excerpt from *A Streetcar Named Desire.*

Rosenman tends toward a more radical bent exemplified in the works of Schoenberg and, more recently, Ligeti. The influence of North and Rosenman upon American film scoring has been substantial; it was through their early efforts that more recent composers working in films, composers such as Jerry Goldsmith and Billy Goldenberg, have been able to pursue their personal styles more fully.

While it is true that David Raksin, with his 1948 score to *Force of Evil,* and George Antheil, with his score for the 1937 film *The Plainsman,* utilized twentieth-century musical idioms, their scores really exerted little influence among their more conservative and cautious colleagues. In addition, the films of the 1930s and 1940s, with their somewhat operatic and unreal plots, simply did not lend themselves to a particularly dissonant treatment and the resulting expressionistic effect of that kind of treatment. This expressionistic effect became more palatable in films by the early-to-mid-1950s owing to Hollywood's movement toward producing slightly more realistic films. This move on Hollywood's part was, of course, partially influenced by the films being produced in Europe after World War II, which had used more contemporary music for their scores (and, many times, no scores at all), almost to a fault.

Leonard Rosenman's first film score was for *East of Eden,* released in 1955. Like Alex North before him, Rosenman had been brought to Hollywood by director Elia Kazan. Rosenman and Kazan would collaborate later in 1955 on another James Dean vehicle, *Rebel Without a Cause.* Figure 5, an excerpt from Rosenman's score to *East of Eden,* demonstrates two outstanding Rosenman traits: a marked taste for the expressive possibilities of dissonance, and a generous sprinkling of contrapuntal textures. As an example of this contrapuntal texture, note the perfect three-part canon beginning in bar 32 (actually a four-part canon if one counts the augmentation of the canonic figure in the violins beginning in measure 34).

Alex North's twentieth-century style shows itself in the previous examples of his score to *A Streetcar Named Desire* (1951). Indeed, the mere choice of a jazz idiom reflects an interest in musical styles of this century. Even within this jazz-oriented score one can find dissonant elements common to later North scores.

In 1955 composer Elmer Bernstein utilized a jazz idiom for the Otto Preminger film, *The Man with the Golden Arm.* One significant difference between the two scores, however, was that Bernstein's Main Title music to the film was to become a popular success away from the film—much like Tiomkin's Main Title song for *High Noon.*

"The score for *The Man with the Golden Arm* is not a jazz score. It is a score in which jazz elements were incorporated toward the end of creating an atmosphere, I should say a highly specialized atmosphere, specific to this particular film." So wrote composer Elmer Bernstein in his repeated attempts to discourage the idea that the score to *The Man with the Golden Arm* is a jazz score. One of the primary reasons it is not a jazz score is that the music is not improvised; improvisation is the lifeblood of jazz. What little improvisation does take place in the score is done by the drummer, Shelly Manne. The art of improvisation does not mix too well with the split-second timing requirements of a film score.

Up to this time the jazz idiom had been used most sparingly in films and the question of why Bernstein chose the idiom of jazz for this film is a logical one to pursue. Bernstein, in an article in *Film Music Notes,* relates the ideas involved in his decision: "I told Otto Preminger, the producer, of my intention after one quick reading of the shooting script. The script had a Chicago slum street, heroin, hysteria, longing, frustration, despair and finally death. Whatever love one could feel in the script was the little, weak emotion left in a soul racked with heroin and guilt, a soul consuming its strength in the struggle for the good life and losing pitifully. There is something very American and contemporary about all the characters and their problems. I wanted an element that could speak readily of hysteria and despair, an element that would localize these emotions to our country, to a large city if possible. Ergo,—jazz."

Upon his decision to use elements of jazz in his score, Bernstein proceeded to gather in the talents of two brilliant jazz musicians, Shorty Rogers and Shelly Manne. Rogers arranged all of the band numbers, and Shelly Manne created his own drum solos where Bernstein had indicated them in the score. Since he had only twenty days in which to write the score he enlisted the talents of the orchestrator Fred Steiner.

Bernstein has made some general comments concerning the content of his score that are worth quoting here. About *The Man with the Golden Arm,* he says, "This is not a score in which each character has a theme. It is not a score which creates a musical mirror for dialogue. Nor is it a score which psychoanalyzes the characters and serves up inner brain on the half shell. It is basically a simple score which deals with a man and his environment. There are only three themes which are exploited in a

FILM MUSIC

Figure 5. Excerpt from *East of Eden,* music by Leonard Rosenman.

compositional manner in the development of the score. These can be loosely identified in the following manner: 1) Frank's relationship to his general environment; his job as a dealer in a cheap poker joint, to his fight against the dope habit, to the pusher who sells him the stuff, to the street itself. 2) Frank's relationship to his home environment; his neurotic wife, who feigns a debilitating illness in order to hold him, to the shabby flat with its 'lower depth' inhabitants, to his own guilty lack of love for his wife. 3) Frank's relationship with 'the other woman,' who is a symbol to him of love, and the better life, such small hopes as he has from time to time, and his chance of making it away from the habit and even the neighborhood and its hold on him."

The music for the Main Title of the film sets the mood immediately. As seen in Figure 6, the repetitive figure in the bass creates a sense of drive and a kind of grinding, grim monotony, while over all of this is the rather hysterical screaming of the brass. The triplet figures in the middle merely continue in a hopeless circle and never arrive anywhere until the very end of the Main Title and then only for a last cry of despair.

The second bit of material, Figure 7, represents Frank's relationship to his wife. Bernstein describes this thematic material as "faintly scented with an aura of romanticism, troubled, never quite going where you expect it to go, striving but never quite comfortable or fulfilled in its cadences."

The last piece of material, as seen in Figure 8, is a treatment of the theme reflecting Frank's relationship with the "other woman" and "is the least disturbed theme although even in this case the first statement in a rather halting 5/4 lest we become too pat or, by making this extremely simple theme too symmetrical, render the relationship with the 'other woman' too easy or ideal."

An especially effective scene occurs when Molly (the other woman) realizes that Frank is once again falling into the narcotic habit, and she leaves him. She runs from the dingy clip joint, through the slum street, and, arriving at her place, hurriedly packs her few possessions as Frank pounds on the locked door. The scene is very effective from a musical standpoint. Bernstein has observed that "This scene presented a tough problem. The chase through the street was not the difficult part but . . . the first part of it [Figure 9] is one of my favorite spots in the score. Being a realist I am forced to the melancholy fact that my solution of the problem is something less than genius; however, the intense, rather nervous

Figure 6. Excerpt from *The Man with the Golden Arm*, music by Sylvia Kaye and Elmer Bernstein.

FILM MUSIC

Figure 7. Excerpt from *The Man with the Golden Arm*, music by Elmer Bernstein.

166

rhythmic piano figures, string bass *pizzicato* and the insistent drumming of Shelly Manne seemed to me to create a kind of grim, driving excitement that suited the scene very well."

The most difficult part of the scene for Bernstein, however, was that portion in which Molly is packing and Frank is pounding on the door. As Bernstein pointed out, the theme for this relationship between Frank and Molly is almost dangerously simple, and certainly devoid of great emotional impact. Aside from the violence of Frank pounding on the door, Bernstein "wanted to use the theme [Figure 8] in this scene and project some of the tears and bitterness of the scene through some use of that fragile motif." The solution to Bernstein's paradoxical dramatic problem can be found in Figure 10. Notice the theme stated in Figure 8

Figure 8. Excerpt from *The Man with the Golden Arm,* music by Elmer Bernstein.

Figure 9. Excerpt from *The Man with the Golden Arm,* music by Elmer Bernstein.

entering in measure 6 of Figure 10 while the agitated rhythmic ostinato continues underneath.

Bernstein's score for this film adds a tremendous amount of atmosphere and drama, and there can be little doubt that Bernstein's choice of the jazz idiom was the right one to make the story more absorbing and the rather heavy-handed social commentary a little less obvious.

But Bernstein could not have foreseen what would happen as a result of his choice of jazz for this particular film. The instrumental Main Title became a popular hit and Hollywood, true to form, began immediate production of a host of imitative scores using jazz elements. Only a few months after the success of his score to *The Man with the Golden Arm,* Bernstein was bemoaning its impact on music in films. Even at that early

Figure 10. Excerpt from *The Man with the Golden Arm*, music by Elmer Bernstein.

date, he was quick to realize the results brought on by his host of imitators. "Now there are a rash of unpleasant films using jazz more or less skillfully. In the future, therefore, it will be difficult, if not impossible, to create a highly specialized atmosphere merely by using jazz elements."

In the same year that Elmer Bernstein wrote the score for *The Man with the Golden Arm*, film composer Leonard Rosenman wrote the first feature-film score utilizing the classic twelve-tone compositional technique of Arnold Schoenberg (although his fine score for the Haskell Wexler film *The Savage Eye* is very definitely atonal). By 1955 Leonard Rosenman had already written one feature film score for director Elia Kazan, for the film *East of Eden*.

The film in which Rosenman employs serial techniques is *The Cobweb*. Rosenman's choice of this particular idiom was not arbitrary. He says his choice was not motivated "simply because I felt it was important to write a serial score. I felt that the film really could have used this kind of treatment. I also felt that it would have set off the film as not simply a potboiler melodrama which happened to center around an insane asylum but rather a film in which this kind of expressionistic music could be, so to speak, mind reading or, as I say, super-real." By that, Rosenman explains, "I simply mean it was not naturalistic. It was my intention not to 'ape' or mimic the physical aspect of the screen *mise en scène* but it was more my intention to show what was going on inside characters' heads."

Rosenman points out that he felt that the function of the atonal score to *The Cobweb* "would be to enter the plot and show something that wasn't immediately perceived on the screen and to try to create a kind of atmosphere that was, in my opinion, conspicuously lacking in the movie. The movie was a very refined and very slick and very well produced film. But I wanted more neurosis; much more of the inner workings of the people which, I think, were a bit lacking in the overt action of the film."

Rosenman accomplished this with a series of motifs using twelve-tone techniques. While he used a large orchestra of 55-60 players for two or three tuttis, the film's music, for the most part, consists of small ensembles treated in a kind of chamber character. It should also be pointed out that the serial techniques employed by Rosenman controlled only the pitches and not other elements in the score. The distinction is important since total serialization was rather popular at that time in the concert world.

The Main Title music to *The Cobweb* is of interest. The music is a kind of piano concerto, whose creation grew out of Rosenman's interest at that

FILM MUSIC

Figure 11. Excerpt from *The Cobweb,* music by Leonard Rosenman.

time in the Schoenberg *Piano Concerto*. Rosenman recalls: "The problem of writing a piece which featured the piano interested me academically because I had just heard, for the first time, the Schoenberg *Piano Concerto* and I was tremendously involved with that piece. As a matter of fact, I taught a seminar in it at that time. I was interested in exploring the whole process of doubling between the piano and orchestra."

A short example from *The Cobweb* Main Title demonstrates, although by no means thoroughly, this process of doubling between the piano and orchestra. The piano is "on mike," or miked separately from other sections of the orchestra. This allows the recording mixer to have total control over the balance between the piano and orchestra. Note in Figure 11 that as the piano enters on the third beat of measure 23, it is doubled by one bassoon. The piano is then joined, on the fourth beat of the same measure, by the clarinets and one horn. This is but one example in this Main Title of the doubling process.

Another point in the Main Title provides one of the most important motivic elements in the score. This material (Figure 12) begins at a dramatically appropriate point: as the title of the film *The Cobweb* comes up on the screen. This motivic idea is stated in the violins, clarinets, oboes, flutes, and piccolo, a rather intense, piercing texture. This particular motive goes through many permutations throughout the score. Two short examples from other cues in the film show Rosenman's use of this motive for entirely different dramatic situations. The first of these examples, Figure 13, occurs early in the film when one of the patients of the mental hospital is undergoing analysis. This example is interesting not only for its development of the original motivic idea, but for its demonstration, once again, of Rosenman's frequent and effective use of the polyphonic devices—in this case, imitation. In addition, the expressionistic quality of the music adds much to a scene that is relatively neutral emotionally. Also note the sparse instrumentation, representative of the "chamber music" quality of the score alluded to by Rosenman. It should be emphasized again that this kind of writing in Hollywood films was utterly without precedent, so much so that Rosenman recalls that he and those musicians working with him on the film were absolutely certain the score would be thrown out by the producers and director. This, fortunately, did not turn out to be the case at all.

The last example from *The Cobweb* is a portion of a music cue used behind a scene wherein Stevie and Sue, two of the patients who are main

Figure 12. Excerpt from *The Cobweb*, music by Leonard Rosenman.

Figure 13. Excerpt from *The Cobweb*.

characters in the film, embrace. While the music is quiet and understated, the predominant dissonant character is still letting us know that these two individuals have troublesome problems within themselves—an example of Rosenman showing "what was going on inside characters' heads."

Figure 14. Excerpt from *The Cobweb,* music by Leonard Rosenman.

In addition to the pop-song craze, the 1950s also saw a rash of biblical spectaculars coming out of Hollywood. The series began with *Quo Vadis?* (1951; score by Miklos Rozsa) and went on to include *The Robe* (1953; score by Alfred Newman), *The Ten Commandments* (1956; score by Elmer Bernstein), the 1959 remake of *Ben-Hur* (score by Miklos Rozsa) and the 1961 epic *King of Kings* (score by Miklos Rozsa). All of these productions were sumptuous spectacles and usually had characters as large as Macy's parade floats. The biblical spectacular was of course not new to

Hollywood. The concept of lavish productions based on religious material (almost always Christian) can be traced all the way back through the silent era. The silent era had produced such epics as *The Ten Commandments* (1923), *The King of Kings* (1927), and *Ben Hur* (1925).

It is logical to ask why there was this sudden influx and interest in religious epics. Probably the foremost reason, as stated earlier, was that Hollywood was feeling the financial pinch created by television and by the Supreme Court's ruling against it in the Justice Department's antitrust suit. Creating large and lavish religious productions might help bring audiences back into the theaters. It was also the era of the Cold War and the blacklist, an era of almost frenzied conservatism. It was an era when just about any subject dealt with in Hollywood films was viewed by the Communist-hunters as possible subversive material. *Esquire* critic John C. Moffitt, for example, saw "picture after picture in which the banker is represented as an unsympathetic man, who hates to give a GI loan." This was an oblique reference to the film *The Best Years of Our Lives,* which explored the problems experienced by returning veterans. It was a time when the Legion of Decency condemned the rather harmless bedroom farce, *Forever Amber.* It was an era when films displaying a social conscience, such as *Force of Evil* and *Johnny O'Clock* were out, and films like *I Was a Communist for the FBI* were in. All of this could only breed an atmosphere of fear in the Hollywood community and, perhaps subconsciously, the filmmakers supposed that only religious subjects were safe.

It is not easy to score a religious epic. The task is compounded if the focal point of the picture is Christianity or even Christ himself. If the composer is to produce a worthwhile score, he must have some feeling for the picture and its subject matter. He is also going to have to produce some sort of musical equivalent for either the concept or the personality of Christ. The difficulties are redoubled when, as is usually the case, any true religious feelings or concepts are subordinated to the more salable commodities of color and spectacle. It is usually understood from the beginning that color and spectacle will dominate the picture; films are, first and foremost, a commercial enterprise, and filmmakers are obliged to make certain concessions to popular taste. The composer's problem is that he is usually limited in his choice of style—the lush romantic style is the only musical style able to match the color and splendor of the decor of such films.

Another factor involved in the scoring of religious epics is the assumed need for the music to denote time and place. This is more of a problem than it might first appear, since it is not easy for the composer to avoid cliché. It is compounded with a musically insensitive producer. Miklos Rozsa, for example, was asked to use *Adeste Fideles* for the nativity scene in *Ben-Hur*. He had to threaten to leave the picture before the idea was dropped.

Rozsa's score for *Quo Vadis?* is probably the best of the group of religious epics produced in that ten-year time span. Rozsa took infinite care in his research for music of the period—more care than anyone had taken in the past or has taken since. He was determined to make the music stylistically as correct as possible while still serving the film dramatically. "As the music for *Quo Vadis?* was intended for dramatic use and as entertainment for the lay public," he said, "one had to avoid the pitfall of producing only musicological oddities instead of music with a universal, emotional appeal. For the modern ear, instrumental music in unison has very little emotional appeal; therefore I had to find a way for an archaic sounding harmonisation which would give warmth, colour and emotional value to these melodies."

For the music to be performed on scene in the film, Rozsa supervised the construction of replicas of ancient instruments. Blueprints of the instruments were drawn up using sources such as Roman statues, antique vases, and bas-reliefs on columns and tombstones. Italian instrument makers constructed the instruments so that they bore an amazing likeness to the real ones and added considerably to the authenticity of the scenes in which they were used.

There are essentially three distinguishable styles of music for the film *Quo Vadis?* The first style is the one used in the music for the Romans. The songs of Nero, the sacrificial hymn used by the Vestals, and the marches and fanfares were all done in this style. Here Rozsa encountered a rather severe problem: no music of the Romans has survived. His solution was a process of deduction, based on the tremendous influence of the Greeks on Roman culture. Since the Romans copied Greek sculpture, poetry, painting, and pottery, it was logical to assume that they copied their music as well. Rozsa chose to base his music for the Romans on Greek examples. With the music of the Greeks the musicologist is on firmer ground, for there is a considerable amount of knowledge concerning Greek music; in fact, the theories of Pythagoras are still valid today. There are several examples of Greek music in existence, such as the "Skolion of Seikilos" (Figure 15). This example of Greek music, dating from around 150 B.C., became the basic idea from which Rozsa developed Nero's first song in the film.

Figure 15. "The Skolion of Seikilos."

The second musical style in *Quo Vadis?* is that of the hymns used for the early Christians. This music also had to be reconstructed through deduction since there are no known examples of music used by early Christians. For this style Rozsa utilized a Gregorian anthem, "Omnes sitientos venite ad aquas," as his point of departure. This particular example (Figure 16) appeared about 400 years after the period depicted in the film. Rozsa also deduced that since the early Christians were partly Jews and partly Greeks, their liturgical music more than likely originated from those sources.

Figure 16. Gregorian anthem, "Omnes sitientos venite ad aquas."

The third category of music in *Quo Vadis?* is that used for the slaves. Slaves of the era were Babylonians, Syrians, Egyptians, Persians, and inhabitants of other nations conquered by the Romans. Most of these nations were Oriental, so Rozsa went to their ancient music in an attempt to evolve a style for the film. He found fragments of old music in Sicily that displayed an Arabian influence, and other ancient fragments in Cairo. He used both in the film. One of these examples, the first "Ode of Pindar" (Figure 17), Rozsa says, "was allegedly found in a Sicilian monastery in 1650. Its authenticity is doubtful, but it is constructed entirely on Greek principles and it is a hauntingly beautiful melody."

Figure 17. "Ode of Pindar."

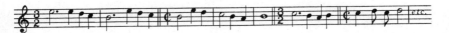

These attempts at stylistic authenticity, tempered by dramatic necessity, were not without their problems, however. Critic Lawrence Morton comments: "I thought it rather curious that the composer sometimes found his way from the conceivably authentic idiom of pagan Rome to the more familiar idiom of medieval Europe. Some of Lygia's music, for instance, suggests *faux bourdon* and the medieval modes. I mention this not as a criticism, for I did not find it in the least bit objectionable, but only as a problem of musical style. Authenticity from the musicological point of view is of course impossible, at least until musicologists discover more than they presently know about Roman music. Cinematically, such authenticity would probably not even be desirable.... Now while I thought it curious ... that Rozsa found his way to an idiom suggesting the medieval, I thought it no less curious that in one scene, that of the street fight between the giant Ursus and the Gladiator Croton, he found his way to an almost modern, twentieth-century idiom. To my ears there was some inconsistency in this."

Another problem for Rozsa was the orchestration of the music that was to appear on scene. Since none of the old instruments were available, Rozsa had to find a modern instrument that might be roughly equivalent to the ancient one. Rozsa used a small Scottish harp, the Clarsach, a "delicate instrument [that] gave a remarkably true likeness to the sound of the lyre and antique harp." This is an interesting observation, since no one knows what the lyre and antique harp sounded like. Perhaps Rozsa should have said, "what the lyre and antique harp *probably* sounded like." In these sequences involving on-scene music, Rozsa avoided using romantic (and hence, chromatic) harmonizations but instead used simple modal harmonizations that more closely caught the character of the music.

In an article entitled "Music in the Hollywood Biblical Spectacular," author Christopher Palmer makes an observation that is misleading, at best, and bears comment. Mr. Palmer is probably correct, in part, when he says that "Rozsa's music is grounded in Magyar folk song." But then Mr. Palmer goes on to say that because Rozsa's music is grounded in the Magyar folk song, it "has a bearing on the enormous success of his scores for *Quo Vadis?* and the later super-spectacles *Ben-Hur* and *King of Kings*. For, melodically speaking, the roots of Hungarian peasant song are in the modes and the pentatonic scale, its predominant intervals are the fourth and fifth and therefore suggest a harmonic treatment derived from these intervals, i.e. parallel chords of superimposed fourths and fifths. Now these are precisely the means whereby an atmosphere of antiquity may be conjured up for Western ears; and, furthermore, there is an element of exotic decoration endemic to Hungarian and all East European folksong which can also lend itself quite readily to an evocation of the Orient of the Ancients. So there was no need for Rozsa consciously to assume an archaic-sounding idiom; the prerequisites were already inherent in his own style. This gives the *Quo Vadis?* score a certain ring of *inner* authenticity as opposed to the *outer* authenticity in which Rozsa's manifold and time-consuming musical researches resulted."

This observation can only be characterized as pop musicology. If we carried Mr. Palmer's too-broad observation to its logical end we would have to conclude that the music of Bartók, another composer whose music has strong Hungarian peasant song influences, contains "precisely the means whereby an atmosphere of antiquity may be conjured up for Western ears." Bartók's music can hardly be regarded as having "an atmosphere of antiquity." Palmer also makes the mistake of confusing *mode* with *scale*. While it is true that scales since the time of Bach have certain harmonic tendencies inherent in their intervallic makeup, modes used by the Greeks were numerous, and their emotional impact was derived from their subtle differences in intervallic structure, or sequences of whole steps and half-steps, not their harmonic implications. This only became the case in the late seventeenth century, with the advent of equal-tempered tuning. Moreover, the pentatonic scale Palmer refers to is really a westernized prostitution of Oriental music; Oriental music has never been harmonically oriented.

Palmer also does Rozsa a disservice by suggesting that the research conducted by him was unnecessary. It is well known in film-music circles that Rozsa's meticulous research for *Quo Vadis?* did not result in other composers' scoring period epics using the same scholarly methods. What Palmer overlooks is that Rozsa set a *style* of composition for religious epics which was to influence other composers dealing with films about the same period. In fact, considering the musical naïveté of film audiences of the time, just about *anything* Rozsa could have written for *Quo Vadis?* would have been "precisely the means whereby an atmosphere of antiquity may be conjured up for Western ears." By his painstaking research, Rozsa at least established a style for such films that was emulated by other composers, which had some basis of authenticity.

More than any other director in the early 1950s, Elia Kazan was responsible for bringing first-rate composers to Hollywood to score his films. In 1951 he brought in Alex North from New York to score *A Streetcar Named Desire*. In 1955 he employed Leonard Rosenman to compose the music for *East of Eden*. Both North and Rosenman have remained in Hollywood and developed substantial reputations based on their fine work in later films. In 1954, however, Kazan called upon the considerable talents of Leonard Bernstein * to create the music for his then latest Marlon Brando vehicle, *On The Waterfront*. The collaboration was less than successful, for while *On The Waterfront* is highly regarded among film historians and theoreticians, the music which accompanies it has several serious flaws. Indeed, the music for this film is discussed here only because of its popularity in film classes and the mistaken idea that, because the multitalented Leonard Bernstein composed it, the score is a brilliant example of film music at its best. Unfortunately, the contrary is true. Bernstein's lack of experience in the area of film composition tends to destroy the effect, in terms of the picture, of what is some very beautiful music. However, the same material as *film music,* becomes, in many places, intrusive and inept-sounding from a dramatic standpoint.

In the opening sequence of the film, for example, the sound track is filled with a crescendo of frantic percussion figures, but the visual merely shows some men coming from a dockside building toward an automobile. The music here is obviously intended to be asynchronous with the picture, speaking as it does to the violent personalities of the men shown on the screen. Without any foreknowledge of the characters of these men, however, the music is confusing rather than enlightening.

---

* No relation to film composer Elmer Bernstein.

Another example of Bernstein's lack of experience in this area occurs when the longshoremen, who have been meeting in a church, are beaten up as they leave the meeting. The music for this sequence is a highly rhythmical brass figure. Moreover, Bernstein made no attempt to write around the dialogue, with the result that his music is repeatedly turned down in volume every time there is a line and then turned back up again until the next line. The dubber had no choice here since the lines had to be heard and, had the music been left at one setting, it would have completely covered the lines.

In defense of Leonard Bernstein, it should be brought out that one of the most inept-sounding music cues in the entire film was a result of Kazan's postproduction decisions rather than a lack of dramatic understanding on Bernstein's part. The scene referred to is the one where Terry (Marlon Brando) asks the girl (Eva Marie Saint) to have a beer with him. Bernstein, in *The Joy of Music,* explains that the scene "was deliberately underwritten, and there are long, Kazan-like pauses between the lines—an ideal spot, it would seem, for the composer to take over. I suggested that here I should write love music that was shy at first and then, with growing, *Tristanish* intensity, come to a great climax which swamps the scene and the screen, even drowning out the last prosaic bits of dialogue, which went something like this: 'Have a beer with me?' (Very long pause) 'Uh-huh.' The music here was to do the real storytelling, and Kazan and company agreed enthusiastically, deciding to do it this way before even one note was written. So it was written, so orchestrated, so recorded.

"But then [in the dubbing room], Kazan decided he just couldn't give up that ineffably sacred grunt which Brando emits at the end: it was, he thought, perhaps the two most eloquent syllables the actor had delivered in the whole script. And what happens to the music? As it mounts to its greatest climax, as the theme goes higher and higher and brasses and percussion join in with the strings and woodwinds, the all-powerful control dials are turned, and the sound fades out in a slow diminuendo."

But Bernstein demonstrates his misunderstanding of film music's function when he says, "sometimes the music would be turned off completely for some seconds to allow a line to stand forth stark and bare—and then be turned on again. Sometimes the music, which had been planned as a composition with a beginning, middle and end, would be silenced seven bars before the end."

This last statement, that the music had been planned "as a composition with a beginning, middle and end," is perhaps the most illuminating when discussing the problems and weaknesses of this score. A composition that has a "beginning, middle and end" implies a composition of a highly linear quality. As pointed out in the chapter on aesthetics, however, most linear music is unsuited to films for it competes with the dramatic action by drawing too much attention to itself. The "love" theme, shown in Figure 18, for example, is a very lovely melody that is played behind several scenes between the two protagonists of the film. This in itself would not be damaging to the film if it were not that one gets the feeling, when watching the film, that Bernstein is going to state the *entire* melody during a scene regardless of what is going on up on the screen. This gives the material an unwanted linear quality that it might not have had had it been handled by a more experienced film composer.

Figure 18. Excerpt from *On the Waterfront,* music by Leonard Bernstein.

Two of the nicest scenes musically occur respectively very early in the film and at the close. The first, Figure 19, entitled "Roof Morning," is a gentle piece of color playing behind a scene between Brando and a young boy as they walk on a rooftop. The second, Figure 20, called merely "Walk and End Title," begins as Terry begins his walk after fighting with

Johnny Friendly (Lee J. Cobb). The other longshoremen have agreed to work only if Terry does and, although severely beaten, he drags himself up to the docks in his own effort to free his compatriots from their crooked union leaders. The music here is absolutely heroic, as it should be, and is so effective that it nearly redeems many of the bad musical moments that seem to predominate in this film.

In 1960 director Alfred Hitchcock made his first "horror" film, *Psycho*. The composer of the unusual score to this film was Bernard Herrmann. Herrmann's association with Hitchcock had begun in 1955 when Herrmann had provided the music for Hitchcock's *The Trouble With Harry*. Thereafter, Herrmann provided scores to *The Man Who Knew Too Much* (1956), *The Wrong Man* (1957), *Vertigo* (1958), and *North by Northwest* (1959). Composer/orchestrator Fred Steiner is probably correct in writing, "No other composer up to that time . . . had so successfully captured, in music, the special Hitchcock mood: a blend of mystery, suspense, the sardonic, and the romantic."

The most notable departure from film-music convention in Herrmann's score to *Psycho* is the exclusive use of a string orchestra throughout the film.* It introduced some additional problems for Herrmann, not the least of which was the limited amount of orchestral color available with that particular ensemble. It also eliminated the possibility of using many of the tried-and-true musical formulas and effects that were considered more or less essential to a suspense-horror film.

In utilizing a string orchestra Herrmann finally brought to the Hollywood film the idea that strings can have an extremely cold and piercing sound. For so many years Hollywood saw strings primarily as creating warmth and vibrancy. Herrmann reinforced his notion when he said, in a 1971 interview, that he used only strings in his score to *Psycho* in order to "complement the black and white photography of the film with a black and white sound."

In the brief analysis that follows I am indebted to Fred Steiner, whose

---

* Much has been made of this fact by aficionados of film music, who have even gone so far as to say that it is the first instance of extensive use of strings alone being used for a film. This observation is not true for as early as 1954, composer David Raksin, for the film *Suddenly*, used an orchestra consisting of four horns, two percussion, and thirty-two strings. There were many sequences for strings alone, the most notable one being a scherzo.

Figure 19. Excerpt from *On the Waterfront*, music by Leonard Bernstein.

Figure 20. Excerpt from *On the Waterfront,* music by Leonard Bernstein.

analysis of the score to *Psycho* appeared originally in his doctoral dissertation and later in the publication, *Elmer Bernstein's Filmmusic Collection.*

Figure 21 contains the opening music to the film and aptly demonstrates Herrmann's motivic approach to composition. In this he has always been consistent. Most of the time the results of this approach, as used by Herrmann, have been brilliant but occasionally it can be taxing. One of Herrmann's lesser efforts in his motivic approach to film scoring is

Figure 21. Excerpt from *Psycho,* music by Bernard Herrmann.

the Main Title music to the 1959 film, *North by Northwest,* wherein the principal motif is repeated ad infinitum and the listener is saved from acute boredom only by the ever-changing orchestral colors. This is, however, the exception. In his orchestrations Herrmann is brilliant, although, as pointed out earlier, his claim to being the only composer working in films who does his own orchestrations is patently untrue.

Figure 21, containing the music that opens under the titles, also states the first principal motive, Motive A. The constant, hard-driving motion of this Main Title music anticipates the primary emotion of the first part of *Psycho:* Marion's fear, verging on panic, during her lengthy flight with the money she has stolen from the realtor's office. Motive A appears in various metamorphoses throughout the score; one example is Figure 22. Here the motive is in a low register, with the second note changed, while the ostinato figure continues above it.

Figure 22. Excerpt from *Psycho.*

A secondary motive, Motive B, is shown in Figure 23. Here the ostinato is momentarily dropped and replaced by a contrasting dotted figure.

Figure 23. Excerpt from *Psycho.*

A third motive, Motive C, is, compared to the previous material, a substantial contrast to the rest of the material. Fred Steiner, in his fine analysis of this score, points out that this particular motive "is the only motive in the entire film which might be thought of as a tune. It imparts a brief hint of lyricism (although the ostinato continues underneath); a strange moment of relief in the midst of all the nervous, fearful, forward motion." This feeling does not last even though this motive appears three times in the Main Title sequence. Herrmann always drops the idea quickly and never develops it in any way.

Figure 24. Excerpt from *Psycho,* music by Bernard Herrmann.

Another example (Figure 25), not only shows further development of Motive A, but Herrmann's subtle dramatic sense as well. Herrmann's title for this cue, "Temptation," refers to the money which Marion steals from her employer in an effort to find happiness with her lover, Sam. This material appears later on in the film when she buys a used car, and again after her arrival at the Bates Motel. Musicians should note the derivative of Motive A in the inner parts (sixteenth notes). The motive appears here in retrograde motion, and the major third changes to a minor third. The outer parts, consisting of whole and dotted half notes, become somewhat important in later scenes and always contain the same dynamic marking of crescendo-decrescendo.

Figure 25. Excerpt from *Psycho*.

In the cue entitled "The Madhouse" (Figure 26), a new leitmotiv is introduced that is associated with Norman and his relationship with his mother. The leitmotiv (F, E-flat, D) is seen in the cellos and basses at the very beginning of the example and then is developed extensively, undergoing many subtle and ingenious changes in the process. In detecting these changes one must admit inversion, retrograde motion, and enharmonic changes; they are indicated in the example with brackets. As Fred Steiner points out about this cue, "this is quiet, unobtrusive, but unsettling music, and as it progresses, we get the first feeling that all is not what it appears to be at the Bates motel." Certain portions of this music

Figure 26. Excerpt from *Psycho*.

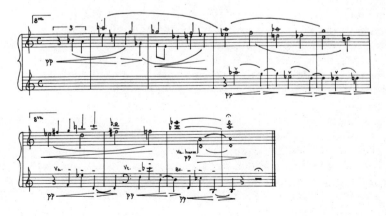

will be used again later in the film: when the detective Arbogast arrives at
the motel for the second time, intending to interview Mrs. Bates; and in
the final sequence when Norman Bates, now the "mother," assures the
audience that she "wouldn't even harm a fly."

Figure 27, "The Peephole," is used behind the scene in which Norman
watches Marion undress, and is a development of the minor second idea
from the previous cue. An interesting musical event occurs in measure 14
of this example: there is a sudden change in both register and dynamics.
The violins suddenly shift to their highest extremity and the dynamics
change to a much greater intensity. Steiner points out the significance of
this shift: "This new effect is unsettling, almost terrifying—like an inner
cry of anger. Norman's face may betray no emotion as he watches Marion
undressing, but here the music subtly suggests the thoughts that must be
flickering through the voyeur's mind." Again one sees the dramatic value
of music running counter to what is depicted on the screen. This
particular cue, in addition, demonstrates Herrmann's inventiveness utilizing a minimum of material. This cue runs more than three minutes and is
based solely on two simple elements: an ostinato and a two-note motive.

Figure 27. Excerpt from *Psycho,* music by Bernard Herrmann.

The next cue we shall look at, one of the most interesting in the film, plays behind the famous murder scene in a shower. Figure 28 contains the deceptively simple-looking music. As Steiner observes: "What could be more primitive in appearance—even naïve—than these reiterated, dissonant, sharp downbow strokes, and the wild glissandos starting in measure 9." The brutality of this sound is heightened by the wide spacing of the diminished octaves and major sevenths, the placing of the notes in the higher registers of the instruments, and the reverberation that was added to the sound track.

It is interesting to note that the music for this scene was not included in the original plans for the score. In his *Filmguide to Psycho,* James Naremore states that "Herrmann says that when he first saw *Psycho* he was told *not* to compose music for the stabbings. Only later, when Hitchcock felt disappointed with the finished film, was the stunning murder music added. Hitchcock, needless to say, was delighted."

Steiner says of this particular sequence that "the effect that Herrmann has created is unique and hair-raising; there is nothing quite like it in the history of film scoring."

Unfortunately the glissando effects shown here have created some confusion. In his fine book *Understanding Movies,* Louis D. Giannetti evidences some of this confusion by discussing these glissando effects under the heading of "Sound Effects." Having incorrectly established these glissandos as "sound effects," Giannetti then compounds his error: "In Hitchcock's *Psycho,* the sound effects of shrill bird noises are used for transitions, for associations, for characterization, and for thematic purposes. A shy and appealing young man (Anthony Perkins) is associated with birds early in the film: he stuffs various birds as a hobby, and his own features are intense and rather hawklike. Later in the film, when a brutal murder is committed, the sound track plays shrill music mixed with bird screeches. The audience assumes the murderer is the boy's mother, but the bird noises have been associated with the boy. One of Hitchcock's recurrent themes is the transference of guilt. In this film, the transfer is rather complex: the boy has dug up his long-dead mother's body and 'stuffed' it. Often he dresses himself up in her clothes. While the audience thinks it sees the mother killing two victims, it has in fact seen the schizophrenic boy as his other self—his mother. The sound effects of the bird noises offer early clue to this psychological transference."

The "bird screeches" Giannetti speaks of are, of course, nothing more

Figure 28. Excerpt from *Psycho*, music by Bernard Herrmann.

than glissandos on the violins. While one might associate the sound of the string glissando with bird screeches, there is no evidence whatsoever that Bernard Herrmann or Alfred Hitchcock intended such an association to be made. Giannetti's observations and correlations, however interesting, are probably less than valid since they are based on an incorrect assumption.

The final cue from *Psycho* discussed here, the "Finale," is used under the last scenes in the picture. Norman Bates, now the "mother," talks to the audience while the camera holds on a close-up of Norman's face; for a moment there is an almost subliminal superimposition of Mother's mummified face on that of Norman's. Then, as the cellos and basses pronounce the leitmotiv refered to earlier (measures 17–18 of Figure 29), "the picture dissolves to the final grisly shot of Marion's car being pulled out of the black muck of the swamp. The picture fades out on a low, heavy, acidulous dissonance in the massed strings—a chord without resolution, a finale without an ending.

A year after the release of *Psycho,* another film composer, Henry Mancini, was to have his first big success in films. Mancini had created a sensation in television with his music for the 1958 series *Peter Gunn.* The 1961 film that proved so successful for Mancini was *Breakfast at Tiffany's.* The title song, "Moon River," has become firmly established in the American pop-music repertoire. It is a position the song well deserves. The effect of the success of the song, however, was to add more reinforcement to the already prevalent argument that what every picture needed was a pop song to accompany it that would, if the producers were lucky, "make the ·charts." With *Breakfast at Tiffany's* we find, as we did

Figure 29. Excerpt from *Psycho,* music by Bernard Herrmann.

with Raksin's *Laura,* Tiomkin's *High Noon,* and later with the Simon and Garfunkel songs for *The Graduate,* that the pop song concept works *in this film.* A close look at the film will reveal that Mancini uses the song, with or without lyrics, only about four times throughout the film. These uses include the Main Title, the time when Audrey Hepburn sings a small portion of it, and then at the very end where it aids substantially in the film's dramatic climax. It is the sparing use of "Moon River" that makes the song so effective in the film. As a contrast to this sensitive use of a theme, one might look to Maurice Jarre's score for *Dr. Zhivago* where his banal "Lara's Theme" grinds on interminably and loses any of its dramatic impact by the end of the first third of the film. *

The song "Moon River" also seems to serve as a kind of gentle character sketch for the film's main character, Holly Golightly (Audrey Hepburn) who, underneath her city sophistication, still has some of the simpleness of the country girl she once was. The simplicity of the song "Moon River" obviously catches this aspect of her character. The song's simplicity is in contrast to all of the other music in the film, which is of a highly sophisticated, polished nature. Most of the other music in the film, incidentally, is not "dramatic" per se; instead, it is either source music or music of a rather light, ironic quality. All of this is in dramatic contrast to the use of the theme "Moon River," which is strategically placed in some of the most moving scenes in the film.

The song "The Days of Wine and Roses," written for the 1962 film of the same name, is a good deal less effective in the film than "Moon River." In *The Days of Wine and Roses* the use of the song in what is essentially a dramatic film seems only a self-conscious attempt on the part of Mancini to repeat his earlier success with "Moon River."

By the mid-1960s the pop-song concept for musical accompaniment for films had settled into Hollywood mainstream thinking. The sound-track album from the film *A Hard Day's Night* made a profit estimated at $2 million for United Artists Corporation by mid-1966. The album's profit represented more than three times the cost of the film itself ($580,000). The use of film music even found its way into advertising with Marlboro Cigarettes paying United Artists "a sum which runs into six figures" for the right to use several bars of music from Elmer Bernstein's *Magnificent Seven* score. The sound-track album of Maurice Jarre's score for *Dr. Zhivago* sold over two million copies and spent seventy weeks on the charts.

By this time bitterness and controversy had understandably set in among Hollywood composers. Jerry Goldsmith, whose fine score to *Patton* is regarded as a substantial achievement, claimed that "The idea is to get a piece that's exploitable and the hell with the drama." Veteran

---

* In fairness to Maurice Jarre, it should be pointed out that he was not responsible for this. The producer, during the production of the film, became so enamored of Jarre's "Lara's Theme" that he threw out much of Jarre's other music for the film and substituted the music of "Lara's Theme."

Max Steiner mourned in 1966 that "Composition is a highly developed art that's now dominated by young men who can only hum a tune." The brilliant Bernard Herrmann simply left town and moved to a more appreciative England, where he scored potboiler horror films such as *Sisters* (1973) and *It's Alive* (1974). His untimely death late in 1975, immediately after completing the score to *Taxi Driver*, was a keenly-felt loss among his colleagues in the industry.

Matters became worse in 1968 with the success of the film *The Graduate*, which contained a string of Simon and Garfunkel pop tunes. Now, it seemed, not one pop tune was enough; there must be a *collection* of pop tunes which, incidentally, create a nice record album. It so happened, as we have seen in the past, that the concept of a series of pop tunes used to accompany the various surrealistic montage sequences in *The Graduate* worked very well aesthetically, but the success of the picture and the accompanying sound track created a host of musical imitators.

This is not to say that there were no significant scores being written during the 1960s. Indeed, this period produced a score that is an unheralded masterpiece. Unfortunately, David Raksin's score for the 1966 film *The Redeemer* is married to a movie so weak in all of its other aspects that the music will probably never receive the critical attention it so richly deserves.

This score is, in my opinion, the finest ever written for a religious picture. *The Redeemer* was produced by the Family Theatre, a film-production arm of the Catholic Church. The film, which is about the last days of Christ, was made in Spain and was originally produced in the form of fifteen half-hour television programs. The film uses Spanish actors, although scenes were shot in both Spanish and English; the Spanish actors learned their English dialogue phonetically. The film was eventually dubbed in a number of other languages. At this writing, *The Redeemer* has never been released as a commercial venture in the United States.

Raksin accepted the job of scoring *The Redeemer* under rather unusual conditions and, it might be added, conditions not often achieved by film composers. Film composers seldom have any say concerning the content of a film they score but, in this case, Raksin was able to exert some influence over certain areas of content. Raksin recalled that "somebody talked the Family Theatre into thinking they could make a movie out of the television segments. I think it was put together at Twentieth Century-

Fox, and they had a score written for it, but the score turned out badly and, as I understand it, the picture turned out to be a mess. So they gave up the whole thing until somebody decided they couldn't have all of that money invested in the film without getting some back. They then brought in a very, very remarkable woman named Maria Luisa DeTeña. She is a Spanish aristocratic woman who became a nun in an order called the Secular Missionaries. She was an incredible woman—fabulously well read and travelled. She came in, and they put the picture together in a different form with the aid of a different cutter. They then started shopping around for a composer. They tried various people but there was nobody there they really wanted. Finally, they asked me to come and look at it.

"I went in and I wasn't sure I wanted to do it because I thought the film was simply a restatement of ancient canards concerning the Jews. I thought it was ridiculous to pretend, on the one hand, that they were being ecumenical and then repeat the old lies. When I said that I couldn't make up my mind whether I wanted to participate in that kind of thing, most of the people in the screening room were horrified, except Maria Luisa. She said she wanted to hear more about it, so I said that if the purpose of the picture was to reconvert the faithful they could leave it the way it was. If not, they had better do some things to it. So they agreed to various suggestions which I made which point out clearly that Caiaphas was not just another 'dirty Jew.' He was a man who was acting because, socially, he was threatened—his whole class was threatened—by Jesus, who happened to be another Jew. If they're going to blame Caiaphas on the Jews, why don't they 'blame' Jesus on the Jews as well?"

Another production aspect over which Raksin was able to exert some influence was the recording of the score. Raksin recalls: "The Family Theatre tried to persuade Maria Luisa to have me record this score in Spain where, apparently, they could get orchestras for peanuts, or in Chile where the same thing was possible. Now, I would have loved to go abroad, but I was not keen on taking work away from American musicians who were already suffering. But, most of all, I thought it would be cheating *them*, the film makers. I said to them, "Do you realize that it might cost you one third less for the musicians, but the recording facilities will surely be inadequate, and we will not get good music tracks. And we will use up all our money anyhow because the musicians will take three times as long to rehearse and record.

"Well, Maria Luisa was sensible enough to see this, and I was so grateful to her that when, eventually, she got around to doing a series called *Prayer of the Ages,* which were little four-minute films, I wrote nine of them for nothing, which is 36 minutes of music."

Not all aspects of Raksin's relationship with the Family Theatre were pleasant, however. The original agreement between Raksin and the Family Theatre concerning Raksin's score for the film included the stipulation that Raksin would retain publication rights to the score he had provided. Several months after Raksin completed the score to *The Redeemer,* the Family Theatre inquired, in a not altogether conventional manner, if they might not, after all, be given the publication rights to the music for *The Redeemer.* Raksin recalls: "Sometime after I wrote the score I was summoned to the Family Theatre by one Father Albert Heinzer. Father Heinzer is the 'legal eagle' of the Family Theatre. I think we had more than one session, and Father Heinzer, in the presence of other people, had the gall to work me over—and it was some job, including the invoking of 'the Lord's work'—how dare I stand in the way of *the Lord's work?* I felt, you know, that it was really not nice to talk that way to a relative of the deceased who hung on the cross. After all, He was one of *my* antecedents, not one of Father Heinzer's. I thought the whole thing was absurd and, of course, I fought him to a standstill. I said, 'I'm not about to do it. This was a part of our agreement, it's a legitimate part, I'm not depriving you of anything and I don't think you need the money, quite frankly.' Father Heinzer has borne a grudge against me ever since and has made it impossible for me to buy a 16mm print of the film." *

Raksin, unlike Rozsa in his music for *Quo Vadis?,* chose not to attempt to connote time and place with his music. An examination of the score to *The Redeemer* will reveal a definite Baroque flavor, or more directly, a style reminiscent of J. S. Bach. Raksin says: "It was an odd thing. While I was watching the picture I kept hearing music in my head—not specific music—and I realized later that it was as though something was telling me that of all the music I had ever heard concerning Jesus, who is a favorite character of mine, the music of J. S. Bach was the most compassionate. I

---

* When I ordered a 16-mm print of *The Redeemer* I was amazed to hear that about three-fourths of the score on that particular print was music from the original television version. About one-fourth of the music was Raksin's. The End Titles (with all of the credits) had been removed. This is not only highly unethical, but probably legally questionable as well.

was hearing a kind of music like the music of Bach. So when I got around to doing the score I decided to see if I could do it as an homage to Bach, without using any of his music."

Raksin uses various harmonic and rhythmic devices to achieve this quasi-Baroque style including dotted-eighth notes followed by six-teenths—a popular rhythmic figure of the eighteenth century—as well as a good deal of use of the Neapolitan chord. Raksin did, however, deliberately avoid "double-dotting" in slow passages. Also included in these various devices is the "Weinen, Klagen" type of sighing eighth-note accompaniment. A brief examination of the score to *The Redeemer* will also reveal a highly contrapuntal style. While such use of counterpoint would seem to be an absolute necessity in a score attempting homage to J. S. Bach, it is also a comfortable device for Raksin. All of Raksin's scores reveal a generous use of contrapuntal techniques. While counterpoint can be dramatically distracting in a film by drawing too much attention to itself, Raksin is so adept at making the music work dramatically with the film that the complexity is evident only to those who wish to listen for it. There are not, however, any full-fledged fugues, as one might expect, in this score. The primary reason for this is that the linear quality of a fugue makes certain time demands that simply do not coincide with the dramatic demands of the picture.

The score to *The Redeemer* is rich in thematic material. Unlike many of Raksin's other scores, it is nondevelopmental, at least in the sense of the German symphonic tradition. Raksin says, "I tried to do things in the *arioso* style which, rather naïvely stated, is one tune after another."

It should be pointed out that, with the exception of the scene of the crucifixion, there is no fast music in the entire score. This is not too difficult to understand in light of the subject matter of the film. The result is that *The Redeemer* is a marvelously lyrical score and a fine manifestation of Raksin's lyric genius.

An additional problem with doing this score in a Baroque style is the difficulty of fitting quasi-Baroque melodies, which tend to be rather square in terms of their phrasing, into predetermined timings. This problem—of writing music that will synchronize with the picture—is, of course, a common one for the film composer. Raksin explains: "The melodies are all varied as required within individual sequences, with meter signatures of 3/4, 2/4, 5/4, and a few others. This is so that the points are made where necessary (cues are hit at proper times) concerning, for instance, the expression of compassion in a face. And these points are made in the music according to where the tension of the melody is at that moment, or where a new musical event takes place in orchestration or thematic material."

Some of the more important and frequently used thematic material from *The Redeemer* is dealt with below. The first piece of material, Figure 30, is heard in the film's opening. It might be characterized as the main theme, since it is used at moments of greatest consequence, such as the march of Jesus to his place of crucifixion and, very dramatically, at the moment of his death on the cross.

Figure 30. Excerpt from *The Redeemer,* music by David Raksin.

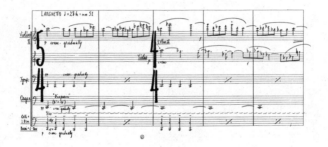

It should be noted that the interval of a minor sixth (C to A-flat) in measure 3 of Figure 30 is sometimes changed to the more dissonant interval of a minor seventh. While within the melody's tonal environment, the interval of a minor sixth is dissonant and requires resolution down to the more stable interval of a perfect fifth (which it does), Raksin saves the minor-seventh interval for only those moments of extreme anguish. This same theme also occurs in canon, as seen in Figure 31.

As sometimes happens, the material shown in Figure 30 was not written specifically for *The Redeemer,* but was initially conceived for another film. Raksin recalls: "I had originally written [the main theme] for another film but they decided to have a completely different kind of score. Subsequently, I gave a producer friend permission to use it as the title theme of a television documentary series. When it came time to do *The Redeemer* I wanted to use this material because it is one of my favorite pieces of music, and seemed so right for the film."

Figure 31. Excerpt from *The Redeemer*.

Another important Baroque device not yet referred to is the use of sequential material. Perhaps one of the most beautiful manifestations of this device in this score is the melody appearing in Figure 32.

Another very important piece of material is a beautiful, lingering melody, much in the style of a vocalise. Like the main theme, this material was also written before Raksin composed the score to *The Redeemer*. This material can be seen in Figure 33. Raksin recalls that he wrote this particular material "on the night of Villa-Lobos' death. I was working on another score to a film, and after I had finished my work I realized something was running around in my head, still unfinished, and so I sat down at the piano wondering what was cooking. Out came this little *aria,* which bears the same relationship to J. S. Bach, I would say, that Villa-Lobos' *Bachianas Brasileiras* does. I called it *A Deus, Villa-Lobos.*"

The fourth piece of prominent thematic material is a little different in character from the previous three in that it has a quality of nobility about

Figure 32. Excerpt from *The Redeemer*, music by David Raksin.

it that contrasts with the pathoslike character of the previous three
melodies. Figure 34 contains this material.

Among small, but interesting, aspects of the score to notice are that
Raksin has used no single reeds in the wind section. Raksin says: "It is a
favorite thing of mine to use double reeds, and I don't just use them in
religious pictures." But in order to cut through the double-reed sound,
Raksin makes use of the Heckelphon, a kind of bass English horn.
Another small point, and one that Raksin is "most pleased with," is the
fact that this religious picture has no "heavenly voices," a point which, in
no small part, adds to the integrity and success of this score. There is one
spot in the film where a lesser composer might have resorted to the
overused device of "heavenly voices:" where Jesus is saying, "I promise
you: This day you will be with Me in paradise." Raksin understates the
moment with the material found in Figure 35.

Note that the cellos, basses, bassoons, and contrabassoon outline a C-

Figure 33. Excerpt from *The Redeemer*.

Figure 34. Excerpt from *The Redeemer*.

major triad in bars 1 and 2 of Figure 35. This C-major triad is stated over the sustained B-minor chord in the rest of the orchestra. The resulting dissonance created by these two keys a minor second away seems to suggest that reality has not left the moment. No flight into other-worldly sounds here. Raksin does not let the agonizing reality of the situation get

Figure 35. Excerpt from *The Redeemer,* music by David Raksin.

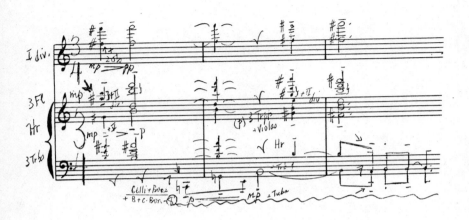

lost in the metaphysics of the moment.

Between December 1, 1971, and February 7, 1972, there was no new motion-picture music written or recorded in Hollywood, because the Composers and Lyricists Guild of America was on strike.

Because the members of the guild could hold out no longer for financial reasons, the composers went back to work—but not without filing suit against the Association of Motion Picture and Television Producers on the day they returned to work. The antitrust action demands settlement of issues dating back to the introduction of sound in motion pictures.

While the dispute covers a number of areas, there are two issues of paramount importance to the film composers. One is the time allowed for a composer to write a score. In the old days a composer was usually given about six weeks to provide a score for a feature film, short enough time in itself. Today, however, with the many low-budget, quickie TV movies or one-hour shows, a composer may be given as little as ten days in which to write and record his score. There are instances of a composer receiving only six days in which to complete forty minutes' worth of music. These kinds of working conditions are what gave rise to the saying in Hollywood about producers' attitudes toward film scores: "They don't want it good, they want it by Thursday."

But the most important issue in the film composer's fight with the producers is the question of copyright ownership. To state it bluntly, film composers do not own their own music. There prevails, in legal circles, the conception that what an artist creates is his. This is not the case in Hollywood, where the studio owns the composers' creative work for its pictures. The ridiculous proportions of the situation are evident in the fact that Twentieth Century-Fox is the "author in fact" of David Raksin's immortal "Laura." Several other examples help illuminate the indignities laid upon the film composers.

In 1971 composer Lalo Schifrin received a request to conduct the music from one of his films in connection with an appearance at a university. He called the studio and asked for the score, but was perfunctorily informed that the music did not belong to him and that if he wanted to play it he would have to rent the music from the studio. Eventually the studio was gracious enough to lend him the music for nothing.

Another well-known film composer, Maurice Jarre, was asked by a major symphony orchestra to conduct his score for *Dr. Zhivago.* Incredible as it may sound, when Jarre asked MGM for the score, he was told that it had been destroyed since MGM needed more storage space.

Film composers are not unaware, of course, of the fact that they do not own what they create for a studio since it is outlined in their contract with the studio.

There have been composers who have had powerful enough reputation to demand half ownership of their music. Henry Mancini, for example, won't do a score for a film unless he gets an interest in the publishing of his own music. Other composers able to demand that right include David Raksin, Burt Bacharach, Leonard Rosenman, and a few others.

Before the Composers and Lyricists Guild's suit was instituted, several producers were ready to compromise on the issues, but one or two studios held out. The problem was compounded when an attorney for the producers said, "When we buy a score, it's as if we are buying a suit of clothes. If we want to hang it in the closet and just leave it there, that's our business." This, as might be expected, did not sit too well with film composers, and the antitrust suit followed.

The composers' position was best expounded by Elmer Bernstein when he stated, "Our position is that what the producers get when they commission a score is the right to use it in that picture, and there it ends.

"We're tired of seeing them take music and lock it up so it can no longer be made available to either the composer or the public."

The suit was eventually settled out of court.

Of the few composers with talent and genius who are extremely active in scoring films today, Jerry Goldsmith must be ranked as one of the most significant contributors in the 1960s and 1970s to the art of film scoring. Goldsmith's creative imagination seems almost boundless, a fact made even more surprising by the Mozartian swiftness with which he produces scores of dramatic significance. His subtle dramatic sense is equaled by only a handful of his colleagues. Like any fine film composer, Goldsmith is aware of the overriding importance of "spotting" music for a film. Goldsmith says, "I think that we are trying to be a little more selective about where the music goes in a film. In the days gone by there seems to have been a liberal sprinkling of music. My preference is that music be used as sparingly as possible. I feel that if there is a constant use of music, or too much music, it will eventually vitiate the needed moments. The music becomes like white sound. It's a little like living in an area that has a high degree of density of traffic noises. Your ear eventually tunes out those frequencies."

On the other hand, however, Goldsmith points out that "the Europeans started a trend in films where it got to be rather *chic* to use no music at all in films. This idea has more or less climaxed in the films of Peter Bogdanovich, which have no formal scores. In *What's Up Doc?*, the leaving out of the element of music, I think, took out a great deal of the humor and a great deal of the relationships between people."

Fortunately, this trend of films *sans* music seems to be changing. Goldsmith has observed that he finds "we are going away from films without scores and this next generation of film directors are suddenly rediscovering the great days of film. These directors seem to now want to go back to the symphonic score again. I think today's filmmakers are realizing that the craftsmen and artists in film 35 or 40 years ago knew what they were doing."

Goldsmith sees his score "as a total piece and not just as a series of sequences. The score is a piece of music. Everything is developed from one piece of material. The most important thing to me is that everything develops out of the initial organic material. All my scores work that way.

If the music has no form, no foundation—no basis from where it came—then why is it there in the first place?" Goldsmith humorously, but truthfully, points out that "this is also one of the problems a composer faces because many producers and directors don't even know why the music is in there in the first place themselves." This problem, of course, is not a new one for screen composers, as we have indicated earlier in the book.

Goldsmith, like Leonard Rosenman, does not hesitate to use a contemporary musical language when it seems appropriate. The excerpt in Figure 36 from the 1974 film *Chinatown,* for example, would seem inappropriate for a film that takes place in the 1930s. Goldsmith's comments on this point are worth quoting, for they point up again the indispensable value of music that is asynchronous with certain physical aspects of a film. Goldsmith observes that *Chinatown* "takes place in the thirties and the producer and director wanted music of that period for underscoring. I told them that I didn't think that that kind of music would be right for the picture in that the visuals already established the setting as 1933 Los Angeles. So I told the producer and director that what we are dealing with in the film are characters and that the time was of little significance. It could be now or 1933." Obviously, Goldsmith's point of view prevailed in this respect, "so that the music in the film is dealing with the relationship of two people as well as providing a certain suspense element. Thematically I tried to write a tune that could have been written during the 1930s [which is first heard in the Main Title] although I orchestrated the tune differently than they would have during those days."

The orchestration of *Chinatown* is interesting for its combination of instruments. Goldsmith recalls that "when I first saw the film *Chinatown* I immediately got a flash as to the orchestral fabric that I wanted. I of course had no idea musically what it was going to be but there was a sound in my mind and I wanted to use strings, 4 pianos, 4 harps, 2 percussion and a trumpet."

It should be pointed out to those with a limited knowledge of music history that all of the instrumental devices seen in Figure 36 have been in the composer's repertoire for a number of years. However, historical precedent is of little importance here since such instrumental devices (plucking the strings of the piano, etc.) are really only a means to an end; using them does not make one an outstanding composer. With Gold-

FILM MUSIC

Figure 36. Excerpt from *Chinatown*, music by Jerry Goldsmith.

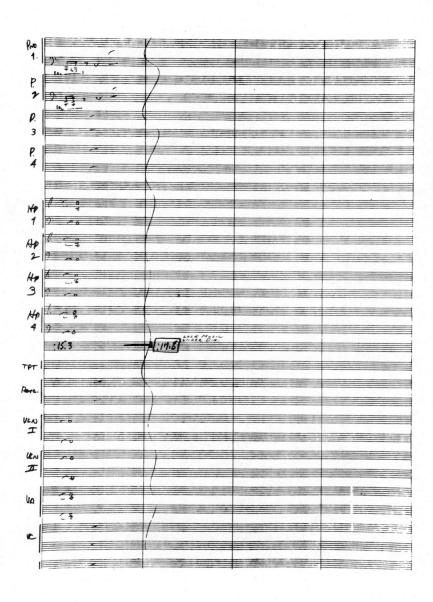

smith, such devices are simply tools with which he creates some very effective and satisfying music. This, of course, must be the final question, after all of the analysis of a work is finished: Is it good music? With Goldsmith, it invariably is.

By way of contrast, as well as a demonstration of Goldsmith's remarkable versatility, is his score to the 1975 film *The Wind and the Lion*. Like Raksin's score for the 1948 film *Forever Amber*, Goldsmith's score is one of a handful of great scores created for large-scale romantic adventures since the days of Erich Korngold.

The Wind and the Lion is a sweeping action drama starring Sean Connery and Candice Bergen. A film of this type of course demanded an entirely different kind of score from the more intimate *Chinatown*. The results are a rich and varied symphonic texture that remains interesting throughout the film. Goldsmith captures the element of place through the use of Moroccan rhythms and scales, which are altered only to the extent of making them playable on Western instruments. There are several places where the use of the percussion alone, or as a featured section of the orchestra, emphasizes these Moroccan rhythms. Figure 37 shows an instance late in the film. This percussion solo plays under a scene where one of the film's main characters, Raisuli (Sean Connery), is attempting to escape from his German captors and is fighting with a German officer.

As to melodic material with a Moroccan flavor, one extended melodic idea is used frequently throughout the score, nearly always behind scenes of great physical action. A portion of this material can be found in the upper parts of Figure 38.

Despite the success of composers such as Jerry Goldsmith and Leonard Rosenman, serious problems still face the sensitive composer working in the film industry. The reasons are not simple. David Raksin, perhaps the most articulate composer to have worked in films, has tried to answer this question. In a May 1974 article for *Variety*, Raksin wrote: "To begin with, there is the state of the Industry; it should be news to no one that many people believe the Industry has been plundered, ruined by incompetence and left to twist slowly in the wind by men whose principal interests—whatever they may be—do not lie in film-making. The disastrous unemployment resulting from this circumstance has become worse as film companies have made more and more pictures abroad; American composers find it difficult to believe that the use of foreign composers is

Figure 37. Excerpt from *The Wind and the Lion,* music by Jerry Goldsmith.

Figure 38. Excerpt from *The Wind and the Lion*, music by Jerry Goldsmith.

not related to the fact that they work for less money. As to the remaining available jobs, they are further curtailed by relegation of the film soundtrack to the humiliating status of an adjunct to the recording industry. In too many cases, the appropriateness of the music to the film is secondary to getting an album, or a single, and the voice of the A & R man is heard in the land.

"All of this has become so much a part of the film music scene that anyone who challenges the propriety or, *perish forbid*, the artistic integrity of the process is sure to start heads shaking with concern for his sanity. Artists and Repertoire tycoons sit in the control rooms (how aptly named!) and freely render judgments upon the viability of film scores as commodities on record racks; these opinions are as freely transferred to apply (as though they were pertinent) to the function of the music *in the picture*, and nobody seems to question the competence of these people to decide what is 'right' for a sequence of a film. Where are the proud directors and producers, formerly so zealous to ensure that all components of their films interacted to fashion the synergistic marvel that is a motion picture?

"There are times these days when I suspect that my students at USC and UCLA are trying to provoke me into 'putting down' Rock and Pop film scores indiscriminately. And I feel absurdly virtuous when I ask them whether they can imagine pictures like *Easy Rider* or *The Last Picture Show* or *American Graffiti* with any other kind of music. The fact is that the music in those films was just what it should have been. But I do not find this to be equally true of all films in which such music is used. For unless we are willing to concede that what is essentially the music of the young is appropriate to *all* of the aspects of human experience with which films are concerned, we must ask what it is doing on the soundtracks of pictures that deal with other times and generations, other lives. It is one thing to appreciate the freshness and naivete of Pop music and quite another to accept it as inevitable no matter what the subject at hand. And *still* another to realize that the choice is often made for reasons that have little to do with the film itself. *One:* to sell recordings—and incidentally to garner publicity for the picture. *Two:* to appeal to the 'demographically defined' audience, which is a symbolic unit conceived as an object of condescension. Three (and to my mind saddest of all): because so many directors and producers, having acquired their skills and reputations at the price of becoming elderly, suddenly find themselves aliens in the land of the young; tormented by fear of not being 'with it,' they are tragically susceptible to the brainwashing of Music-Biz types. What is one to think of men of taste and experience who can be persuaded that the difference between a good picture and a bad one is a 'now' score that is 'where it's at?' "

It is difficult to tell when the old American movie became the new American cinema. Gerald Mast points out that *Bonnie and Clyde* "was perhaps the first full statement of the new cinema's values." But with the influence this film exerted on American film values with its innovations also came merely a new set of conventions and clichés. Among these clichés is the use of music in as stereotyped a manner as its Strauss-symphonic counterpart in the 1930s and 1940s—only the Strauss is now replaced by the pop, and the symphonic by the Fender bass.

Producers, directors, and writers about the cinema are as unaware as they always have been—perhaps even more so because of their youth—of the potential of music in films. Gerald Mast makes the observation that "the new American cinema does not ask to be taken as reality but constantly announces that it is artificial." This is well and good, and one is immediately tempted to surmise that if the new American cinema does not ask to be taken as reality then the "unreal" aspect of dramatic music on a sound track should not be bothersome. But Mast merely ignores this distinction, for soon after his pronouncement about the unreality of the new American cinema, he says about the new American film: "Gone is the old principle of studio scoring—to underscore a scene with music that increases the action's emotional impact without making the viewer aware of the music's existence. In new films there is little of this kind of background music. If there is music it must be clearly motivated (i.e. playing a radio or record player nearby). . . ." If this observation sounds familiar to the reader it is because this attitude of music "clearly motivated" is the same one held in the infancy of sound. American cinema has, musically, experienced an aesthetic regression.

At another point Mast claims that the new American film "purposely emphasiz[es] emotional continuity at the expense of linear continuity." Film music has almost always been nonlinear, which apparently makes it a perfect match for today's American film. Music in films continues to be as misunderstood as it ever was.

From January 23 to January 30, 1977 the American Broadcasting Company aired the eight-hour mini-series, *Roots,* based on the book of the same name by Alex Haley. While the series garnered the highest viewership (until that time) in the history of American television, its real significance is that it was the first example of a new form for television, the multi-hour mini-series.

The length of these projects can range anywhere from four hours (such as *Anastasia,* discussed below) to the 1988 thirty-hour *War and Remembrance.* While the amount of music required can seem overwhelming to the composer (the eight-hour *Peter the Great* for NBC had over three hours of music), projects of this length present certain advantages to the composer. Laurence Rosenthal, one of the finest composers working in this form, has stated that, ''One of the nicer things about the mini-series is that [the mini-series form] is usually of sufficient length to enable you to develop and expand musical material into a kind of tapestry that is often not possible even in a feature film.'' Rosenthal's screen credits include *The Miracle Worker, Becket, A Raisin in the Sun,* and *Requiem For A Heavyweight.* His many television credits include *Peter the Great, Anastasia, On Wings of Eagles,* and *Mussolini: The Untold Story.* His work has brought him two Academy Award nominations as well as three Emmys and five Emmy nominations.

Besides the enormous amount of music involved in most mini-series, the medium of television creates other problems for the composer as well. Rosenthal points out that, ''One of the principle differences between television and theatrical films is that, in television, there is less time and less money. Not that I consider a large orchestra *per se* better than a small one, but the composer is limited in rehearsal time and in certain orchestral luxuries that are very often available in the budget of a feature film. In television, the pressures of a tight composing schedule are also extreme, and I find that one is somehow urged to be less subtle owing to the producer's chronic terror that the viewer will switch channels. Even though these shortcomings of working in television are obvious and often painful to a composer, the fact is that the medium, by its nature, requires an awful lot of musical material, and a composer likes to feel that he is producing something that is needed.''

For the film student the study of music for television is a bit more difficult owing to the lack of availability, on videocassette, of much of the material produced for the medium. Most networks broadcast mini-series or films for television on an average of twice per production. They are then released to the overseas market but are seldom released, at least at this time, on videocassette. Despite this problem I would like to discuss three examples of Mr. Rosenthal's work for the medium of television. Each example addresses a distinct problem in writing music for motion pictures that has not been thoroughly covered in previous examples.

The first, from the 1986 mini-series, *Peter The Great,* is what Rosenthal describes as "minimal music" for a scene. The term should not be confused with the current trend of "minimalist" music in vogue in the concert world. Here the term implies the somewhat complex relationship between music and picture discussed in Chapter 6. The music for this example is in Figure 39, entitled "Further Questioning." The scene it plays has Peter torturing and questioning his son about suspected plots against the throne. The son is hanging from his wrists in a dark cell. The instrumentation chosen by Rosenthal contains only a deep bell, tam-tam, bass drum, the bottom strings of the piano being strummed while holding down the *sostenuto* pedal, a small, muted piano, a very low note of the timpani, and a low note on the harp. Obviously the dark quality of the scene suggested these comparable orchestral colors. More important, however, is the thematic treatment (or, more correctly, nontreatment) that Rosenthal has chosen. Note the total lack of thematic movement in the cue which, on the surface, seems quite simple and direct; but when this cue is placed against the picture, something much more complex takes place. Rosenthal says, "The scene was so intense and horrible that any music that moved in any kind of melodic way would tend to soften and modify the impact. The music had to be implacable and almost like a series of nervous shocks—it is absolutely compelling when that happens. I find this to be often true in film music: that a melody can take on an almost dialogue-like quality and there are times when you really don't want that at all. For a scene such as this one a melody, no matter how agonized, atonal, and angular, would still, in a certain way, sentimentalize and weaken the scene. The particular effect I used here reminds me of the kind of device I heard when I went to performances of Japanese theater: the use of a simple low drum would act as a kind of emotional counterpoint to the scene. You would only hear it about every ten seconds and after a while you knew it was coming and the effect had something terrifying about it."

This example is compelling in its manifestation of the "symbiotic catalytic exchange-relationship" described by Leonard Rosenman in Chapter 6. Here, certainly, the film is enriched by the music and the music is enriched by the film.

FILM MUSIC

Figure 39. Excerpt from *Further Questioning,* music by Laurence Rosenthal, from the mini-series *Peter the Great*. Copyright © 1986 Dejamus California, Inc. (3500 West Olive Avenue, Suite 200, Burbank, CA 91505). All Rights Reserved. International Copyright Secured.

Another example, Figure 40, is from the 1985 television mini-series *Mussolini: The Untold Story,* starring George C. Scott. The first two pages of the cue, "Mourning Family," are reproduced here and exhibit one of Rosenthal's most unique gifts in writing for motion pictures: his masterful treatment of scenes involving dialogue.

The music reproduced here plays behind the scene where Mussolini visits the site of a plane crash which killed one of his sons. The dialogue consists of a monologue by Scott in which he imagines his son's thoughts as he tried to land the out-of-control aircraft. The delivery of the lines is soft and emotional, a very difficult situation to score effectively. As Rosenthal observes, "One of the ways of scoring dialogue while at the same time keeping the music interesting is to utilize the transparency of the strings. I used to think it was a matter of the tone color itself, and it is, to a certain extent. But I now think that it has also to do with being out of the way of the register of the voices in the scene. In addition, some voices can really absorb more music than others. Richard Burton, for example, could cut through anything. Many women's voices, on the other hand, require the music to absolutely tiptoe behind them in a scene. Generally speaking, sustained sounds work best but that depends on the kind of dialogue, of course."

Figure 40. Excerpt from *Mourning Family,* music by Laurence Rosenthal, from the mini-series *Mussolini: The Untold Story.*

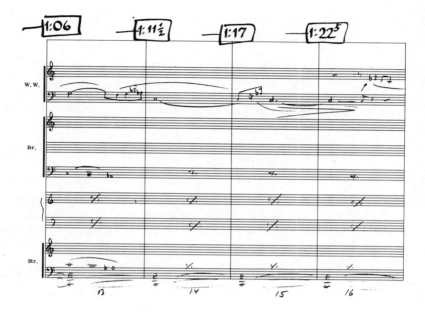

The opening of the cue involves the closing of the scene where Mussolini is viewing his son's body, and then a slow drive-up to the crash sight. Dialogue begins just before bar 11 of the example. The bassoon solo in bar 12 gently answers the first line of dialogue. Note how Rosenthal has incorporated both the sustained quality (in the strings) mentioned earlier, as well as fragments of thematic material to keep the music interesting while still contributing to the emotional impact of the scene. The real challenge when scoring dialogue is to balance sufficient thematic interest and emotional support for the scene with the unobtrusiveness of the music. Rosenthal's scores abound with brilliant solutions to this problem of delicate balance.

The final example, Figure 41, is from the 1987 mini-series, *Anastasia*. While this example, "Berlin Bridge," is a bit more utilitarian in its dramatic intent—a deeply depressed Anastasia jumps from a Berlin bridge and awakens in a mental ward—its true interest lies in its musical style. The style, that of the Viennese atonal school of the 1920s, and the dramatic requirements of the scene (mental instability) created an interesting confluence of necessities. Rosenthal points out that this "is an example of using a certain kind of music to suggest a total mental disorientation while at the same time evoking a particular period in history, and, incidentally, a certain parallel period in the history of music. In this strangely bittersweet atonality, even the harshest dissonances can sound pretty.''

There is no question that Rosenthal succeeds on all three counts even though much of the audience is probably not aware of the more subtle aspects of the music which only the trained ear would recognize and appreciate. This example is also important in revealing that, despite the richly deserved reputation of film and television being the most commercial of enterprises, they still attract composers of the highest caliber in both talent and training. This small circle of composers working in film and television, despite many commercial necessities, still have moments of brilliance deserving of the same level of attention given the work of their concert-hall colleagues. It should not be forgotten that these film composers, owing to film's relative infancy when compared to other art forms, daily confront compositional problems that have never really existed for composers before. This fact, coupled with the enormous pressure of schedules which pay no heed to the muse, will hopefully help us to begin to recognize the unique and rich contribution these composers are making to the culture and history of music.

Figure 41. Excerpt from *Berlin Bridge*, music by Laurence Rosenthal, from the miniseries *Anastasia*.

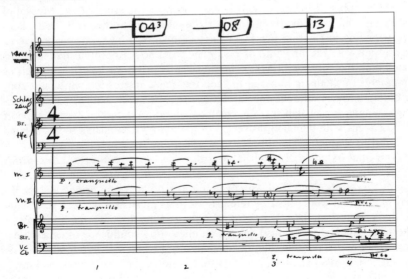

5

Music in the Cartoon
and Experimental Animated Film

If the neglect of and misunderstandings about music in feature films have been unfortunate and unwarranted, the total inattention given music in cartoons verges on the criminal. With the exception of one substantial article on cartoon music by composer Ingolf Dahl, who early on was aware that something of significance was happening in this genre, there has been nothing of any real importance written about music in cartoons. Even so-called film-music aficionados have chosen to by-pass cartoon music in their writings in favor of the more glamorous feature-film scores. It is evident that these aficionados find it far more captivating (and pretentious) to discuss the heroic sweep of a Max Steiner score than to talk about the crazy and delightful machinations of a Scott Bradley score to a Tom and Jerry cartoon. As in the case of its big-brother counterpart, the feature-film score, the neglect of cartoon music by scholars is perplexing.

Cartoon music since the advent of sound has had much the same fortunes as feature-film scores. Unlike feature-film scores, however, music for cartoons took a little longer in discovering its potentialities. For a considerable time the primary type of music used to accompany the sound cartoon was well-known popular and folk tunes. For example, Figure 1, wherein Scott Bradley makes use of the tune "Rock-a-bye

Figure 1. Excerpt from *The Lost Chick*, music by Scott Bradley.

Baby." This example is drawn from the score to the 1931 cartoon, *The Lost Chick*. Composer Scott Bradley is probably the preeminent composer for cartoons and an examination of his career and work reflects as good a cross-section of the development of music in cartoons as one is likely to find, as he is responsible for many of the musical innovations in this film medium.

Bradley's career in films began around 1929 in Los Angeles. He had been the conductor at radio station KHJ in Los Angeles and started his career in cartoons by playing piano in the then tiny Walt Disney Studios. Bradley recalls that Disney took an extremely active part in the recording of the scores to these early cartoons. He recalls, "Disney would come in and stand with the percussion section." Disney's attention to detail continued throughout his career. Bradley worked for Disney during that short period when "actual" recording, or recording without benefit of postproduction dubbing, was still in use. Bradley recalls: "In those days we had to get everything on one track—there was no cutting. You had to get the sound effects, dialogue and music all at the same time."

By 1934 Bradley was scoring cartoons for the Harman-Ising organization (the horrible musical pun was intentional). During his tenure with this group he continued to write material of the same nature, namely, popular and folk songs familiar to everyone. Bradley's standard orchestra during this period was seventeen to eighteen players, slightly more in later years.

In 1938 Bradley went to work for the Metro-Goldwyn-Mayer Studios as a composer and conductor of cartoon music. During the earliest days of that studio's work in cartoons (Bradley came to them at the beginning of their production of cartoons), Bradley was forced to write in much the same manner as before. At one point he decided, "It seemed to me that almost anybody could collect a lot of nursery jingles and fast moving tunes, throw them together along with slide whistles and various noise makers and call that a cartoon score, but that didn't satisfy me and, I felt sure, wouldn't really satisfy the public. So I set about to work out musical scores that would add significance to the picture, that would be musically sound and would be entertaining."

This new approach was only possible through Bradley's own initiative. Dissatisfied, Bradley finally went to his executive producer, Fred Quimby, and told him of his ideas concerning cartoon scores. Bradley emphasizes, however, that "the writer-directors (Hanna and Barbera) always suggested the type of music to be used which was usually 'vetoed' by me if it was a corny song. But we respected each other and after Quimby resigned in 1953 due to ill health, Hanna and Barbera turned all of the musical matters over to me." After his conversation with Quimby, Bradley recalls, "Mr. Quimby . . . allowed me complete freedom to score the cartoons as I wished." Bradley also remembers that after this meeting with Quimby he also had the opportunity, quite often, "to do a score *before* the animation was done."

It is interesting to note that in the 1930s cartoons tended to follow musical structure more closely than cartoons produced in the '40s and '50s. Ingolf Dahl, writing in *Film Music Notes,* pointed out in 1948 that "Seeing old cartoons again we realize how much the medium has changed. The procedure used to be one of fitting humorous story and action to cheerful, zippy, bouncy music which hovered in style between Gilbert and Sullivan and Zez Confrey. The music was rhythmically defined, symmetrically constructed in eight bar phrases, somewhat on the order of a dance tune, and its changes of mood ('chases,' 'danger,' 'villain,' 'heroism,' etc.) were modified by the structural symmetry of popular music and its inherent simplicity. The cartoons represented in essence a kind of humorous 'choreography' to catchy music. This analogy can even be carried into details: just as the dancer reserves his more spectacular tricks for the cadences at the end of musical phrases, so the cartoonist, probably out of instinct, achieved some of his funniest effects by placing outstanding action (be it the bounce of a ball or the impact of a pie in the face) on the same cadential accents with which in popular music every eighth measure ends."

The symmetry in the action of these early cartoons is understandable since animators worked with a definite tempo in mind. This particular tempo, the one most prevalent at that time, was known as a "twelve tempo," * or the equivalent of 120 beats per minute. These beats were then evenly divided into groups of four or eight. This partly explains composer Dahl's observation that the music to these early cartoons "was rhythmically constructed in eight bar phrases. . . ."

---

* A twelve-frame click track. It should be mentioned here that Scott Bradley came up with the concept of a click track at about the same time as Max Steiner, if not before. Steiner is purported to be the inventor of the click track. See chapter 8 for a complete discussion of click tracks.

By the early 1940s the style of cartoons had changed and the composer had to change with it. Dahl points out that by the '40s the music in cartoons "is added to a pre-determined course of hectic events and is in many cases required to do nothing more than duplicate the action by synchronous illustration, taking the role of sound effect together with the role of musical characterization. It attests to the stubbornness of some few composers that in spite of this more or less mechanical application of their art they still try, here and there, to invest their 'sound tailoring' with some musical meaning. 'Realism of action' (whatever that can be in drawn images) has become more important than rhythmic stylization. This is clearly reflected in the average present day cartoon score: when we look at the music we see that it makes sense only if considered as 'recitative accompaniment' to an action in pantomime."

Dahl rightly points out that this "recitative accompaniment" is not a new musical form: "To quote just two of the most famous historical examples: Beckmesser's pantomime scene in the 3rd act of 'Meister-singer,' as well as the opening scene of the 3rd act of 'Fledermaus.' Both are accompanied by such a direct anticipation of cartoon music tech-niques that once more they give one cause to reflect: have technical advances of our new media called for and developed commensurate musical advances?"

But Dahl's observation about "recitative accompaniment" not being a new musical form can be carried further. When viewing cartoons produced by the major studios during the 1940s and early 1950s, one is struck by the freshness and audacity of their music. The instrumental resources are usually small and the musical idiom employed is very much into the twentieth century. As pointed out earlier, dramatic feature films tended to shy away from any sustained use of twentieth-century musical idioms, a policy justified in part by the type of dramatic films then being produced. But why the solid and sustained use of twentieth-century musical language in cartoons? Because, as Dahl suggests, with its incessant and lively motion, the cartoon really represents a kind of dance; the cartoon, like the ballet, was a perfect outlet for the neoclassic movement of the twentieth century represented in many of the works of composers such as Stravinsky and Milhaud. It is no accident that some of the greatest works to come out of the neoclassic movement were ballets; because of the cartoon's dancelike quality, the neoclassic style was well suited to it as well.

The relationship of cartoon music to neoclassicism is better understood if we trace the neoclassic movement back to its model, the classical period, and to one of the most successful dramatic creations of the classical style, the comic opera, or *opera buffa.* There are several important and fundamental similarities between eighteenth-century comic opera and twentieth-century cartoons, as well as the music used to accompany them. These similarities suggest a direct link between the classical *opera buffa* and cartoons: the neoclassical movement of the twentieth century.

On a fairly superficial level, cartoons require the viewer to suspend physical reality to a far greater degree than do dramatic films of the same period. *(The Roadrunner* cartoons are a good example of this: all sorts of catastrophes befall the poor coyote, but his ability to survive springs eternal.) The element of disbelief was important to the eighteenth-century comic opera as well. The Venetian composer Carlo Gozzi, who influenced Mozart's comic operas, realized the dramatic importance of the suspension of belief in the comic opera. Some of his comments on his own works read like a description of the cartoon. Writing in his *Memoirs of a Useless Man,* Gozzi says of his "dramatic fables" that they should have, above all, "the great magic of seduction that creates an enchanting illusion of making the impossible appear as truth to the mind and spirit of the spectators."

Charles Rosen, in his book *The Classical Style,* points out that *"opera buffa* has conventions as artificial as those of any other art form: one must accept the idea that it gets dark enough outdoors for a valet to disguise himself as his master by the mere exchange of cloaks; that a young man can go unrecognized by his fiancee if he puts on a false mustache; and that if someone is to get a box on the ear, it is almost always somebody else standing nearby who receives it by mistake." In cartoons we can, of course, see these same sorts of conventions at work although the ease with which we accept those conventions, as well as suspend our rational mentality, is probably increased by the fact that we are watching what are very obviously drawn, and in many cases, animal characters.

The elements of the classical style which suited *opera buffa* so well and the *opera seria* only with partial success are also the same elements that make the neoclassic style of the twentieth century so successful in cartoons. Again we turn to Rosen for specifics: "The style that Mozart inherited and developed was only applicable to the tragic stage with difficulty, and the sense of strain is inevitable. The classical style was, indeed, one which dealt clearly with events, and its forms were anything but static, but its pace was too rapid for *opera seria.* . . . Although the principal modulation within late eighteenth-century style is conceived as an event, there is no way that this event can be evaded for any length of time without the delaying action of a considerable amount of chromaticism, and Mozart's language was essentially diatonic, at least in its long-range aspects . . . the pacing of the classical style worked supremely well for the comic theatre, with its quick changes of situation and the numerous possibilities of accelerated action."

At another point Rosen makes an observation that is pertinent to the pacing of the cartoon. "The speed of the *opera buffa's* large-scale rhythm," he points out, "and its emphasis on action in place of dignified expression of *opera seria* enable [Mozart's *Indomeneo*] to move at a dazzling pace from aria to ensemble. . . ." The comedy of situation, the preeminent dramatic substance of the *opera buffa,* is also endemic to the dramatic elements of the cartoon for there is little, if any, "dignified expression" in the short cartoons of the 1930s, '40s, and '50s.

The point of all this is simply that the cartoon, because of its very nature, demanded, as did the *opera buffa* of the eighteenth century, a style of composition suited to it. In dramatic films of the 1930s and '40s the chromaticism of the nineteenth century was appropriate because of the music's tendency to deemphasize small-scale musical events, thereby drawing the listener's attention to a larger sense of movement. Cartoons, on the other hand, are usually nothing less than frantic movement consisting of a series of small-scale events, and the music in cartoons usually plays at least an equal role with the animation and story in establishing the humorous success of events. The cartoon composer needed an idiom that would allow him to move musically in the same rapid-fire fashion as the visual. The neoclassical style, with its articulation of phrase and form that gives a work the character of a series of distinct events, was what the cartoon composer instinctively looked to. This is certainly what happened to Scott Bradley when he sensed the need to get away from nursery jingles as musical accompaniment for cartoons. His cartoon scores very quickly moved into a far more daring harmonic idiom and took on many elements of the neoclassic style.

One unusual precedent set by Bradley in the early '40s was the scoring of a cartoon before the animation was done. The advantages to the composer working in this manner should be obvious: he was able to write and record his score using to a far greater degree than normal such musically expressive devices as *rubato, accelerando,* and *ritardando.* Bradley first did this in 1944 with the cartoon *Dance of the Weed.* He later employed this technique using arrangements of well-known classical works. By recording the music first he was able to give those classical works the expressive qualities they deserved. One such cartoon, *The Cat Concerto,* utilizes the *Second Hungarian Rhapsody* of Franz Liszt. A page from Bradley's arrangement of this work for the cartoon can be seen in Figure 2. The arrangement has the left hand of the original version assigned to one piano, and the right hand of the original given to the solo, or featured, piano. The solo part in the film was played by the late John Crown, former head of the Piano Department at the University of Southern California. Note the use of devices such as *rubato* as well as the free, florid cadenzas so common to Liszt's piano music. These devices would be very difficult to execute had the composer had to work within predetermined timings. By recording the score first, and then doing the animation, the composer was able to do justice to the music, whether his own or another's work.

Another significant contribution of Bradley's to the art of cartoon music was his use of what he calls "shock chords." Shock chords, according to Bradley, were conceived as a means of getting away from strictly mechanical sound effects. The chords are used at points in the action where natural sound effects would seem logical—and unimaginative. Just such a chord can be found in Figure 3 in measure 208, the last measure of the example. On the second beat is a slightly dissonant chord providing the necessary sound for Tom the cat's bouncing on the floor.

The concept of "shock chords" was not a late development for Bradley. As early as 1937 it was reported in the *Pacific Coast Musician* that Bradley used "a minimum of mechanical sound effects and achieves the desired effect by use of the orchestra. For example, in a scene where [Little Cheeser] is made to slide on a deck of cards, instead of using the slide whistle that everybody else seems to use for a like scene, Bradley uses his harp in glissando, thus preserving the tonality already established and arriving at what is, in fact, a more realistic effect. Another example of this is a recent picture where a sort of Rube Goldberg mechanism is used to start the machinery which 'manufactures' spring weather, by the dropping of water into a cup, etc. Instead of using a bell or some mechanical noise

Figure 2. Excerpt from *The Cat Concerto*. A portion of Bradley's arrangement of the *Second Hungarian Rhapsody* of Franz Liszt.

to denote the dropping of water, Bradley uses a little octave figure for the celeste, which finally becomes an important part of the general music which underscores the whole big scene in which spring is actually being manufactured."

Scott Bradley was by no means the only talented composer working on cartoons for the Hollywood studios of the '30s, '40s, and early '50s. Among other composers who were doing some fine work during this period were Oliver Wallace, Paul Smith, and Leigh Harline, all of the Disney Studios; Carl Stalling of Warner Bros.; and Winston Sharples of Associated Artists Productions.

In order to familiarize the reader with the process used to score cartoons during this period, we will take a closer look at some of the work of Scott Bradley, whose career spanned the entire length of studio-produced cartoons. Bradley retired in 1958 when MGM closed out its cartoon department.

Once the animation was completed, the composer was provided with a number of items. He was given a rough cut of the cartoon, known as the "pencil reel." The pencil reel is a black-and-white version of the cartoon. With this he could refresh his memory of details by running the print through a moviola machine. He was also given a "detail sheet," an example of which is shown in Figure 3. The detail sheet was covered with all kinds of signs, figures, multicolored words, directions, and descriptions. The composer's job, then, was to fill in the empty staff with music. In the example shown, this job has already been completed by Bradley. Composers were generally given about two weeks in which to compose, orchestrate, and record such a score. Before this, the composer had not seen the cartoon and knew the script only in general outline. However, if a cartoon was to contain any song and dance numbers, they had to be recorded in advance of the drawing stage of the production so that the animation could fit the timing of the music. The detail sheet contained a complete breakdown of all items of action; these timings were tabulated according to a regular number of frame units on which the animation was based. When this frame unit was translated into music it became the metrical beat from which the composer worked. His bar lines were then set according to the metric scheme in which he wanted to group several beats. All of this was eventually translated into a click track for purposes of recording.

The reason for scoring and recording the music after the animation was done was that most cartoon directors were not musical and would have had some difficulty in building their action to fit musical patterns. Consequently, the music had to shift to the rapidly changing image. The composer's almost overwhelming task in this situation was to create some sort of coherence and structure to the music. With problems like these expediency was the rule. Musical illustration of the action was another required element and the degree to which the composer was able to lift such illustration above the purely mechanical depended solely on his talent and inventiveness. Another problem was the extremely short time given the music to make its point, to indicate changes of mood and character and changes of expression. Ingolf Dahl pointed out that "this calls for constant flexibility in the handling of thematic material and the ability of applying the variation technique to phrases of aphoristic brevity. One sustained melodic note on the violin may consume four feet of film, not to speak of the whole of such a melody. There is little chance for musical extension of any kind."

Other hazards for the composer included the constant preoccupation with a metronomic beat from which he could not escape. The preoccupation could impart a certain rhythmic squareness to the phrases; it took a good deal of conscious effort on the composer's part to overcome this. The composer was, to an extent, shackled to the bar line. "But if, on the one hand, he has to fight the constraining influence of the squarely regular time unit he has to try, on the other hand, to create musical *symmetry* where the cartoon lacks it." The needs for this symmetry constructed in the music can be found in the fact that cartoons, at least the commercial productions, are a very extroverted and direct form of entertainment. The problem for the composer, however, is how to supply this musical symmetry when the direction and form of the cartoon has been conceived outside of musical considerations.

There are, to be sure, certain compensations for the composer of cartoon music. Music can give definition to screen action and it can invest the drawn characters with personality.

As he wrote his music, the composer of the studio-produced cartoons had to keep in mind that his orchestra would consist of anywhere between sixteen and thirty musicians. Scott Bradley, for instance, usually had at his disposal four violins, one viola, one cello, one bass, one piano, one percussion player, one flute (doubling piccolo), one oboe, one bassoon, three clarinets (doubling saxophones), three trumpets, and two trombones. In the hands of an imaginative composer that can be more than enough instruments to achieve a satisfactory result.

The cartoon selected for illustration is the 1948 MGM cartoon *Heavenly Puss.* The directors were William Hanna and Joseph Barbera and the music is by Scott Bradley. The detail sheet from this cartoon (Figure 3), was selected for its demonstration of a wide variety of elements and illustrates within a limited space all of the important parameters of cartoon music technique of the 1930s, '40s, and early '50s.

The dramatic action for this example is this: Tom the cat is attempting to get into heaven. Before he can be admitted, however, the ticket agent on the "heavenly train" demands that Tom obtain a Certificate of Forgiveness from the little mouse, Jerry. In order to let Tom know what is in store for him without the certificate, the agent lets him have a peek at hell, the image of which fades at measure 199 of our example. Tom is reminded by the agent that he has only one hour in which to get the certificate.

The tempo of this sequence translates, from the click-track tempo, into MM = 88 to the half-note. Over the music can be seen a detailed description, at their exact places, of all the action going on in the cartoon. Reading upward from the music the following information is provided: 1) Length of action, measured in frames. 2) Dialogue. 3) Description of action. 4) Measurement of additional action. 5) Description of additional action. There are no sound effects on this particular page but there is a space provided for it.

Note the onomatopoeia of the words used to describe some of the action: "Phoom" (bar 193), "Eaa" (202), "Plop" (208). These are not audible sound effects on the soundtrack but, rather, vivid verbal descriptions of gestures, expressions, and happenings. They are included in the detail sheet for the benefit of the composer.

It should be pointed out that where the *unit* of measurement changes the composer will start a new recording sequence. These various sequences are then connected to one another by the sound editor.

Points of action that are to be emphasized musically are indicated on this detail sheet exactly where they occur; the composer will then place his musical accentuation on the equivalent metrical subdivision of the measure. It is at such points in the action that Bradley uses the "shock chords" discussed earlier.

It is interesting to note that Bradley does not, in measures 193–200, "mickey-mouse" every action down to the batting of an eye—a trait extremely common to cartoon music—but, instead, writes a kind of mock-Wagnerian hell music to represent the scene.

FILM MUSIC

Figure 3. Excerpt from *Heavenly Puss,* music by Scott Bradley.

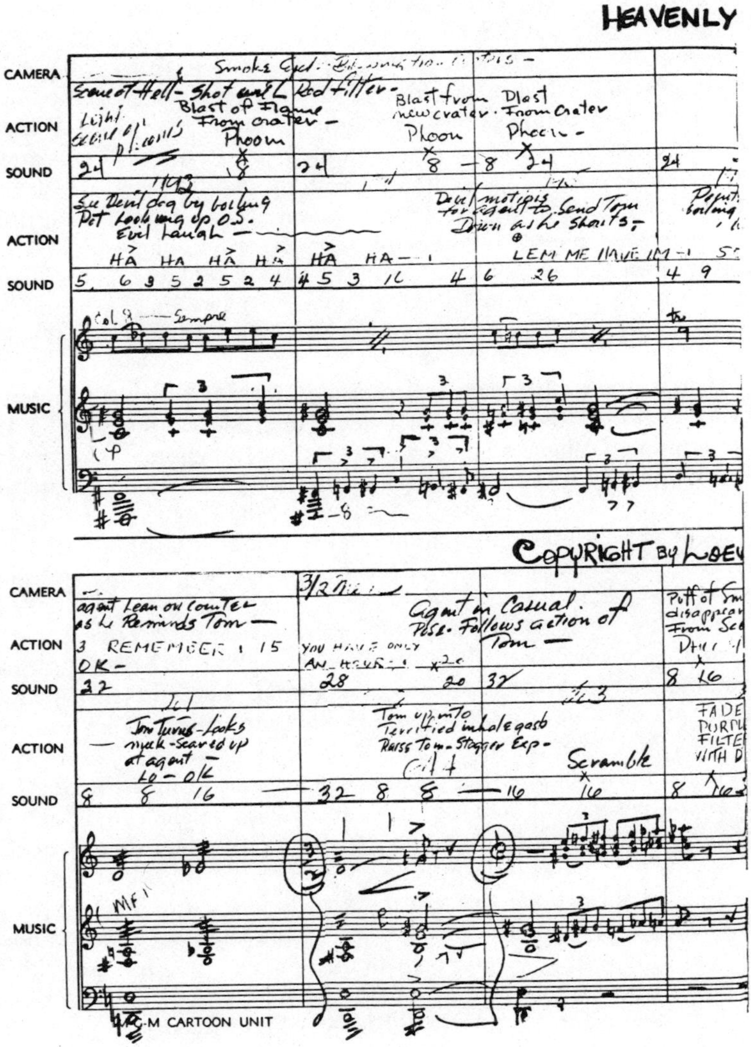

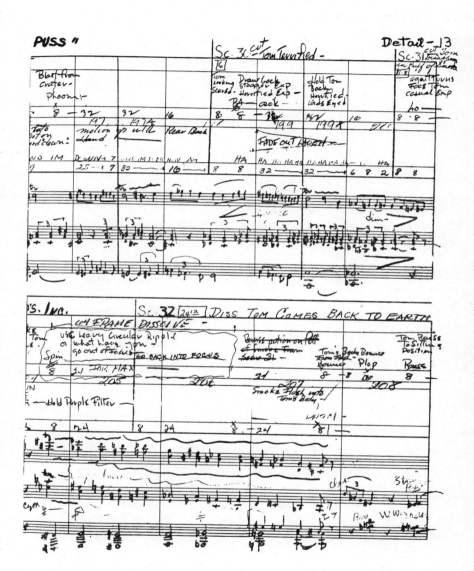

The music changes, however, with the measures that follow. Here the music must take us out of the hell music in one measure (measure 200). In rapid succession the music takes on the following functions: In measures 201-202 the music acts as background in the dialogue of the agent; beginning on the third beat of measure 202, which is Tom's startled gasp, the music reflects Tom's scramble to get away; measures 205-207 indicate Tom's body spinning within a cloud; measure 207 indicates a smoke flash and the landing of Tom's body on the floor; finally, his bouncing back is reflected in the music in bar 208.

The above deals only with the technical and functional aspects of the music in this sequence. The musician should notice some of the compositional devices Bradley has employed as well. Note the whole-tone and augmented structures in measures 193, 196, and 208. Also observe the sudden relaxation of harmonic tension for the background to the agent's dialogue in measure 201 and 202 as well as the use of descending seventh chords over an ascending chromatic bass in measures 205 and 206.

Another example proves even more daring in its harmonic idiom: it utilizes the atonal, twelve-tone technique of Schoenberg. Figure 4 is from the cartoon *The Cat That Hated People*. This cartoon dates from 1947 and the serial technique used by Bradley for portions of this cartoon would not find their way into feature-film scoring until Leonard Rosenman used them in his 1955 score for *The Cobweb*. In this particular example the piccolo and oboe represent Jerry Mouse in a twelve-tone row, which is stated twice. The bassoon, on the other hand, represents Tom the cat. The

Figure 4. Excerpt from *The Cat That Hated People*, music by Scott Bradley.

bassoon part is the same row in retrograde (backward).

In the early 1950s United Productions of America (UPA) began producing cartoons considerably unlike their commercial predecessors. The comic figures were drawn in a highly stylized manner reminiscent of some of Picasso's early work. The characters' movements were also stylized, reducing human actions to the simplest possible rhythms. Among UPA's most outstanding work were *The Unicorn in the Garden,* the *Mr. Magoo* series and, one of their most delightful creations, *Gerald McBoing Boing.*

Gerald McBoing Boing contained a score by Gail Kubik, a concert composer who had scored some documentary films during World War II, as well as several Hollywood productions after the war.

The main character of the film, Gerald, is the despair of his parents for he is unable to talk; he can only speak sound effects with the characteristic "boing" of the cartoon world being the most formidable effect in his arsenal. The music to the film, as might be expected, is highly percussive and very much in keeping with Kubik's own compositional style at that time. A short excerpt from the opening of the cartoon suffices to give the reader some idea of the type of music written for this delightful cartoon. Note especially how the music is set in a twentieth-century harmonic idiom and how it follows the general pattern described earlier in this chapter, i.e., a series of distinct musical events manifested in a precise articulation of phrase.

Figure 5. Excerpt from *Gerald McBoing Boing,* music by Gail Kubik.

It is also worth noting that, as Scott Bradley had done before on occasion, Kubik wrote the music before the animation was done.

It was just such independent organizations as UPA that began to replace the large studio cartoon units. As the studios began to fade in the early 1950s, so did their cartoon production units. MGM, for instance, closed its cartoon unit in 1958. The market for cartoons in theaters also seemed to slacken and the independent producers of cartoons began to gravitate toward television work where there was a growing demand for their services.

The music for cartoons discussed above is typical of the better music of mainstream cartoon music during Hollywood's studio years; however, one area of music and animation was never sufficiently explored on a commercial level. This was the potentiality of animation reflecting some of the abstract or absolute qualities of music.* As early as 1946, a studio animator named Chuck Jones (now head of ABC television's Children's Programming) advocated just such an approach to music and animation. Writing in the *Hollywood Quarterly,* Jones advocated the use of abstract drawings to accompany abstract music. He wrote: "I believe that the best solution to interpretation of abstract music is to go along with it; that is, to be abstract graphically. . . . it is possible to find abstract sounds and abstract images that are sympathetic." He then goes on to demonstrate his point with some interesting examples.

The two abstract words "tackety" and "goloomb" are illustrated by the following abstract shapes:

Abstract drawings on pp. 196–98 by Chuck Jones. Copyright © 1946 by The Regents of the University of California. Reprinted from *Film Quarterly* I/4 (July 1946) 364–70. Used by permission.

With sounds approaching the qualities of music he uses the sound, "oooooooooooomp," which he represents as follows:

---

* In contrast to this concept is the full-length animated film *Fantasia. Fantasia* reflects the programmatic and coloristic aspects of music rather than music's abstract qualities.

And another sound, "pooooooooooo-o-":

Jones then moves into pure music and asks, "Which of these is the bassoon, and which is the harp?"

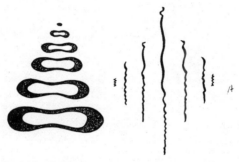

Using the same method, *andante* becomes:

"Abandon":

Crescendo might be graphically illustrated in this way, according to Jones:

And its converse, *decrescendo:*

While Chuck Jones's concepts never found fruition in the commercial film industry, there have been film experiments in the area of sound and music since the earliest days of the sound film. These experiments have centered on the creation of sound using nonmusical means. There is little doubt that pure sound can take on many of the dramatic functions of music. The sound track to the Hitchcock film *The Birds* is a good example of this.

This idea of "music" created without benefit or in complement with traditional Western musical instruments is not new to the musician. George Antheil, who later wrote for Hollywood films, led a group of composers in Paris during the 1920s in an avant-garde musical movement. Their musical creations were called *musique concrète,* one of their more famous works being Antheil's *Ballet Méchanique.*

In the realm of film, however, this idea was manifested in what is called "animated sound." This technique, as applied to the sound track of a film, is closely allied with the techniques employed in the production of animated films. Animated sound's most famous exponent has been the Canadian filmmaker Norman McLaren, but experiments in the field go back to as early as 1922.

It was in 1922 that I. Moholy-Nagy published some articles in Holland and Germany that discussed the possibility of the synthetic production of sound on film. Later, Ernst Toch, the German theoretician and composer, suggested the direct writing of sound without using the usual performers.

The available evidence seems to indicate that the first body of investigation and practical work in this area was done in Russia at the Scientific Experimental Film Institute located in Leningrad. It was here in 1930 that the musical theorist and mathematician A. M. Avraamov worked with two animators, N. Y. Zhelinsky and N. V. Voinov, on what they called "ornamental animation in sound." This same work was later carried on at the Leningrad Conservatory by G. M. Rimsky-Korsakoff and E. A. Scholpo. It appears that this group's work was rather extensive and pursued a number of different lines.

Avraamov used a frame-by-frame method that utilized a standard animation camera. Geometric figures such as rectangles and triangles were photographed; these were the basic units for his sound waves. The pitch of the sound was controlled by bringing the camera either closer or farther away from the drawings, or by preparing separate drawings for each pitch. The volume was controlled by varying the exposure. Harmony and counterpoint were achieved by multiple exposures, or by subdividing the sound track length-wise into sections, or by an extremely rapid alteration of several tones. *Portamento* was achieved by a rapid series of micro-tones.

Avraamov's chief aim was the freeing of his music from the restrictions of the twelve-tone well-tempered scale. He wished to create a new tonal system assimilating the many scales of the traditional folk music of the Eastern and Southern Republics of the U.S.S.R. He was able to achieve very accurate control over pitch and volume although his range of timbres was more limited. It should be pointed out that Avraamov was not looking for flexibility of timbre but rather for a limited number of new tone qualities that would arise naturally from the geometric shapes.

Soon thereafter Scholpo and Rimsky-Korsakoff began creating sound tracks for films by assembling small units of film and editing the music and sound effects into a whole.

At about the same time another Russian, B. A. Yankovsky, working in Moscow, developed a system in which he abandoned the frame-by-frame shooting on a standard animation camera in favor of continuously moving patterns. He was able to obtain these patterns through the use of rotating wheels with cog patterns.

Of all the Soviet animated sound techniques developed, animator N. Voinov's system is said to have been the most practical. Voinov had a library of eighty-seven drawings. These were graded in semitones covering a little over seven octaves of the twelve-tone, equally tempered scale but using a fixed tone quality of great purity. With this system he produced an interpretation of Rachmaninoff's "Prelude in C-Sharp Minor" as well as Schubert's "Moment Musical."

At about the same time as these Soviet experiments, a Munich electrical engineer by the name of Rudolph Pfenninger began work on his own system of animated sound. Pfenninger's system was similar to the Russians' although he apparently had no contact with them and developed his own system independently. Pfenninger also had a library of

cards with each drawing being of a single pitch and graded in semi-tones
over a wide pitch range. These drawings were used as the basic unit for
sound waves, sine-curves and saw-tooth forms. Pfenninger was able to
achieve great control over dynamic nuances. One of the best examples of
his work is the documentary film *Tönende Handschrift*, which was
produced in the early 1930s.

During this same period and again in Germany the Fischinger Brothers
in Berlin began photographing geometric shapes on the sound track. I.
Moholy-Nagy was using alphabetical letters, people's profiles, and
fingerprints as the basic graphic material for sound waves.

In 1933 a New Zealand musician, Jack Ellit, working in England,
experimented along the same lines as Pfenninger and was the first to
actually draw the sound directly onto the celluloid without the use of a
camera.

In the United States during the early 1940s John and James Whitney
created a prize-winning set of five films, entitled *Five Film Exercises,*
which utilized the concept of animated sound. The sound tracks for these
films were created by the filmmakers themselves using a pendulum device
invented by John Whitney. Figure 6 is a photograph of this device.
Whitney explained the technique: "The natural swing of the pendulum is
literally a subsonic audio device, the swing of a pendulum being no
different than the 'swing' of a string on a musical instrument. It was
simply a matter of adapting that natural phenomenon of an array of
pendulums and recording [photographing] their motion. It was a matter
of recording the pendulums' motion and translating it into a variable area
type of pattern on motion picture film. The motion picture film would be
exposed, correspondingly, subsonic. That is, the film would be moving
approximately 60 times slower than its playback speed."

After this initial effort in creating his own sound track, Whitney set
aside the idea of creating his own music. Whitney recalls: "There were
some inherent shortcomings to the pendulum device in that original form
as an optical device. The biggest problem was the signal-to-noise ratio.
There was always an inherent soundtrack noise that seemed to be
technically impossible to reduce. We were unable to follow any of the
procedures for noise reduction then being utilized by the commercial film
industry because our system was essentially a mechanical one."

By this time Whitney had found that "the visual problems were
comprehensive and enormous. I felt constrained to devote my entire
attentions to the visual design problems."

Figure 6. The machine on the right is the pendulum device invented by John Whitney. The device on the left is a visual one. Photo by John Whitney. Used by permission.

Whitney has, of course, continued his work in film; a discussion of some of his more recent work appears later in this chapter.

The person to devote the most time to this aspect of the sound track has been Norman McClaren, assisted by Evelyn Lambart, under the sponsorship of the Canadian Government. McClaren's system differs little from that of the Voinov and Pfenninger systems in that it uses a library of cards, each bearing the representation of sound waves. McClaren has streamlined the operation, however, to a point where it has become a simple and economic operation. He describes the process he uses in creating sound waves:

"There are many different ways of producing [sound waves]. For instance, it would have been possible to make them by recording (i.e.,

photographing) 'live' musical sounds on to film sound-track, then tracing
the resulting patterns from the track. However, to do this would be as
pointless and creatively stultifying as to make animated cartoons by
photographing live actors and tracing their outlines. Instead, in the films
under discussion [*Love Your Neighbor, Now is The Time, Two Bagatelles,
Twirligig,* and *Phantasy*], a non-naturalistic approach was taken, with no
particular attempt to imitate natural sounds or traditional musical
instruments. New kinds of sound waves were made by using simple and
easily drawn shapes.

"The drawings consist of a basic figure or simple shape, that is repeated
over and over to form a patterned band. The figure may be no more than
a white line on a dark ground or a single gradation of tone from light to
dark, but, by virtue of its identical repetition, it builds up into a series of
sound waves having a definite tone colour.

"Each card in the library of drawings carries one such band of repeated
patterns on an area 1 inch wide and 12 inches long. On some cards the
basic figure is repeated only about four times within this area and this,
when photographed on one frame of film, will sound as a musical note of
a fairly deep pitch (about two octaves below middle A). For midpitches
there are from twenty to thirty repetitions of the basic figure on each card,
and for very high pitched notes as many as 120.

"There is one card for each semitone of the chromatic scale, and in all,
for the sound tracks of the five films mentioned, sixty such cards were
used, covering a range of five octaves, from two octaves below middle A
to three octaves above.

"These sixty cards were labelled with the standard musical notation
and arranged systematically in a small box to form a kind of keyboard.

"When the music was being shot, the box was placed beside the camera
so that the composer (who would also operate the camera), desiring a
particular pitch, would select from the box the required card and place it
in front of the camera.

"To get notes of a very deep pitch, the music was shot twice as fast as
finally desired, and in the process of re-recording slowed down by half,
and thus dropped one octave in pitch.

The Mosaic Nature of Music

"Because of the fact that a *picture* camera takes film intermittently by
the frame (rather than running continuously as in the ordinary sound

recording equipment) the sound-track has a mosaic nature; in other words it builds up out of small units each 1/24th of a second long.

"If the duration of a note is desired longer, several successive frames of the same card are shot, thus building up a sustained effect, by a very rapid repetition of the same note, as in a harpsichord, a mandolin or xylophone; for a very short note, just one frame or at most two frames suffice.

"For rests and pauses a black card is photographed.

Dynamics

"Before exposing the film, however, the composer has to determine the precise volume or dynamic level of that note. This is one of the important new factors in animated music for, in the past, dynamic markings have never been written into traditional music scoring with any degree of precision.

"The standard *pp, p, mf, f, ff,* etc., indicate relative, approximate amounts of volume, and are never applied to every single note in a score, and their final determining is left to the interpreting artist; but in creating animated music the precise dynamics of every note in the score is the job of the composer; in other words the composer must also be the interpretive artist.

"To this end, 24 degrees of dynamic level were used (representing a decibel scale) and opposite each note in the score the number representing the desired dynamic level of that note was written.

"For instance, 0, 1, and 2, represent three differing degrees of *ppp;* 9, 10, and 11, three shades of *mp;* 12, 13, and 14, three degrees of *mf;* 21, 22, and 23, three degrees of *fff,* and 24 represents *ffff.*

"Subdivisions of these 24 degrees were constantly being used (particularly in crescendos and diminuendos) but were seldom written into the score. In local or rapid crescendos and diminuendos only the starting and finishing dynamic marks were written and the type of crescendos and diminuendos (such as 'arithmetical' or 'geometric') were indicated by a small sketch.

"The volume was controlled sometimes by manipulating the shutter or diaphragm of the camera and so affecting the exposure (variable density control) but more often by covering up the 1 inch-wide drawing until only ½ inch, or ¼ inch or other fraction of its width was visible (variable area control). Whichever method was used, the calibration was in decibels.

Tone-contouring

"Not only did the composer have the last and precise word on dynamics but he was also forced to specify the exact tone-contouring of each note; that is, what sort of attack, sustention and decay each tone was to have.

"This is important because even more than the basic tone quality of the note, the contouring of the note affects the "instrumental" effect. In traditional musical sounds, for instance, a piano note has a very rapid attack, no period of sustention, but a long period of decay; its contour is like a mountain peak with one very steep side, and one gently sloping side. A typical organ note has an abrupt attack, a prolonged sustention and a rapid decay; a contour rather like a plateau with a precipice at one side and a steep slope at the other. A tap on a wood block has a sudden attack, no sustention and a very rapid decay. Wind instruments are capable of much less abrupt forms of attack than percussion instruments. A violin, like the human voice, is capable of almost any kind of attack, sustention and decay.

"And so the composer, by giving a particular contour to each note, affected what would traditionally be called its instrumental quality. In practice this was done by placing black masks of varying shapes in front of the selected pitch card bearing the drawing of the sound waves; in this way we obtained about six kinds of tone-contour.

Tone Quality

"In the sound-track of *Love Your Neighbour* the range and variety of sound effects and tone qualities were considerably enlarged by using several supplementary sets of drawings, some of which had rising and falling pitches for portamento and glissando effects. Some drawings, though very simple to the eye, had a very complex sound wave structure, rich in harmonics, thus giving very strident and harsh sound qualities.

Harmony

"For several simultaneous musical parts either in harmony or counterpoint, three different methods were used. Either different drawings were superimposed on each other by several separate exposures, or the sound-track was divided lengthwise into several parallel strips and the different drawings shot alongside of each other in each strip. Alternatively each musical part was shot on a separate film and the various parts mixed together during re-recording.

Acoustic Quality

"Animated sound produced by this method is normally 'dry,' or without resonance or echo. To achieve more resonance and to add acoustic quality two methods were used. The first, mainly for specific notes and localized or momentary effects, was done by shooting the same note on a rapid series of diminishing volumes (that is, the same drawing in smaller and smaller sizes); this simulates the natural effect of the sound waves bouncing back and forth from the walls of an instrument, room, hall, or cavern. The degree to which any particular note in the score can be placed in such an acoustical environment is controlled during shooting by the number and nature of diminishing replicas of the original drawings of that note.

"To obtain the general or overall acoustical environment, varying amounts of reverberation and echo were added, either electronically or acoustically during a re-recording.

". . . it has been found in several cases more economical to make animated rather than live music, particularly for animated visuals. Close synchronization with previously completed visuals presents no problems, and subsequent changes and alterations to parts of the music can be made without the need to re-do the whole score, simply by re-shooting the particular notes affected."

Work with animated sound has not been carried significantly further (if that is indeed possible) in recent years and one finds filmmakers like John Whitney going back to traditional music or onward into computer technology. Whitney's film *Matrix,* for instance, uses some of the piano music of Antonio Soler. Whitney has, however, carried forward his concepts concerning similarities between the visual and aural arts. "At the outset the similarities obtain only in a visual world that is completely dynamic," he emphasizes.

During the late 1940s Whitney was awarded a Guggenheim Fellowship for two years. "During that time, [I] developed some spontaneous real-time animation techniques. I could manipulate paper cut-outs to music. I was working with jazz music that had no pretentions and none of the complexity and subtlety of structure of traditional Western art music. I was finding ways to satisfy my own concepts regarding the dynamics of visual motion by ways that avoided the tedium, stasis, and the restrictions that you have with any cell animation or any conventional techniques. I was manipulating cut-outs and working with fluids, very much as they were later to be used in the light shows. I had an oil bath on a level tray with the light below. I put dye into the oil until it was deep red, and then used red-blind film in the camera. With my finger or with a stylus, I could draw on this thin surface of oil; drawing would push the oil away and the light would shine through so I could draw caligraphic, linear sequences very freely; and by selecting the weight and thickness of the oil, I could control the rate at which the line would erase itself, so that it was constantly erasing with a constantly fresh surface to draw on—the ultimate Tabla Rasa. I was doing that and manipulating paper cutouts, and then doing a lot of direct etching on film as McLaren had done. I made, during that time, half a dozen little films to classic jazz recordings such as Will Bradley's.

"At that time I was building much of my own equipment including a selsyn interlock system. The sound track was previously recorded, and it could be run backward and forward in interlock with the camera. The only cue I had as to my progress in making a film was what I could hear along the soundtrack; so I would rehearse two or three riffs of a piece, plan it more or less spontaneously right there and then shoot it; then back the film up to work another section or over the same section, or make a superimposure over that. Accumulatively, I was painting a complex moving image on film. I'd shoot complete three minute films in one afternoon's work."

The important thing about Whitney's work in this area was that it pointed to a kind of spontaneous performance—much like improvisation in music. Whitney points out that this system "pointed to something else: to give up film techniques entirely and begin to explore video techniques. I made a proposal in the early fifties at UCLA that we set up an arrangement with six or eight video cameras and six or eight performers using these various manipulation techniques—the cameras were to be mixed electronically—then we'd perform a real-time graphic experience as an ensemble. The very idea of an ensemble to 'perform' a visual art is quite valid. I think and hope it will happen some day."

In a film entitled *Permutations*, Whitney has consciously carried the consonance-dissonance (relaxation-tension) concept of music into the visual arts through the imaginative use of computers. Speaking of the dots that create the graphics of the film, Whitney points up the similarities of the effect, created by the graphic figures, to some of the tensional effects created by music. Whitney says: "Every one of the points in *Permutations* is moving at a different rate and moving in an independent direction in accord with natural laws as valid as Pythagoras' while moving within their circular field. Their action produces a phenomenon which is more or less equivalent to musical harmonics. When the dots reach certain numerical (harmonic) relationships with other parameters in the equation, they form elementary many-lobed figures [see Figure 7]. Then they go off into a non-simple numerical relationship and appear to be random again. I think of this as an order-disorder phenomenon that suggests the harmony-dissonance effect of music. Graphically, as a static illustration in a book, it may not be as striking as it is to perceive the dynamics of the experience on film."

Whitney does, however, see the inherent fallacy of trying to invent a technology that would produce a musical counterpart to graphics or vice versa. For him, "music is sort of a narrow road I'd like to try to steer my own way through. I don't want to go in either of two directions. For example, I don't want to be mechanistic about art. And yet I'd like to begin to work with parallels which abound within the computer system for sound and image. Let me add, I am not composing music right now simply because I have my hands full with what I'm doing about the graphic formal problems."

Whitney rightly observes that creating some sort of musical score that would simultaneously generate a graphic countervoice would be "just as arbitrary to do as to invent a machine whereby I might compose the piano part while the machine does the violin part of a duo musical work. Yet all in all the great music of the future may well be heterosensuous."

In his more recent films Whitney has been trying to achieve the same kind of control that the composer has with music. I see the composer as an intuitive architect creating and manipulating aural material which has the effect of producing distinct feeling states on the listener. However, Whitney "agrees with Stravinsky that the problem of music is essentially one of architecture. A kind of spatial architecture. The emotional response is solely a by-product or a natural, inevitable development from that."

Whitney draws this concept into his film work, believing that "it is possible to create a spatial architecture that the eye can perceive and that has the same kind of potential for emotive consequences as the most profound music."

Whitney also feels that he is gaining more and more control over the effects he wishes to create. He says: "I do have a cautious, unfolding confidence in being able to predict effects that I know will affect you. But one technical development that is urgently necessary is production in real-time. I think as soon as we have computer graphic systems that produce the kind of fluidity I'm presently able to generate, being generated in real time, then we're going to be able to achieve something fantastic. . . . Then we're going to really begin to make exciting film experiences. And I'm sure these developments will have revolutionary consequences for the composer and musical audiences though all this may be inconceivable to us right now. For example, we do not even clearly understand the relationships between the spontaneous and the cautious, the contemplative and the planned in musical art."

Whitney sees another relationship between the graphic structure of his film *Permutations* and musical structure: "Notice that in music, frequently the first hearing of a piece of music is not transparent to you. In fact, with better music, often enough (it is a truism), if you're not totally familiar with the composer, the sections that you'll like most in the long run will be those which are hardest for you to appreciate upon the first hearing. I would argue that, with my recent films there is this quality: if you see a film again and again you will discover more structure. It will become more revealed to you that the whole work is a structure possessing its own kind of pattern integrity. It is unfortunate that our film viewing conventions do not permit the repetition we allow with music."

As advanced and sophisticated as Whitney's theories and films are, he clearly perceives that his art is, in many ways, still in an embryonic stage. He asks: "What if eight tones of the musical scale hadn't been discovered yet? What if our composers had only four tones to work with? And . . . what if the pianist had to wait twelve hours before he could hear the keys he had played? And, on the other hand, what if we could buy and play in our home these new visual compositions as freely as we play music recordings? Probably we will soon. And I expect we'll soon find the missing notes."

Figure 7. Selected here are some frames from the film *Permutations*. They might represent a much longer time sequence; being each one only the twenty-fourth frame, or one sampling every second of time. The order-disorder dynamics are explicit.

This sequence could as well be a schematized illustration of a melodic figure of music. (Read top to bottom.) Used by permission of John Whitney.

PART II

Aesthetics

6

The Aesthetics of Film Music

What is it, exactly, that music contributes to a film? David Raksin has written that music's avowed purpose in films is "to help realize the meaning of a film." Aaron Copland has said that a composer can do no more than "make potent through music the film's dramatic and emotional value." Both observations approach a general answer to the question. We shall divide this question further into five rather broad areas, taking a detailed look at each. The main headings are Aaron Copland's, drawn from his article in *The New York Times* of November 6, 1949; the discussion that follows each heading is the author's work.

"Music can create a more convincing atmosphere of time and place."

There are a variety of ways of achieving an atmosphere of time and place, or, musically speaking, "color." In a broad sense, musical color may be taken to represent the exotic or sensuous aspects of music, as distinct from musical structure, or line, which might be considered the intellectual side. Although admittedly an oversimplification, this distinction has a good deal of validity in terms of film music. Film music is overwhelmingly coloristic in its intention and effect. This is always true when a composer is attempting to create an atmosphere of time and place.

213

Color is associative—bagpipes call up images of Scotland, the oboe easily suggests a pastoral scene, muted brass connotes something sinister, rock music may imply a youthful theme, and so on. Also, color is not intrusive; it does not compete with the dramatic action. This is especially important for film music. The effect of color, moreover, is *immediate,* unlike musical thematic development, which takes time. In addition, color is highly flexible and can be brought in and out with relative ease by the experienced screen composer. An important quality of color, given the short amount of time the composer usually has to write a feature score, is that color is easier to achieve than musical design. Finally, and probably most important of all, color can be readily understood by a musically unsophisticated film audience.

Musical color can be achieved in a variety of ways. One is to use musical material indigenous to the locale of a film. Thus Adolph Deutsch employed sea chanteys in *Action on the North Atlantic,* and Alfred Newman used street songs and hurdy-gurdy music in *A Tree Grows in Brooklyn.* A related technique is the use of musical devices that are popularly associated with foreign lands and people; for example, using the pentatonic idiom to achieve an Oriental color. The "Chinese" music written for a studio film of the 1930s and '40s is not, of course, authentic Chinese music but rather represents our popular Occidental notions of what Chinese music is like. The Western listener simply does not understand the symbols of authentic Oriental music as he does those of Western music; therefore, Oriental music would have little dramatic effect for him.

Along the same lines, there is the problem of stylistic integration. This arises when composers are required to use set pieces of music for purposes of color within the larger framework of their score. Such set pieces can include folk songs, music for fairs, street cries, dances, and so on. It is far better for the composer to arrange these pieces himself so that they conform stylistically with the rest of his music for the picture. The folk-song arrangements of Bartók indicate ample precedent for this. The problem can be avoided entirely if the composer creates his own atmosphere music. An example of this is Bernard Herrmann's hurdy-gurdy music for *Hangover Square.* The film's climax includes the performance of a piano concerto written specially for the film and Herrmann simply took one of the concerto themes and transformed it into the hurdy-gurdy music.

Stylistic parody * is another coloristic device, and one that has been only slightly cultivated in film music. Examples can be found in Hugo Friedhofer's score to *The Bishop's Wife,* wherein he uses a concerto-grosso style, and in David Raksin's score to *Forever Amber,* in the pseudo-Handelian music for the amusing scene in the king's antechamber (a portion of this music can be seen in Figure 1). Few composers are capable of carrying off stylistic parody, for it takes an intimate sense of another's compositional style.

Figure 1. Excerpt from *Forever Amber,* music by David Raksin.

This emphasis on color does not mean that musical line should or does go unused, however. The primary reason film composers have traditionally stayed away from complex line and structure in music is that such complicated structures cannot successfully be emphasized without competing with the dramatic action; i.e., it is bad film music. The answer to the problem of color and line, as it applies to film music, is that musical color can, to an extent, be created just as effectively by the confluence of

* Parody, as used here, refers to the musical procedure common in the latter part of the sixteenth century and exemplified in such works as Josquin's Mass *Malheur me bat.* The somewhat unfortunate term, of 19th-century German coinage, refers only to a method of composition and is not intended to have a pejorative meaning.

individualized lines (a more contrapuntal texture) as by the arbitrary piling up of dissonance in a chord. Examples of this kind of contrapuntal coloristic writing abound in the scores of both David Raksin and Hugo Friedhofer. Raksin's score for the little-known film *The Redeemer* is full of canons and fugatos; Friedhofer's score to *Joan of Arc* has several highly contrapuntal sequences.

> *"Music can be used to underline or create psychological refinements—the unspoken thoughts of a character or the unseen implications of a situation."*

Frequently, music can imply a psychological element far better than dialogue can. This use of film music is perhaps most effective when it is planned well in advance—when the film is in the scripting stage. Far too often, however, this possibility is passed over and music is not allowed to speak. Copland has observed that music "can play upon the emotions of the spectator, sometimes counterpointing the thing seen with an aural image that implies the contrary of the thing seen." Although music in film can be most effective in such instances, composers are given little chance to use it.

One of the classic examples of this kind of writing is found in David Raksin's score to *Force of Evil,* discussed in some detail in chapter 3. In the final scene the main character, Joe (John Garfield), is seen running in the street, then along a great stone wall and down a huge flight of stairs. Yet the music here is not "running" music—Raksin has scored the emotional rather than the physical character of the scene. Joe has been running, figuratively, throughout the film; it is only now, as he begins the search for his dead brother's body, that he finds any sort of quietude. Raksin reflects this psychological point in his slow music for this sequence.

The ability of music to make a psychological point in film is a subtle one, and perhaps its most valuable contribution. Yet film theoreticians appear not even to recognize music's possibilities in this area. For example, George Bluestone, in his book *Novels into Film,* states that "the film, being a presentational medium (except for its use of dialogue) cannot have direct access to the power of discursive forms. The rendition of mental states—memory, dream, imagination—cannot be as adequately represented by film as by language. . . . The film, by arranging external signs for our visual perception, or by presenting us with dialogue, can lead us to infer thought. But it cannot show us thought directly. It can show us characters thinking, feeling, and speaking, but it cannot show us their thoughts and feelings. A film is not thought; it is perceived."

This quote demonstrates the typical naïveté of most film theoreticians concerning the possibilities of music in films. If by the word "film" Bluestone means a total work (i.e., visuals, dialogue, sound effects, and music) then his statement is totally invalid, for music can and does serve just this function better than any other element of film.

Composer Leonard Rosenman has pointed out that "film music has the power to change naturalism [in films] into reality. Actually, the musical contribution to the film should be ideally to create a *supra-reality*, a condition wherein the elements of literary naturalism are perceptually altered. In this way the audience can have the insight into different aspects of behavior and motivation not possible under the aegis of naturalism.

"Film music must thus enter directly into the 'plot' of the film, adding a third dimension to the images and words. It is an attempt to establish the *supra-reality* of a many-faceted portrayal of behavior that should motivate the composer in the selection of sequences to be scored and, just as important, the sequences to be left silent."

While music certainly does have the catalytic ability to change the audience's perception of images and words, it is worth pointing out that there is a corollary: the effect of the image and words upon the music. A simple recollection by composer Leonard Rosenman should suffice to make the point. Rosenman says, "There is a symbiotic catalytic exchange-relationship between the film and the music that accompanies it. I have personally had the experience of hearing musically unenlightened people comment positively and glowingly on a 'dissonant' score after seeing the film. I have played these same people records of the score without telling them that it came from the film they had previously seen. Their reaction ranged from luke-warm to positive rejection. . . . ."

"Music can serve as a kind of neutral background filler."

Aaron Copland has said of "background" music: "This is really the kind of music one isn't supposed to hear, the sort that helps to fill the empty spots between pauses in a conversation. It's the movie composer's most ungrateful task. But at times, though no one else may notice, he will get private satisfaction from the thought that music of little intrinsic value, through professional manipulation, has enlivened and made more human the deathly pallor of a screen shadow. This is hardest to do . . . when the neutral filler type of music must weave its way underneath dialogue."

This can sometimes be the film composer's most difficult task for it calls for him to be at his most subordinative. At times one of the functions of film music is to do nothing more than be there, "as though it would exist as sound rather than as 'constructed' music." Even though it is filling a rather subordinate role to other elements in the picture, "filler" type music is in fact a very conscious dramatic device. Hugo Friedhofer's score to *Broken Arrow* offers two outstanding examples of how this can be masterfully handled.

Figure 2. Excerpt from *Broken Arrow,* music by Hugo Friedhofer.

The first example (Figure 2) is the underscoring for a scene at the beginning of the film. In this scene the film's star, James Stewart, is riding on horseback through the Western desert. Pictorially the setting is spacious, immobile, and quiet. The slow gait of the horse is the only sign of life; the hero is meditative, and a narrator starts the story on its way. Even though the inner parts are extremely simple, they still make music by themselves. There is just enough harmony in the outer parts to keep the solo clarinet from competing with the narrator's voice, and just enough mobility in the inner parts to counteract the rather static monotony of the double pedal.

The other example (Figure 3) of Friedhofer's from *Broken Arrow* is music accompanying a wedding ceremony. The tender, delicate melody, cast in the aeolian mode, is so well suited to its purpose that Lawrence Morton was moved to say that it "shows how it is possible to avoid the pitfall of an Apache *Lohengrin.*"

Figure 3. Excerpt from *Broken Arrow.*

There are times when music accompanying dialogue can take on a definite foreground character. An example of this is in the film *The Heiress* (see chapter 3). Generally, such music is treated musically in a

Figure 4. Excerpt from *Will Penny*, music by David Raksin.

recitative style reminiscent of the opera: blank spots in the dialogue are filled with fragments of music, which come to the foreground momentarily to comment on the dialogue and then drop back into the background when the next line is said. All of this has to be done, of course, by the way the composer writes his music, not by the simple turning of knobs in the dubbing room. Dimitri Tiomkin's score to *High Noon* has several prominent examples of this kind of writing, especially in the scenes involving the sheriff and his deputy. Another example, again by David Raksin, and from the film *Will Penny*, clearly demonstrates how a composer writes around dialogue (see Figure 4).

In this example Raksin has treated the dialogue operatically, that is to say, in the manner of a recitative. The small "x's" above each staff of music indicate the "clicks" of the click track.* Note that Raksin has written in the dialogue spoken by Preacher Quint exactly where it will occur in relation to the clicks. The dialogue begins in bar 7 with Preacher Quint's invocation, "Beware the wrath of the Lord." The music drops out when there is a line; this "clears" the dialogue without the dubber's having to drop the music level down when mixing it with the dialogue track. The time space between Quint's lines is filled with declamatory music. Note, too, Raksin's notation of the rhythm of the delivery of the lines "Life for life" and "eye for eye" in bars 11 and 12:

Figure 5.

Vocal rhythm:

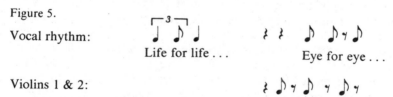

Life for life . . .   Eye for eye . . .

Violins 1 & 2:

The importance of this masterful attention to detail can be seen especially in bar 12 where the strings play a pizzicato figure, the third note of which (D-flat) fills the eighth rest in the dialogue.

"Music can help build a sense of continuity in a film."

Music can tie together a visual medium that is, by its very nature, continually in danger of falling apart. A film editor is probably most

---

* For a complete discussion of click tracks see chapter 8.

conscious of this particular attribute of music in films. In a montage, particularly, music can serve an almost indispensable function: it can hold the montage together with some sort of unifying musical idea. Without music the montage can, in some instances, become merely chaotic. Music can also develop this sense of continuity on the level of the film as a whole. This idea is discussed in greater detail in chapter 7.

"Music can provide the underpinning for the theatrical buildup of a scene and then round it off with a sense of finality."

Music has a way of bypassing the human's normal, rational defense mechanisms. When used properly, music can help build the drama in a scene to a far greater degree of intensity than any of the other cinematic arts. It is of little significance whether the scene involves an intimate love relationship or a violent fight; music evokes a gut reaction unobtainable in any other way. On the other hand, this can be one of the least effective uses of film music if not handled properly. In fact, many producers and directors seem to feel this is film music's only function in a film—especially if the film is inherently weak. Every composer who has worked in film has, at one time or another, been asked to provide music for a weak scene in the hopes that the music will somehow make the scene stronger. It simply cannot be done, and it is then the composer who usually but unfairly receives the critic's blame for a scene poorly executed.

One wonders if some of the objections to music in films is that it is *too* effective. We tend to react to music whether we desire to or not and if we don't wish to be moved by it, we resent its presence for making us begin to lose control of our rational, "sophisticated" defenses.

Of course, there are times in a film, perhaps even entire films, when any kind of music is inappropriate. One critic, writing about the film *Sunset Boulevard,* said: "The plain fact is that the script of *Sunset Boulevard,* with its use of both narration and dialogue, and its realization through the camera, is so complete as to leave music not much to do." This certainly *can* be the case, but it is not true of most films. Films usually lack music because a producer or director did not want it. To them, music impinges on a sense of "realism." "Where's the music coming from?" is the oft-quoted question. This question was raised during Hitchcock's filming of *Lifeboat.* On hearing that Hitchcock had asked, "But where is the music supposed to come from out in the middle of the ocean?" composer David Raksin replied: "Ask Mr. Hitchcock where the cameras come from." * The answer, unfortunately for the film composer, demonstrates more intelligence and perception than the question. The film composer must understand more about every other aspect of the filmmaker's craft than any other individual involved in the production. Since the composer is usually called in on the project after the film is complete, he must know what the director, cinematographer, actors, and editor are all trying to say dramatically. Without this dramatic sense for film, the composer is lost and his contribution to the film will be negligible.

A famous example of what purports to be a totally fused relationship of music and picture is the "audiovisual score" constructed by Sergei Eisenstein of a sequence from *Alexander Nevsky*. Because this example is used frequently in film classes and because the assumption that it is a totally fused relationship of music and picture is wholly incorrect, a critique of its essential points are in order.

Figure 6 shows that Eisenstein has constructed a diagram of the "picture rhythm" as well as the "musical movement," for he considers the two to be identical. "Now let us collate the two graphs," he writes in his book *The Film Sense,* "What do we find? Both graphs of movement correspond absolutely, that is, we find a complete correspondence between the movement of the music and the movement of the eye over the lines of the plastic composition. In other words, exactly the same motion lies at the base of both the musical and the plastic structures."

Two areas in this "correspondence" between picture and music are highly questionable. The first is the relationship of the rhythm of the music to the rhythm of the picture. The identification of musical and visual rhythms is dubious because in the plastic arts the concept of rhythm is largely metaphorical. Here the problem for Eisenstein is compounded, as his graphs refer to single shots, not to the time relation between them.

The second area in which Eisenstein's views are questionable deals with the idea that the graphs are supposed to prove that the actual movement

---

* In my research I have seen this famous reply attributed respectively to David Raksin, a sound technician, Lionel Barrymore, and someone in the studio music department. Some checking with those present at the time, however, proved beyond any doubt that it was Raksin who came up with this famous comment.

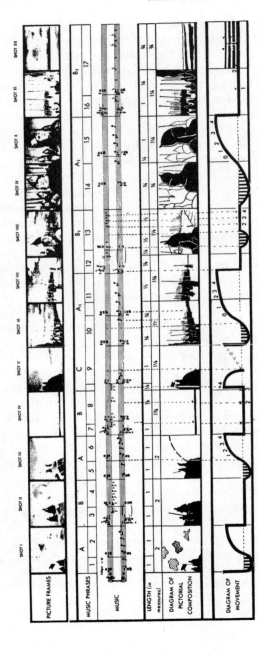

Figure 6. "Audiovisual score" from *Alexander Nevsky*, directed by Sergei Eisenstein, music by Sergei Prokofiev. This oft-used example of what purports to be a totally fused relationship of music and picture is seriously flawed. Excerpt from *The Film Sense* by Sergei Eisenstein. Translated and edited by Jay Leyda. Copyright 1942, by Harcourt Brace Jovanovich, Inc. and renewed 1970 by Jay Leyda. Reprinted by permission of the publisher.

of the music is similar to the sequence of pictures. In reality, what the graph proves is that there is a similarity between the *notation* of the music and the picture sequence. This is an extremely important and crucial distinction upon which the whole of Eisenstein's premise rests. But Eisenstein's comparison is a bogus one, for musical notation is merely a graphic fixation of actual musical movement, "the static image of a dynamic phenomenon," according to Hanns Eisler. Music is an art that moves *through* time, an art that cannot be perceived instantaneously; whereas, in Eisenstein's graph, the pictures are perceived instantly. And while it is possible for the film director, through the composition of his shot, to control somewhat the direction of the viewer's eye movement across the frame, there is no way to control the rhythm or pace of that movement. In shot IV in the diagram, two flags are visible on the horizon. Eisenstein correlates these two flags to two eighth notes in the music. Because these two flags are vertical images and in direct conflict with the primary horizontal composition of the shot, they are recognized instantly by the eye. The music, however, is quite another matter. Using Prokofiev's tempo marking of Largo ♩ = 48, it takes approximately 4 seconds from the time shot IV appears on the screen to the appearance of the first specified eighth note on the sound track. It is another 2½ seconds before the second eighth note is heard. The point is that the recognition of the metaphorical picture rhythm of shot IV is instantaneous, while the musical rhythm that Eisenstein claims corresponds to the picture rhythm takes 6½ seconds to be perceived.

Another example of this sort of faulty comparison can be seen in Shot V. The music supposedly imitates the steeply sloping rocks by descending down a triad. The descent down the triad in the music actually has the appearance of a precipitously falling curve in the notation. But the problem here is that in the music itself the fall occurs *in time,* while the steeply sloping rock in Shot V is seen as unchanged from the first note to the last.

A further objection has to do with the development of the sequence and the music. If we are to accept Eisenstein's thesis of a correspondence between the music and the picture, then we can assume that the musical development will match that of the motion picture. The music then should show some distinction between the close-up and the panoramic views of the film.

However, a close examination of both music and picture will reveal that just the opposite is true, for here the picture moves on while the music merely marks time. For instance, there is a clear difference in the stage of development between the first three shots, which show a good amount of detail, and shot IV, which is a general view of the battle line. But an examination of the music will show that measures 5 through 8 literally repeat measures 1 through 4. In this instance Eisenstein's repeated suggestion that picture and music should correspond in movement goes unnoticed. Alluding again to shot IV, the two eighth notes representing the flags also are heard in the music accompanying shot II, which does not show any flags. If Eisenstein wishes to be so pedantic in translating picture details into music, he should at least make the pedantry consistent. Instead, Eisenstein seems to practice such pedantry one moment and then forgets it in the next.

What Prokofiev seems to be doing with the music at this point is catching the general tension of this pre-battle moment. In other words, the music is speaking to the psychology of the moment (i.e., apprehension, fear) in terms of the characters involved rather than to any abstract notion of shot development or metaphorical "picture rhythm."

Film theoreticians refuse to give up their idea that this example represents the ultimate wedding of music and picture. For example, John Howard Lawson in his book, *Film: The Creative Process,* decries the fact that "the experimental work initiated by Eisenstein and Prokofiev in *Alexander Nevsky* has not been appreciated in theory or utilized in practice." This support of Eisenstein's concept of an "audiovisual score" on the part of film theoreticians is a result of their highly limited and superficial knowledge and understanding of music.

7

Film Music and Form

Of the many criticisms leveled at film music, a major charge is that it lacks cohesive form. Naïve at best, such criticism betrays a total lack of understanding concerning the function of film music and its intimate relationship with other elements of the film. Even a composer as towering as Stravinsky failed to understand this crucial point about film music. When he was hired by Columbia Pictures to do a score for *Commandos Strike at Dawn* Stravinsky, unbeknownst to the producer, proceeded to write some sketches for the picture—without having ever seen the film, which had not been completed at that time. Obviously, the sketches were unusable for that film; Stravinsky later adapted them into what is now known as *The Four Norwegian Moods.**

A good film composer must be chameleonlike both with his compositional style and, perhaps more importantly, with the form and shape his music takes in relation to the dramatic developments on the screen. It is a cardinal rule for the film composer that the visuals on the screen determine the form of the music written to accompany it. A composer

---

* Composer David Raksin recalls another case: "When Villa-Lobos was here to do the film *Green Mansions* he told me that he had already finished the music—orchestration and all. (The film was still shooting, but he had written the music without reference to its timings.) After he returned to Brazil, Bronislau Kaper adapted the music to fit the picture."

encounters similar problems when he sets about the task of creating a song from a given text. In this case, the *poet* has already grappled with the problem of form (just as a director has already dealt with the form of a motion picture); for the composer then to impose his own different *musical* form on the poem is asking for confusion, at the very least. Likewise, the film composer must take into consideration the form and rhythm of a scene established by the visuals. To do otherwise is to invite argument not only from the film itself but from the producer and director as well.

This problem of formal continuity between music and picture need not be resolved by having the music merely "ape" the action on the screen ("mickey-mousing"). While "mickey-mousing" is appropriate, even expected, in cartoons, it can be out of place and in poor taste in the dramatic film when it is not handled subtly.

There are, however, some brilliant and imaginative examples of music that take their form from the visual and dramatic structure of a scene. An eloquent example of visual-dramatic-musical formal continuity can be found in a small scene from William Wyler's film *Carrie*. The composer is David Raksin. At one point in the film, George Hurstwood (Laurence Olivier) has left his wife and his job as the manager of a sophisticated restaurant, and has run off to Chicago with Carrie (Jennifer Jones). Hurstwood learns that the knowledge of his theft of $10,000 from the owner of the restaurant where he had been employed has caught up with him and he will be unable to gain the kind of high-paying employment he has had in the past. This portion of the scene takes place in the hall of the hotel where he and Carrie are staying. The musical material used for this scene consists of two elements: a slow, plaintive bassoon solo and an elegant waltz tune. The waltz tune is first heard earlier, in the scene where Hurstwood and Carrie first meet in Hurstwood's restaurant. In the later scene, the waltz music is used primarily to evoke the elegance and sophistication of the restaurant. As the film progresses, however, the little waltz tune takes on dramatic importance and is used to recall those times between Hurstwood and Carrie when their problems did not involve mere survival.

When Hurstwood learns that his theft has been discovered the slow bassoon solo begins, giving the viewer an indication (along with Olivier's superb acting) of what must be going on inside of Hurstwood at the time. As Hurstwood goes back into the hotel room, he sees Carrie, very elegantly dressed and obviously very happy, and the slow waltz begins as Hurstwood looks longingly at her. He knows it is the last time they will know such a relatively carefree time. Carrie chatters on about nothing as Hurstwood looks on; this lasts for about 45 seconds. Then Carrie asks, "George, what is it? What's wrong?" At this point the slow bassoon solo returns, with its plaintive call indicating a return for Hurstwood, and now Carrie, to the reality of their plight. Dramatically the scene is a simple (although subtle) A-B-A form. Raksin structured his music accordingly: A = solo bassoon, B = waltz tune, and A = solo bassoon.

Another example demonstrating this formal principle is from the film *Joan of Arc,* with a score by Hugo Friedhofer. This music does not have the formal symmetry of the Raksin example since the dramatic structure did not call for it. The music for this sequence can be seen in Figure 1.

On the basis of screen action, this cue is divided into three sections. The first section covers bars 1–19, the second bars 20–33 and the third section bars 34–39. The sections are not related thematically; each has its own melodic material. The sections are, however, unified by texture, style, and the continuity of the action. This scene takes place at the French court, where, in order to test Joan, it has been arranged to have a courtier pose as the Dauphin. Joan senses the deception, and her "voices" lead her to single out the true Dauphin from the crowd of assembled courtiers.

As any musician will realize, the texture of the music is contrapuntal, for the most part. The opening phrase is answered in bar 9 in canon at the octave. In bar 13 the strict imitation is abandoned in order to begin a brief crescendo. In the next bars, as far as bar 20, the materials are still presented in two-part counterpoint and are almost completely derived from what has come before. This process represents a tiny development with fragments being piled atop each other in a more and more compact fashion. This intensification is increased still further by a rise in pitch and by the sudden change in bar 16 to a relatively homophonic structure. Also, the crescendo does not culminate in the expected climax but, rather, uses the device of a negative accent by going to a *subito piano* (suddenly soft). The *subito piano* in bar 20 begins the second section, which is a canon in three parts at the unison for treble voices. These voices in the score represent Joan's "voices." The orchestral accompaniment at this point should be regarded as no more than coloristic accompaniment, secondary to the vocal parts. Now ensues the delayed climactic passage, with the alto voices, horns, and trombones swelling into rich harmonies.

Figure 1. Excerpt from *Joan of Arc*, music by Hugo Friedhofer.

This climax is placed approximately in the third quarter of the piece, which, while serving the dramatic needs of the picture, also proves advantageous to the symmetry of the music. The remainder of this cue, from bar 34 on, is a musical and dramatic tapering off from the climax; it ends with a quiet theme in canon at the fifth below.

Of incidental interest is the fact that this cue uses the Dorian mode on G and that it employs a characteristic contrapuntal element of sixteenth-century counterpoint in that the melody never leaps a greater interval than a minor sixth. The range of the melody, however, does go beyond the restricted range of the ninth. The harmonies are also unobtrusive since there is nothing more complex than a triad. The progression of triads in the climactic section are definitely "contemporary" but the listener still perceives the section as predominantly modal in character. This particular sequence, while not the most complex in the score, is one of the most effective.

Thus far we have looked at the relationship between visual/dramatic form and musical form only in the context of individual scenes. What of the entire picture? Is there some sort of cohesive form at work within the picture as a whole, and, if so, should the music reflect this underlying formal structure of the entire film? The answer to both questions is undeniably yes, but with certain qualifications where the music is concerned. Unlike the visuals of a film, which are ever-present and, as a result, have the opportunity for smooth organic growth, music is not one of the ongoing elements of a film. Good film music is used sparingly and only at those moments where it will be most effective. This important dictum of good film music presents a unique formal problem for the composer. Form in absolute music, such as sonata-allegro or rondo, depends a great deal on the principle of repetition and contrast, but repetition and contrast in a relatively short time span and without interruption. With film, on the other hand, there may be long sections with no music at all, in which the audience has plenty of time to forget whatever musical material it may have heard earlier. Knowing this, the film composer has several general formal resources at his disposal to achieve some sort of formal unity in his music.

The first and most common resource is the leitmotiv, which had its flowering in the operas of the nineteenth-century composer Richard Wagner. Film composers picked up on the basic idea of having a different melody or motif for each character in a film. The advantage of the leitmotiv score is that the musical material is more easily recognizable by the audience. Max Steiner insisted that "every character should have a theme." The melodies or motifs of a leitmotiv score can be restated in various forms each time the character appears. Alterations in the melody's character (e.g., sinister, loving, excited) can give the listener some indication of that character's state of mind at any particular point. This device can become very valuable if the scene itself is emotionally neutral; the music can add something not already present on the screen. While this definition of leitmotiv is an oversimplification, it is not far from the mark. There are, to be sure, many bad examples of the leitmotiv score but there are also many fine examples of the concept being used in a highly subtle and unobtrusive manner. There are films where a motif has been used to express a single, recurring psychological state. One such is the film *The Lost Weekend,* with Ray Milland. The picture, which deals with alcoholism, was scored by Miklos Rozsa. In this score Rozsa makes use of a Theremin, a forerunner of present-day electronic music synthesizers invented by Leon Theremin. It is the sound of the Theremin playing a particular motif (see Figure 2) that helps suggest Ray Milland's craving for alcohol throughout the film. Neither the instrument nor the melodic material is used at any other time in the film; so when they appear on the sound track, they have a rather stunning dramatic impact. In this instance the sound of the Theremin is in itself part of the motif that suggests a psychological state.

Figure 2. Excerpt from *The Lost Weekend,* music by Miklos Rozsa.

Most composers working with leitmotiv scores tend to treat the melodic material as variations. In other words, a motif varies and develops alongside a character or dramatic situation. Easily one of the finest scores in this category is Hugo Friedhofer's score for *The Best Years of Our*

Lives. The 1946 film was rather lengthy for its time—it ran 170 minutes—and the score won Friedhofer a well-deserved Academy Award.

The Canadian film composer Louis Applebaum observed that in this film Friedhofer "chose to work on the development, juxtaposition and superimposition of leitmotifs more or less in the Wagnerian tradition. The material itself is definitely not Wagnerian in character, but the manner of its handling derives from the Wagner of the Niebelinger [sic] Ring." There are only five basic motifs from which Friedhofer draws his material for the rest of the score. Such economy of material is a tribute to Friedhofer's inventive genius. See chapter 3 for a more complete discussion of Friedhofer's score.

A second, and much overused formal device, is the monothematic film score, in which a composer uses *only* one tune (usually popular in nature) for an entire score. This compositional device had its classic expression in David Raksin's score for the Otto Preminger film *Laura.* The subsequent popularity of the haunting song derived from the score (with words by Johnny Mercer), along with the misapplication of the monothematic concept by producers, makes the score an early landmark in the variety of reasons for the slow demise of intelligent and sensitive film music.

In the case of *Laura* the monothematic score works because the film almost *demanded* such a score. The film deals with a pragmatic, tough detective-type who finds himself slowly falling in love with a girl he believes to be dead. The melody "Laura" has an important dramatic role in the film: for the better part of the film, the music *is* Laura. Film composer Elmer Bernstein touched on this dramatic function of the music when he said, "The film portrayed a man falling in love with a ghost: The mystique was supplied by the insistence of the haunting melody. He [the detective] could not escape it. It was everywhere. . . . We may not remember what Laura was like, but we never forget that she *was* the music." Never in the course of the film does Raksin use the theme to manufacture love interest between the detective and Laura (who, in the end, is really alive—a case of mistaken identity). Nor does Raksin overuse the theme—an important consideration in the success of the score.

There is a third type of formal structure for film scores; it bears some resemblance to the leitmotiv score and is perhaps best called a *developmental* score. The formal procedure of a developmental score could be loosely compared to the classical sonata-allegro form of the eighteenth-century but only insofar as developmental procedures are concerned. In many instances the Main Title music in a developmental score serves the function of the exposition in classical sonata-allegro form in that it presents the musical material to be used throughout the score. Here any *structural* resemblance to sonata-allegro ends, there being no definite sequence of formal events in a film score as there is in a sonata-allegro movement. There are altered and unaltered recapitulations of material in a film score but these are decided more by the film's dramatic necessities than by any inherent musical considerations. Among the numerous examples of this type of film score is David Raksin's score to *Forever Amber*. We will use it to demonstrate the kinds of transformations a theme or themes can go through in a score.

Figure 3. *Passacaglia* figure from *Forever Amber*, music by David Raksin.

Figure 3 is the original *passacaglia* idea from which all the other material of the score is derived. Figure 4 shows material derived from the *passacaglia* figure and which proves to be a durable thematic source throughout the score.

The reader should notice the ostinato idea in the bass. This motif is later used as a thematic idea in its own right when it becomes a cantus-firmus of a scherzo sequence.

The little theme shown in Figure 4 becomes, in a new guise, Amber's theme (see Figure 5).

Figure 4. Excerpt from *Forever Amber*.

Figure 5. Excerpt from *Forever Amber*.

Figures 6, 7, and 8 show the material in Figure 4 developed into several new short phrases:

Figure 6. Excerpt from *Forever Amber,* music by David Raksin.

Figure 7. Excerpt from *Forever Amber.*

Figure 8. Excerpt from *Forever Amber*.

Figure 4 then becomes a fast string passage in a scherzo, with the ostinato in the bass:

Figure 9. Excerpt from *Forever Amber*.

The metamorphosis continues with the last few notes of Figure 9 being used as a rhythmic figure in Figure 10.

Figure 10. Excerpt from *Forever Amber*, music by David Raksin.

The first few notes of Figure 9 then become a new motive found in Figure 11.

Figure 11. Excerpt from *Forever Amber*.

In the course of this scherzo movement the fast string run and the ostinato are simultaneously inverted, as seen in Figure 12.

Figure 12. Excerpt from *Forever Amber*.

Raksin has said of his score to *Forever Amber:* "There are enough canons in this score to start a minor Balkan uprising." One of these canons is developed out of the original material found in Figure 4. The same ostinato in the bass accompanies the canon:

Figure 13. Excerpt from *Forever Amber*.

Figure 14 shows the first three notes of the original theme in a transformation into another short melodic phrase.

Figure 14. Excerpt from *Forever Amber*, music by David Raksin.

Figure 15 shows the same three notes from the original theme inverted for use as a climactic figure.

Figure 15. Excerpt from *Forever Amber*.

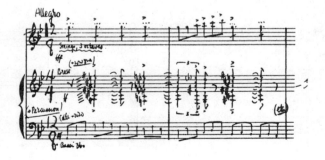

Figures 14 and 15 are then used together to form yet another new phrase, alternately bitter and sympathetic:

Figure 16. Excerpt from *Forever Amber*.

The original theme of Figure 4 becomes, at one point, a chorale, with an elaboration of the ostinato running through it:

Figure 17. Excerpt from *Forever Amber*, music by David Raksin.

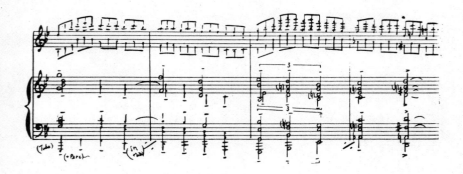

Finally, the string passage found in Figure 9, the ostinato of Figure 4, and sundry other material is moved into the key of the relative major in Figure 18.

Figure 18. Excerpt from *Forever Amber*.

Figure 19 contains the material that ends the prologue of the film and that accompanies the beginning of the story. The key is B-flat major at the beginning of this example but, by the end, has shifted back to the original key of Figure 4, G minor. Raksin has humorously dubbed this particular example a *Quasicaglia* because "it managed to avoid being either a *Passacaglia* or a *Basso Ostinato* while combining the worst features of both."

Figure 19. Excerpt from *Forever Amber*.

Raksin's humorous self-criticism is perhaps a little harsh. The meta-morphoses of one single theme, as shown in the previous examples, demonstrates a highly fertile imagination as well as a great deal of technical facility.

In closing it should be pointed out that there are instances where composers have the opportunity to apply conventional musical forms to film. One of the more common musical forms to be found in the cinema is the *scherzo*, which is a fast and usually exciting piece of music. This musical form has been used innumerable times in music accompanying chase scenes in films. In fact, the scherzo has been used with such frequency that it allowed Burt Bacharach to do something rather imaginative in his otherwise dismal score for *Butch Cassidy and the Sundance Kid.* The most effective place musically in the film is a portion that has no music at all. There is a rather lengthy scene where the two heroes (Paul Newman and Robert Redford) are being chased by the law across the plains. Rather than employ the usual *scherzo* at this point—an almost unbreakable tradition in Westerns—Bacharach chose instead to create a kind of negative accentuation by avoiding music altogether.

Another musical form occurs in one of the more famous montage sequences in all of cinema. It is a theme and variations, employed by composer Bernard Herrmann in his brilliant and flamboyant score for the great Orson Welles film, *Citizen Kane.* The famous montage sequence brilliantly shows the dissolution of Kane's marriage to his first wife. It begins with Kane and his young wife very much in love. Herrmann employs a gentle little waltz tune through this first portion, and as the montage proceeds, he writes a variation on the waltz tune for each sequence of the montage, the variations reflecting in mood the change in the relationship between Kane and his wife.

The opportunity for employing strictly musical forms in pictures is a rather rare one for film composers, and when musical forms are used, it should only be in those instances where the scene allows for it or, as in the montage sequence from *Citizen Kane,* the scene almost demands it.

In any attempt to describe what is basically a visual-aural experience through the medium of words, much is lost in the translation. Unlike sonata or rondo form where the listener has certain preconceived formal expectations concerning the music, with film music there cannot be any real formal expectations in the traditional sense of the word simply because there are none. Each film has a unique form, each scene its unique underlying rhythm, and it is these elements that a sensitive film composer tries to capture in his music.

While it would be possible to cite more examples of visual-dramatic-musical continuity of form, it is enough to alert the reader that form is operating at various levels within a film. Music is most certainly one of them.

PART III

Technique

8

Synchronizing Music To Picture

The first thing a composer does before scoring a picture is, of course, to see the picture. He usually does this when the film is in what is known as the "final cut," meaning it will be released to the public in much the form he sees it at this initial screening. In an extremely rare instance, a composer will be consulted during the making of a film. Alfred Hitchcock's long and successful relationship with Bernard Herrmann is one example of a director consulting with a composer even before a film gets to the shooting stage, but this is most certainly the exception. Composers normally only get involved during the shoot if dance music or some other "source" music must be written before a sequence is actually filmed. This situation is created when music is needed for actors to dance and / or sing as a scene is being photographed. Recording the music before photographing the scene enables the music and picture to stay in synch throughout the editing and post-production process. When such music is played on the shooting stage for the actors the procedure is called "playback."

Once the composer has seen this initial screening to get a sense of the film, he then runs the picture reel by reel, stopping and re-running a scene if needed, deciding where music should begin and end within the picture. This procedure is known as "spotting" a film and the participants normally include the producer, director, composer, and music editor.

The discussion which takes place at this session is primarily aesthetic in nature and, aside from the actual composing of the score, is probably the most critical aspect in the process of providing music for motion pictures. The results, if they have been handled with good taste and judgment, are one of the most subtle areas of music in motion pictures.

The decision to start music at the top of a scene or within a scene is always based on the details of that particular sequence and situation. Therefore, there are no hard and fast rules about where music should begin. There are, however, certain conventions that have persisted. These include initiating music at the end of a pivotal line of dialogue or on a hard cut to an action sequence. Music will sometimes begin on a bit of action by a character in the film or a sudden, violent move such as a car pulling out in a "chase" sequence. Since, unlike opera, film music is constantly entering and disappearing, composers sensitive to this area of spotting are very much aware that when music does make an entrance it is immediately noticed by the ear. Because it has been absent from the soundtrack, music's presence is more acutely noticed at this point than might be expected. Composers, of course, exploit this fact by occasionally maintaining silence for a longer period of time than usual in order to add even more emphasis to an important music entry.

The weight of musical entrances ranges from crashing beginnings to moments where music "eases in" as quietly as possible. There are, of course, many shades in between these two extremes which can be exploited, as can these very conventions themselves. This phenomenon is always one of the primary considerations in the decision of start points for music in a picture. Another important consideration is the pacing of the music throughout the film. Questions such as "How much time has elapsed since the last cue ended?" and "How long was the last cue?" are frequently asked during spotting sessions. Unlike earlier periods when music in films tended to be "wall-to-wall," current practice tends toward a more sparing use of music throughout a picture. I do not mean to infer any judgment about the two approaches but wish only to present the observation that music in films, as any other art form, is in a constant state of reaction and flux.

Once the motion picture has been spotted the music editor, who has taken detailed "spotting notes" during the session, now proceeds to generate for the composer what are called "timing breakdown notes" or, simply, "timing notes" or "breakdowns" (see Figure 1). Note that the breakdown is a detailed description of the scene requiring music. The music editor creates these from a copy of the film which is provided to him by the production company. Most composers work from these timing notes but there have been some notable exceptions, including Aaron Copland and Erich Wolfgang Korngold. Aaron

Figure 1. Timing breakdown notes for the Laurence Rosenthal cue *Land Rovers*, from the mini-series *On Wings of Eagles*.

```
-----------)                                    <---------- 11/14/90
NAME        START       On Wings of Eagles - (Drop Frame)
                                                            PAGE 1
2-5M-1      42:47:10    Cue begings EOL (End of line) "...to the Turkish
                        border, my friend."
```

CUM TIME	TIME CODE	NOTES:
0:00.00	42:47:10	EO1 above as he turns and moves towards the door.
0:02.56	42:49:27	The three men with rifles begin to move in towards the businessman.
0:06.33	42:53:20	He starts to back away.
0:08.10	42:55:13	CUT to a MS of businessman.
0:09.47	42:56:24	CUT to MS of three men as they continue to move in on him.
0:11.01	42:58:10	CUT to MS of businessman as he trips and falls.
0:11.97	42:59:09	CUT to a CU of telephone lines.
0:14.01	43:01:12	CUT to a FS of man climbing down telephone pole.
0:16.98	43:04:11	He hits the ground.
0:18.38	43:05:23	He bows to the others.
0:19.01	43:06:12	CUT to a FS of rest of group with Lancaster in the foreground.
0:21.22	43:08:18	Lancaster says, "No encores, let's keep moving."
0:22.88	43:10:08	EOL above.
0:27.06	43:14:13	CUT to FS of aircraft sitting on runway.
0:31.03	43:18:12	CUT to interior of aircraft and tense passengers.
0:33.83	43:21:06	CUT to CU of American passenger.
0:36.03	43:23:12	CUT to CU of other American passenger.
0:38.37	43:25:22	CUT to MS of thrid American and his wife.
0:42.00	43:29:11	CUT to overhead FS of Lancaster group driving on road.
0:44.97	43:32:10	CUT to CU of one of group in vehicle.
0:47.04	43:34:12	CUT to MS of two others.
0:48.94	43:36:09	CUT to Lancaster driving in other vehicle.

Cue: 2-5M-1   Project: On Wings of Eagles   PAGE 2

0:52.25   43:39:18   CUT to overhead LS of vehicles moving along the road.

0:58.99   43:46:10   CUT to a FS of one of the vehicles as it slows for a
                     turn.

1:07.86   43:55:06   CUT to FS of vehicles as they turn onto a dirt road.

1:14.67   44:02:02   CUT to FS of vehicles as they move slowly along dirt
                     road.

1:19.34   44:06:22   CUT to MCU of two of the men in vehicle.

1:21.74   44:09:04   CUT to a low FS of vehicles coming around a corner.

1:27.68   44:15:02   CUT to a FS of vehicles with large, snow-covered
                     mountain in background.

1:35.86   44:23:07   CUT to CU of Iranian in vehicle, chasing the Lancaster
                     group.

1:37.59   44:24:29   CUT to overhead FS of Iranian vehicle moving along the
                     road.

1:41.50   44:28:26   CUT to a FS of Lancaster group vehicles coming around
                     a corner.

1:50.17   44:37:16   CUT to a FS of an approaching flatbed truck.

1:53.01   44:40:11   CUT to a FS of approaching Lancaster Land Rovers.

1:56.54   44:43:27   CUT to a MS of Lancaster and group in vehicle.

1:58.58   44:45:28   CUT to a POV shot of approaching truck.

1:59.51   44:46:26   Cut to a MCU of Lancaster as he says, "Holy Toledo,
                     look at that idiot!"

2:00.55   44:47:27   EOL above and CUT to a POV FS of approaching truck.

2:01.25   44:48:18   CUT to a MS of Lancaster and group as they swerve to
                     avoid collision.

2:01.68   44:49:01   CUT to a POV FS out windshield as they swerve off the
                     road.

2:02.35   44:49:21   CUT to a FS of vehicles as the swerve off the road
                     into a ditch.

2:06.72   44:54:02   CUT to a MS of driver of Land Rover as it settles to a
                     stop.

2:08.92   44:56:08   CUT to a FS of scene as truck drives off. Music
                     should be tailing at this point.

Copland preferred to run a scene over and over again on a moviola while he tried out various musical ideas with the picture. Erich Wolfgang Korngold would sit in a projection room with a piano and improvise while a projectionist ran the film for him. The advent of the home videocassette recorder has now provided for all composers the luxury of trying out their musical ideas ''against picture'' or of reviewing a scene to refresh their memories. It is now common practice for production companies to provide composers with a videocassette of the show they are working on.

Methods of work vary with each composer, of course, but, generally, once the composer is satisfied with the musical ideas for a given scene, he then proceeds to ''lay out'' the score onto score paper. At this point there is no composition involved to speak of, only the notation of meters and bar lines— a sort of beat-by-beat layout reflecting the exact elapsed time of the scene and those moments within the scene the composer wishes to ''catch.'' This is a meticulous and time-consuming process whereby tempos and the number of beats needed within those tempos must be determined if the music is to stay in exact synch with the picture. Figure 2 is a completed ''short score,'' but in its initial stages it consisted of only bar lines and meter signatures which were determined by the ''click'' tempo (the tempo of the ''click tracks'' discussed below) and the number of beats in a given period of time created by that tempo. The tempo, in turn, was determined by the type of musical ideas being presented.

The breakdown notes in Figure 1 are the composer's reference throughout this tedious process. From them the composer gathers all of the timings for events he deems important to reflect in the music. In the past, composers were greatly aided in this process by referring to several books which contained elaborate listings of timings and click numbers, and described where a particular beat might fall at any given timing. With the advent of the home computer, however, a number of programs have appeared which have considerably expedited this process. Some of these programs, once given the appropriate information, will even print out a simple score page layout of the cue— minus the music, of course.

Once this score page layout has been completed the composer then proceeds with the actual writing of the music for the scene. Figure 2 is the compositional solution for the scene described in the breakdown notes of Figure 1.

Figure 2. Excerpt from *Land Rovers*, music by Laurence Rosenthal, from the miniseries *On Wings of Eagles*.

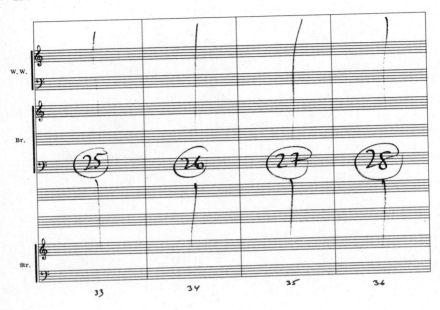

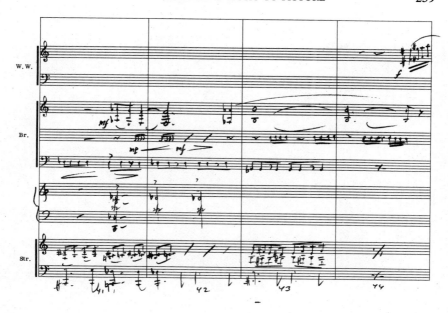

Click Tracks

In effect, a click track is a metronome, a device that emits steady ticks, much like a loud clock. The rate of speed of these ticks can be adjusted from 40 beats per minute to 208 beats per minute. The ticks enable a musician to maintain a steady tempo, or speed, during practice. The device also enables composers to indicate how fast or slow a piece should be played. A symphony conductor can be compared to a metronome as he coordinates the musicians by the movement of his baton. A click track, as it relates to film, is a synchronous metronome that is locked to the picture, thus enabling the music to stay in synch with the picture. The fact that it is synchronous means that a composer can predetermine what timings he wishes to catch with his music. Film runs through the camera and projector at a rate of twenty-four frames (or separate pictures) per second. The material used to record music for films is called magnetic track (or "mag track") and looks exactly like standard 35 mm film, except that it is coated with an oxide surface like that found on commercial sound or videotape one purchases for home use. Magnetic track has the same number of sprocket holes (four per frame) as optical film, and the machines that play this magnetic track (they are called playback "dummies" because they merely follow the film projector) move the track over the sound head at the same rate of speed at which film passes through a projector: twenty-four frames per second.

Click tracks used to be created on what is called opaque leader. Holes would be punched in this leader and, as these passed over an optical playback head of an audio film machine, a "pop" would be heard. In more recent years a digital metronome known as a "Urei" (an acronym for the name of the manufacturer, United Recording Electronics, Inc.) has become the standard in virtually all film recording studios. One can set the tempo on this device through the use of dials which are calibrated in film frames and eighths of frames. It is normally operated at the recording session by the music editor who sets the tempos based on the composer's specifications for the cue being recorded. Since 1984 even more advanced, computer-generated click track systems have been introduced, giving the composer far more flexibility in this area than has ever before been available.

A simple example will demonstrate how a film composer uses a click track. A composer decides that he wants a tempo of one beat per second (60 on the metronome). Knowing that film passes through the projector and all film-related sound equipment at the rate of twenty-four frames per second, the composer selects a twenty-four frame click tempo. Now suppose that in the film somebody gets hit over the head at precisely six seconds into the music cue. Since film passes through the projector at twenty-four frames per second, the hit on the head in the picture should arrive on the 144th frame of the picture ($6 \times 24 = 144$) and the seventh click, or beat, of the click track. It is on the seventh click because the first click is the very begining of the cue (:00 on the breakdown notes). The second click occurs at one second into the cue, and so on. The composer, knowing that all speeds will remain constant, will write the cymbal crash to indicate the hit on the head on the seventh click or exactly six seconds into the cue.

If a composer wants a faster tempo he merely selects a click tempo involving fewer frames. A twelve-frame click tempo would be twice as fast as the twenty-four frame tempo just discussed as the beats would be falling every half second rather than every second. Most of the time one sees click tempos such as a $10 + 5$, or 10 and ⅝ths of a frame. Occasionally a "variable click track" is requested. This usually occurs if a dance sequence has been shot without reference to a pre-recorded playback. The result of not using a playback during the shooting of such a scene is that the tempo, understandably, fluctuates. This makes it almost impossible to later record music for the sequence as the conductor has no way of anticipating where these fluctuations in tempo are going to occur. The problem is solved by having the music editor construct a variable click track, by hand and at the moviola, beat by beat, until he has created a matching and continuous click track for the sequence. This is a very tedious and time-consuming process which can take days to create for a sequence of only several minutes. Again, the advent of the computer has seen a number of devices created to handle such a task in only a few minutes.

The major advantage of a click track is that it provides a fast way to record a score for the picture, since it takes the pressure off the conductor in catching specific cues. For certain types of cues, however, usually "action" cues, the click track can be indispensible in catching required moments, and even the best of conductors use click tracks at these times. The primary disadvantage of solely using click tracks to record an entire film score is that it allows the composer little in the way of freedom and elasticity. It is difficult for the tempo of a cue to "breathe" when the tempo is locked to a click. With the click track maintaining a constant and exact tempo, there is little room for those musical devices that make a piece of music more expressive. It is possible to create accelerandos (gradually speeding the tempo up) and ritardandos (a gradual slowing down) by the use of a variable click track, but this is a rather mechanical substitute for a function some composer-conductors are able to do intuitively.

Figure 2 on pp. 254–62 is a typical example of the use of clicks for a cue. In this case the composer, Laurence Rosenthal, has requested two different click tempos within the cue with the two tempos being separated by a short "free-timing" section. This particular cue is from a television mini-series entitled "On Wings of Eagles" which tells the story of the escape of some businessmen from Iran during the revolution of 1979. Figure 2 is the breakdown of this scene, and a close examination of the breakdown will reveal that the music covers a number of different shifts in mood. Note that the scene opens in an apartment and then, at :11.93 into the cue, we cut to another, entirely different scene, and then again at :27.00 to still another scene. Finally, at :41.93, we cut to an overhead shot of some land rovers moving down a road. Each one of these short scenes is rather different in character and the music must reflect those differences. Mr. Rosenthal decided that the shift in music should reflect those cuts, and that is the primary reason for his selection of a click track.

Note that in the upper left-hand corner of the first page of the score is the indication of the click tempo—an eleven-frame click. Also note that he has requested eight warning clicks before the actual downbeat of the cue. These warning clicks provide the conductor and the orchestra with a preview of the tempo they will be performing before they actually begin playing.

At this particular tempo the timing of :11.93 occurs on the 27th beat in the score. The :27.00 timing occurs on the 60th beat. Note the changes in the music at these points and, especially, how well Mr. Rosenthal has made the shift from one mood to another without abruptness, mending the scenes together smoothly. In bar 20 of the score he begins a new click tempo of 11 + 3 and, in bar 21, he catches the timing at :41.93, the cut to the overhead shot of the land rovers. Again, note the shift here in the music with the strings supplying the necessary energy required by shots of the moving vehicles. He utilizes clicks throughout the rest of the cue and only stops them at the very end of the scene in bar 67. It would have been extremely difficult and time consuming to have attempted to record this cue without clicks and, in many respects, irresponsible.

Click tracks are used heavily in recording music for television shows. This is primarily due to the "time-is-money" factor that imbues all filmmaking but is especially true in television. Another reason, and not an insignificant one, is the lack of expert conducting ability among many composers working in the film industry. The use of the click track effectively removes from the conductor any responsibility for maintaining synch as a cue is recorded. However, it should be noted that conducting an orchestra to a projected picture is one of the most difficult areas of this art form to master.

Using clicks is really no problem and is usually preferable in fast, action-type cues but in slower, more rubato-like moments the music definitely suffers when clicks are employed. For these slower moments something called "free timing" is often employed.

Free Timing

Free timing refers to the process of recording music to picture without the use of a click track. This process involves the use of a large "sweep" clock at the conductor's stand and a print of the film that has been marked by the music editor. The markings placed on the film by the music editor consist of "streamers" and "punches" (see Figures 3 and 4). Streamers are created by scraping the emulsion off the film on a diagonal line. The line usually covers three feet of film which is equal to two seconds of time when the film is projected. The length of streamers can vary according to the composer's needs in any particular music cue. Slower streamers of three or four seconds duration, for example, are used for cues involving slower tempos. When the film is projected, the visual effect of a streamer is a vertical line panning across the screen from left to right. When the line arrives at the right-hand side of the screen it indicates to the composer the exact "synch point" he wishes to catch. A punch is always placed at the end of the streamer to indicate this synch point. "Punches" are holes which are literally punched in the film using a standard paper punch. The effect of these punches, when projected, is a flash of light that can be seen on the recording stage without even looking at the screen. Punches without an accompanying streamer are generally used as "internal timings" by composers. Internal timings are those points in a cue that a composer uses only to make sure he is where he should be, in time, as he records the cue. They are not used to catch hard synch points because the streamer, as it moves across the screen, allows the conductor to anticipate the upcoming synch point and give the orchestra an appropriate downbeat.

To better illustrate the difference examine bars 16–21 in Figure 2 on pp. 255–56. In bar 16 the clicks are stopped which means the conductor now has no aural reference (clicks) with which to lead the orchestra. The block with a line attached at the top of the score in bar 17 is the way most composers

Figure 3 (left). Demonstration of the principle of the streamer. The diagonal line is made by actually scraping the emulsion off the film; it will appear as a vertical white line moving across the screen from left to right when the film is projected. The punch on the first frame of the new shot is used to indicate the "dead cue." Most streamers are scraped to cover three feet of film which projects a streamer two seconds in length. The length of a streamer can be altered to suit the specific needs of the composer. This particular strip of 35mm film is, for reasons of space, considerably shorter than would be used in actual practice.

Figure 4 (right). This 35mm film strip is a static representation of what a streamer looks like when it is projected. It warns the composer, as he leads the orchestra through its music cue, that the embrace shown in the new shot is about to appear. The punch on the first frame of the new shot gives off a bright flash of light on the recording stage and indicates to the composer that the music he has written to go along with the embrace should now be sounding. After the cue has been recorded the engineers will rewind both the film and the audio and can then immediately play both back for the composer.

indicate to the music editor that they want a streamer at that particular timing. If you compare this timing, :30.96, with the breakdown notes in Figure 1, you will see that at that moment in the scene we cut to the interior of the plane. Mr. Rosenthal begins to move the music just a bit at this point. The streamer provides him with some warning before this timing and thus allows him to give the orchestra the downbeat at precisely that moment. He is, of course, watching the screen during this time. In bar 18 note the box with a "+" over it. This is a standard symbol indicating a punch without an accompanying streamer. As mentioned earlier, composer / conductors use a punch as a reference only. In this particular example Mr. Rosenthal would hope that, as he arrives at the downbeat of bar 18 with the orchestra, he will also see a punch appear on the screen. If the punch occurs before he hits the downbeat of bar 18, then he knows he is moving the tempo too slowly and must pick it up before he nears another definite synch point he wishes to catch. If the punch occurs after he has already gone beyond the downbeat of bar 18, then he knows he is moving too quickly and must slow down if he intends to "stay in synch" with the picture over the full length of the cue.

While the example in Figure 2 represents only a small portion of a cue in free timing it should be sufficient to demonstrate the technique. Many cues are done completely with this free timing technique. It generally takes a little longer to record a cue using this system, but the musical results are well worth the extra time involved.

The Scoring Session

The scoring session, where all of the music for a film is recorded, is one of the most enjoyable of all the activities involved in the making of a film. It is also one of the most pressure-filled. The pressure arises from two areas: the costs of the session and the principals involved.

The average television film will require four three-hour sessions of recording time in a studio that will cost between $400 and $500 per hour. On an average there will be thirty musicians or more for a single three-hour session and from fifteen to twenty musicians required for the remaining three three-hour sessions. These musicians, in Los Angeles or New York, will cost approximately $290.00 per player (in 1990 dollars), per session. Principal players receive a "double," meaning twice the $290.00 rate, as will any player who performs on more than one instrument (such as a flute player who also plays piccolo). There are also cartage costs for the percussion and synthesizer gear that is being used, as well as a fee for the contractor who has booked the orchestra. All of this, over the course of the two days of sessions, can add up to figures in the $40,000–$50,000 range. Large orchestras will, of course, cost considerably more. Needless to say, the composer / conductor is very much aware of this fact when he steps up to the podium to record the score. While this kind of pressure is obviously not paralyzing, it does color the composer's decisions as to whether or not to try another take of a cue that he might not be completely satisfied with. The length of the sessions themselves are rigidly controlled by the contractor, to the minute. So while they are concerned about the quality of the performances being recorded, composers have the additional concern of whether or not all of the music will be recorded in the specified period of time. Experience, of course, teaches a composer about how much time is required to record a given amount of music. The musicians' union also allow only five minutes of usable music to be recorded per hour. This means that during the course of a three-hour session only fifteen minutes of the recorded music may be used in the picture. More music will have been recorded, of course, as there are bad takes of a cue which are not used.

The second area that creates pressure for the composer is the possible reactions of the production company representatives to the music created for the picture. The producer and director are almost always present at the recording session, for obvious reasons: in addition to paying for the session, as well as the composer's fee, the motion picture is their creation, so they have a legitimate professional concern about the music to be used. Concerns about the composer's ability, the general direction the music is to take, etc., have usually been settled long before a note of music has been written. Producers are generally well aware of a given composer's style and reputation when they engage him for the project. As mentioned previously, a detailed discussion of all the aesthetic aspects of the music needed for the picture takes place during the spotting session. However, the leap from conceptual discussion to notes on the score paper is a long and difficult one with the possibility for many misunderstandings to occur. This is especially true when dealing with a producer and / or director who is uninformed or inarticulate in the area of music which is, more often than not, the situation the composer confronts.

Once music is actually being recorded it is not at all unusual for a producer or director to request a change in a cue, usually while the composer is rehearsing it. Criticisms can range from "I have the music—it doesn't work" to "Could we maybe lose the piccolo, it's a little shrill." Understandably this puts a good deal of pressure on the composer. He must then try to rework the cue, right at that moment, to satisfy the request for a change. This can involve omitting or adding various instruments, thinning or thickening a harmonic texture, or adding or deleting beats or bars if it is suddenly decided that the cue needs to be longer or shorter. In some cases the alterations required are so radical that even these "head arrangements" from the podium will not suffice. In those cases the cue will be rewritten, usually that night. In the worst cases entire scores are thrown out, a new composer employed, and a new score is written and recorded. Understandably this is an extremely expensive move and, therefore, is not a frequent occurrence.

Requests for a change in the music can, and do, elicit objections from the composer. The nature of the exchange which takes place depends in large part on the relationship between the composer and the producer and director. Almost always these discussions are intelligent and professional, with the primary consideration being the resolution of the problem to everyone's satisfaction. Rarely do egos conflict with one another. A salient point, however, is that an employer / employee relationship does exist between the producer and the composer, and both are always aware of this relationship.

The recording studio where all this takes place is usually a large room specifically designed for the recording of music utilizing a picture source. Figure 5 is a photograph of Evergreen Studios in Los Angeles. Note the large conductor's podium at the left of the photograph, and the large "sweep" clock attached to the left of the podium. This clock, as well as the click machine, is operated by the music editor who is usually seated at a smaller desk. Also note, at the center, the large screen where the picture is projected while the music is being recorded. With the advent of videotape, a video monitor is usually placed just forward of the conductor's podium and is then used as the picture source rather than the film screen.

The recording engineer is another key factor in the recording process, as he is the person who achieves the actual mix of the sound of the orchestra. World-class mixers number only in the handful and include Dan Wallin and John Richards, both of whom work in Los Angeles although John Richards established his reputation in his homeland, England. In London, Eric Tomlinson is highly regarded as is Adrian Kerridge, although Mr. Kerridge's reputation lies mainly within England. In Munich, West Germany, which is fast becoming a major scoring center for films, Malcolm Luker (yet another Englishman) is quickly being recognized as belonging to this small group of professionals.

Figure 5. Recording stage at Evergreen Studios in Burbank, California. Photo used by permission.

Tracking

Tracking is a term used to describe the process of putting existing music into a picture in place of a specifically written score. There are two instances when this technique is used. The first is when a motion picture is in the final stages of editing and there is a need to exhibit the film before a score has been written. These screenings are usually held for investors, studio or television network executives, distributors, etc.—anyone with a vested interest in the outcome of the project. In order to make the film as attractive as possible at this point, the director and editor usually ask the music editor to find and edit some music for the more important moments in the film. Since this is only "temp" music, the editor can draw on virtually any source he or she desires without concern for copyright or residual payments as the music selected will not appear in the final release of the film. If a composer has already been engaged for the film he will sometimes assist the music editor in this process. If handled well the results can be very effective.

These "temp tracks" can pose a serious problem for the composer, however. Having heard the temp track a number of times, those involved in the film can become quite attached to the music. When the composer arrives on the scene he is confronted with the problem of trying to overcome the familiarity and affection for the temp music which he is about to replace with his own. Occasionally certain pieces used in a temp track are retained in the final version of the film.

One example of this is in the 1981 film, *Caddyshack*. There is a montage scene wherein a vicar is playing golf at the height of a violent storm—and having the best game of his life. For the temp track the music editor used a piece from the Elmer Bernstein score to *The Ten Commandments* which included a "heavenly choir." The effect was rather humorous and the satirical element was immediately latched onto by the director, Harold Ramis. Once the score, by Johnny Mandel, was recorded, it was all dubbed into the picture, except for one cue: the one written for the golf montage scene. The director preferred the one from the temp track and this is the cue that appears in the picture. The use of this one short piece of music ultimately cost the production company over $15,000 in re-use fees.

The second instance where tracking is used occurs when there is no budget for an original score. In this case, the music editor is left with the not-insubstantial responsibility of locating and editing to length all of the music for the film. There are professional music libraries available for this purpose where, for a relatively small fee, the production company is able to buy the rights for whatever pieces of music they select from that library. While tracking is certainly not the best way to provide music for a picture, in the hands of a skilled music editor the results can be quite satisfactory. To the uninitiated listener, tracked music for a picture can often sound as if it had been scored.

Dubbing

The term "dubbing" refers to the process of blending the numerous dialogue, sound effects, and music tracks into a single balanced mix of those elements. Dubbing stages where this activity takes place, like scoring stages, are specifically designed and built for this sole function. They consist of a large motion picture screen and a mixing console, or "desk," where three individuals each handle various tracks. Each "mixer" primarily handles one area and they are referred to as the dialogue mixer (generally in charge of the mixing crew), the effects mixer, and the music mixer.

If the recording of the music is the most enjoyable and rewarding aspect of the composer's job, the dubbing of the music along with the numerous other soundtracks for the picture can be the least rewarding and most frustrating. It is on the dubbing stage that the film composer sees much of his music lost in the melee of other tracks.

Dialogue rules supreme on a film soundtrack. Composers are very much aware of this fact and write their music accordingly, making sure that they don't overpower the dialogue with their music but, rather, "write around" the lines. Music cues will occasionally be dropped after they have been heard against all of the other sound elements, or it will be decided that the music is a secondary element on the soundtrack and will be mixed very low in relation to the other tracks.

The length of time required to dub a picture depends on the length and complexity of the show as well as the budget. A typical two-hour television movie will be dubbed in three to four days. A feature can easily take two or three weeks and more. Composers do not attend dubs as a general rule, but will drop in from time to time to try to get a feel for the way their music is being mixed into the picture. Usually they are already working on their next project, however, so attending the dub is impossible. All they can do is hope that their substantial efforts will be heard.

9

Music for Television: A Brief Overview

While it would require another book to properly discuss the use of music in television, it is important in this work to at least touch on some relevant points concerning the differences in the use of music in television and feature films.

In television's dramatic one-hour series, made-for-television movies, and mini-series, it has obviously adopted the entire film language as it has existed in feature films. The very structure of American television, however, imposes a number of fundamental differences in the kind of motion pictures produced for television and the ones produced for theatrical release.

On the largest level is the editorial pacing of a television show. Even a casual look will reveal that the pace of the television film is usually far more rapid than most theatrical films.

For example, a scene involving someone leaving a house with a friend, getting into their car and driving off, followed by some dialogue in the car might be edited in the feature as follows: begin with a full shot of the house as we see two people coming through the front door. We see the front door close behind them as they walk to the car, get in, and drive off. Cut to a full shot of the car moving down a street, then cut to a medium close-up of the two people in the car as the dialogue begins. This whole sequence, up to the dialogue, might take twenty or thirty seconds in a theatrical film whereas in television the same scene is likely to be edited in the following manner: begin with a full shot of the house as we see two people coming through the front door. We see the front door close behind them and, just as the door closes shut, we cut to a medium close-up of the two in the car, driving down a street, as dialogue begins. Suddenly, what was a leisurely twenty- or thirty-second sequence is now a rapid-fire ten- or twelve-second sequence. Why the considerable difference in the pacing of the two? I think the answer lies in the overall nature of television's perception and use of time which is reflected in the rhythm of the product that is produced for the medium. As I pointed out earlier in this book, the identification of musical and visual rhythms is dubious because in the plastic arts the concept of rhythm is largely metaphorical. I would, however, like to discuss visual rhythm exclusively, because of its effect on the pacing of a film and how that is reflected in the music. In order to do this it is necessary to step back and view television from its broadest commercial aspects, as these are reflected directly in the rhythm of films produced for the medium.

The critical element to remember is that, first and always, the primary purpose of American network television is to sell. And while network representatives will speak about their responsibility to the public, their primary responsibility is a commercial one: profit. Putting aside the essentially simplistic moral issue, if profit is the primary motive then garnering viewers is a network's primary task. The general wisdom that has matured into petrification (with some reason) is to "grab" your audience as quickly as possible and, even more importantly, to hold them for the entire show. One important way to achieve this is to continually deliver something "new" to the viewer lest he or she become bored. Referring back to the comparative example of editing portrayed earlier, the television version is a result of this idea that the plot must keep moving with no delay. Film editors who edit television shows respond to this need by eliminating anything that is not absolutely essential to the forward movement of the plot and action. Little time, obviously, is allowed for some of the more subtle aspects of filmmaking. This editing technique, incidentally, grew in part out of television commercials themselves which have only a few seconds to sell the product being advertised.

The problems this creates for the composer are mainly related to time, specifically, having enough time to allow music to achieve some effect in a scene. In the example under discussion it would be no problem for a composer to write a cue for the feature version with the music starting as the people came out the door and then ending (or "tailing") under the dialogue. This would allow for a cue of twenty or thirty seconds duration which is a perfectly acceptable amount of time for music to make a contribution to a scene.

The television version, conversely, is a far more difficult situation. Music moves through time and, because of this, needs a certain amount of it to express something. Even if we leave thematic statement aside and consider only musical color, the ten to twelve seconds allowed for music in the television version is little time indeed. The music at this point becomes what is called a "bridge," a somewhat predictable and over-used device in television, especially in "sit-coms" (situation comedies) which originated in the days of dramatic radio shows (see Figure 1). About the only positive contribution the music provides in this situation is a kind of aural seam to connect one scene with the next. It is interesting, however, that feature film makers avoid this device like the plague for fear of "sounding like TV." There is a growing trend among composers working in television to try to avoid this device, and generally, in the spotting session, they will appeal to the producer's desire for his show to be "different" by suggesting that avoiding bridges will contribute to a more unique outcome. It is always amusing to attend a music spotting session for a television show when the producer has announced that his show is "different" and he doesn't want it to have a typical "TV feel," and then proceeds to suggest music spotting that is identical to every other show on the air.

Another, formal, aspect of television which affects its rhythm is a direct result of the need for commercial breaks. Television shows, whether they are one-hour series, two-hour movies, or mini-series, are divided into "Acts." These acts have beginnings and endings and these "Act-ins" (beginnings) and "Act-outs" (endings) have traditionally been accompanied by music (see Figures 2 and 3). As with the bridges, these are very short and present the same difficulties for the composer as the bridge cue. The problem is compounded by the fact that, more often than not, the act endings occur at some terribly climactic moment which requires the music to suddenly thrust itself into the situation with several brief, dramatic statements and then exit just as suddenly as the screen goes to black for the commercial. The resulting effect can be a little overwrought. One way to address this problem of the Act-out is, of course, to have no music at all. Unfortunately the scene has usually been cut by the editor with the idea that there will be music at this point. The result is that, after the last dramatic line of the scene where music would usually enter, the editor has placed a series of "reaction shots" (usually a long hold of the camera on one of the characters) which creates a lengthy "stage wait." This stage wait usually will not hold up very well on its own and really does cry for music. There are times, though, when such a stage wait is very effective without music.

Figure 1. A "bridge" of about 10 seconds duration from the television series, *Dallas,* music by Jerrold Immel.

Figure 2. An "Act-in" for the television series, *Dallas*. The music here has so little
time to achieve anything that it serves only as a sort of muted fanfare to let the audience know, in an auditory sense, that the story is continuing.

Figure 3. A typical short ''Act-out'' from the television series, *Dallas*. More tasteful than many, this one does not reach beyond a *mezzo piano*.

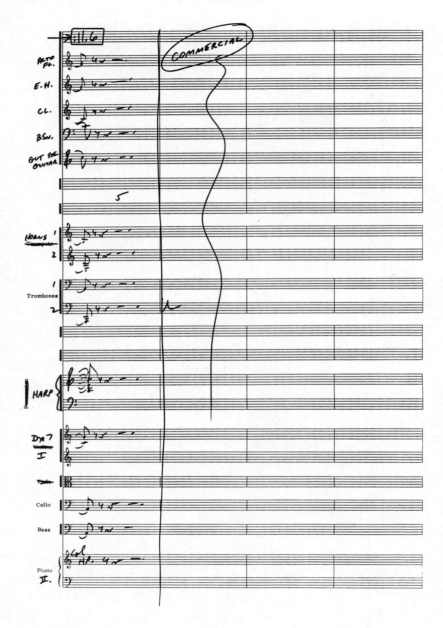

Another solution which works very well involves starting the music somewhere earlier in the scene. Usually one looks for a point, however small or subtle, where the scene shifts slightly. This could be a change in the subject of the dialogue where one idea is complete and a new one begins, or one character finishes speaking and another begins. By introducing the music before the climactic moment a more subtle and tasteful effect is created since the music is already an element in the scene (see Figure 4). This same solution, incidentally, is also used for the bridges discussed earlier.

The Act-in is less of a problem for the composer in that, dramatically, the device tends to be somewhat innocuous. "Establishing shots" such as a shot of an office building or house followed by a dialogue scene in the interior of the building are common Act-ins. In this case the music is usually much more neutral in character although the generally short length of the cue (eight to twelve seconds, at most) tends to make the music seem somehow gratuitous or irrelevant. As with the Act-out, many composers are attempting to avoid the device when possible.

Finally, there is the "bumper." This is the five-second picture of the show's logo which is placed midway through a commercial break and is invariably accompanied by music (see Figure 5). It is also often placed at the end of an Act-out and before an Act-in. This placement is especially disconcerting because it generally collides with either the incoming or outgoing cue for a less-than-stellar effect. The music for these is usually based on one of the more dramatic thematic ideas in the score and is written and recorded specifically for this use. On occasion, however, the music editor will create one by editing a short piece from a longer cue in the show.

It is difficult to determine why the bumper came into being or the reason for its continued use. The one used midway through the commercial break could, I suppose, be an attempt to hoodwink the audience (which may be in another room, away from the television, at this point) into thinking the show is beginning again in the hopes of drawing them back to the screen for the commercials that will follow. The others, at the beginning and end of the act, can have an effect of "bookending" the act—a somewhat dubious value.

The musical styles employed for television are as varied as the program material. A nighttime dramatic series (less decorously known as "nightime soaps") such as *Dynasty* employed a fairly traditional acoustic orchestra, whereas another nighttime dramatic series such as *Airwolf* utilized synthesizers to a great degree.

Figure 4. A longer, more subtle "Act-out" from the television series, *Dallas*. Note the quiet, sparse entrance as well as the *mezzo-piano* dynamics until the crescendo in the last bar of the piece. Being the end of an episode such a crescendo is nearly mandatory and quite dramatically correct.

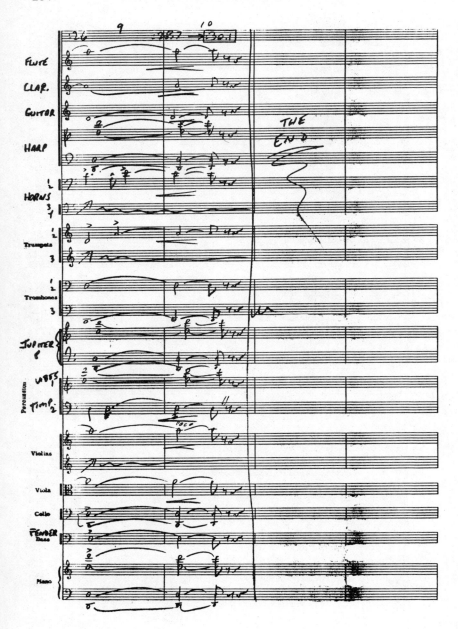

Figure 5. A "Bumper" from the television series, *Dallas*. It speaks for itself.

The use of pop music is re-emerging thanks to the success of the show, *Miami Vice*. As pointed out in an earlier chapter, using pop music in television and motion pictures is a recurring practice. The producers of *Miami Vice* used current pop tunes of various recording artists rather than creating their own tunes for the show. This practice can be very expensive as they not only have to purchase the publishing rights for the use of the songs, but the synchronization rights from the record companies and artists. The high cost of purchasing these rights has spawned a minor industry of singers and musicians who will create what are known as "sound-a-likes"—recordings of songs with unknown singers and musicians who sound very similar to the original artist on the original recording. This small industry was generated primarily by producers wishing to emulate the *Miami Vice* success but without the same budget. While this technique of sound-a-likes has been quite successful for those involved, it has already elicited a legal response from some of the artists being imitated. These artists claim that since the singers and bands are attempting to sound like them it may just as well be them on the recordings and, therefore, they should be paid accordingly. This legal argument is apparently so strong that most of the major studios who were indulging in this practice have recently been advising their producers to avoid it.

While the use of current pop tunes by the latest groups gives a show a very "hip" sound, such a soundtrack also becomes dated very quickly. Normally this wouldn't be a problem in first-run network television but many programs only make money for their producers when they go into syndication. One wonders what the effect of a show such as *Miami Vice* will be in several years when pop music styles have, as they always do, changed considerably. Unfortunately most of the *Miami Vice* imitators have missed the fact that while pop music worked for that particular show it is not necessarily a concept that can be spread onto any show format like so much butter. In short, the use of pop music was not the only reason for *Miami Vice*'s success.

Finally, there remains the question of the dramatic value of using pop songs under dramatic situations in a film. Many times the songs bear little or no relation to what is on the screen and are obviously gratuitous attempts to pander to a certain trendiness. Even when an attempt is made at some correlation between an independently conceived pop song and a scene in a film the results can be questionable. One of the sillier examples of this occurred in the television show, *Misfits of Science*. The episode in question concerned a fellow who thought he was communicating with beings from outer space. During one scene where the character thought he was guiding a rocket to earth the Elton John tune "Rocket Man" was used. Another example is in a television movie *Help Wanted: Kids* wherein the tune "Jump" was used in a basketball-playing sequence.

The work schedule of the composer writing for television is almost always more severe than for the composer writing a feature film score. It is not unusual in episodic television for a composer to have to write twenty to thirty minutes of music in four or five days and sometimes less. In fact, the composing schedule for episodic television is very reminiscent of the schedules composers working on "B" movies in the 1930s and '40s had to contend with.

The scoring session for a one-hour episodic television show generally runs from one to two three-hour sessions, depending on the amount of music to be recorded. A two-hour movie for television generally requires four three-hour sessions over the course of two days.

The sheer amount of product required for television provides a substantial pool of work for composers in the United States (primarily Los Angeles). And even though the schedules can sometimes be mind-boggling, it does provide a lucrative training ground for composers. Owing to television's native conservatism, opportunities for the composer to experiment musically are rare. Conversely, when a musical risk is taken and is successful, the networks are deluged with imitators trying to duplicate its popularity. This particular phenomenon persists and will undoubtedly never change.

PART IV

Contemporary Techniques and Tools

10

Video Post-Production Techniques

Video post-production came into existence soon after the development of the first videotape machine in 1956. Until the creation of such tape machines all programs appearing on television were either "live" or on film. Live shows had to rely on whatever sound effects or music could be provided during the actual broadcast, and film shows, of course, were produced in the traditional fashion. The videotape machine created the ability to edit and "sweeten" (add sound effects and music) the videotape product itself. While this process increased in sophistication during the past thirty years, it never achieved the level of detail and aesthetic quality realized in the film medium. This was primarily due to the fact that most of the material produced in the videotape format never required the level of quality expected in film. The unfortunate result was that craftsmen working in the videotape post-production area developed an entirely different set of standards from craftsmen working in the film area. Another almost insurmountable problem was the vast difference in the technology of the two disciplines. This resulted in two different working "languages," or sets of terms for various activities, which widened the gap even further. When the concept of doing film-style post-production on videotape began emerging with some force in the early 1980s, this was the situation confronting those trying to bring it about.

The primary motivation to handle post-production on videotape is one of cost savings. The motion picture and television industries are labor intensive, meaning that labor is very expensive and critical to the production of product.

Film is essentially a mechanical medium while videotape is primarily electronic and computer oriented. Herein lies the advantage of videotape: it is considerably faster to work with and therefore saves labor costs without any sacrifice in the quality of the end product. For example, to prepare a picture (stream and punch and calculate various click starts) for a scoring session for a one-hour dramatic television show being done on film it would take a music editor about six to eight hours to complete at a moviola. That same show, if done on videotape and using the computer-based "VideoScore" system developed by The Music Design Group (a music editing company), can be completed in about thirty minutes, at the most. In addition, the cost of magnetic 35 mm film stock is three times the cost of the equivalent magnetic tape stock used in the videotape post-production process. In a cost-conscious industry it is difficult to argue against such dramatic savings.

To develop the technology and techniques required to execute film-style post-production on videotape a number of different companies, each addressing different areas, worked in loose cooperation over several years to create a small network of services that were technologically compatible. One of the earliest developers of a video-based sound-effects system was the now-defunct Neiman-Tillar Associates who created the ACCESS system. Developed in the mid-1970s, this digital editor was well ahead of its time and is still in use at two locations, one in Hollywood and one in New York. Another system, the "PAP" system, which was developed at about the same time by Glen Glenn Sound, has proven to be the real workhorse in this area. A major reason for this is Glen Glenn's long experience in the film area as both a sound-effects editing and a mixing facility. They were also one of the earliest facilities to move into videotape when it was first developed. This combination of film and video experience under the guidance of Joe Kelly and, later, Tom Kobayashi, made them a natural incubator for the development of video post-production.

While development of equipment and techniques was occurring in the late 1970s in the areas of sound effects, dialogue replacement, foley (footsteps, clothes rustle, etc.), and mixing, music was left languishing for lack of interest and funds. The music editing facility would be the most likely candidate to create systems and techniques to accommodate the new videotape medium as it applied to music scoring. Unfortunately, there are only a few independent music editing facilities in Los Angeles and their size, relative to facilities such as Glen Glenn Sound, is small, so their financial resources for research and development are limited. In addition, the incentive to invest in such development is substantially diminished by the natural human inclination to resist change, especially since these independent houses were so swamped with film work that the move to video seemed years away and of little concern at the time.

One company, The Music Design Group, pursued the development of these techniques with a good deal of success. The systems and techniques they have developed fall into two areas: pre-scoring / scoring and the assembling of tracks for the dubbing session. Traditionally, in film, these areas were all handled at the moviola using a 35mm picture as a reference. The music editor created breakdown notes for the composer by running the picture on the moviola and taking the timings required from a counter placed on the moviola. For the scoring session, the music editor streamed and punched the picture on the moviola. This meant that if a cue began 351 feet into a reel, the editor would have to put up the reel and run down to that footage—a process that would take five or six minutes. Likewise, at the scoring session, each time picture was requested for recording a cue, the projectionist would also have to run down to that footage, although the music editor provides a "rundown start mark" on the film itself to expedite matters. To assemble the recorded music tracks for the dub, the music editor returns to the moviola and cuts the music so that it is in synch with the picture for the dubbing session.

In video, while essential music editing tasks remain the same, the method of dealing with them is considerably different. As mentioned previously, film is primarily a mechanical medium while video is an electronic one. This merely reflects the larger evolution that one sees generally in society as it moves from the industrial revolution of the last few hundred years into the electronic revolution now well underway.

The picture source for video is, of course, videotape. The audio portion is recorded onto audio recording tape, either two-inch twenty-four-track or half-inch four-track, depending on the number of tracks needed. The picture and sound are synchronized, or "locked up," through the use of SMPTE time-code (SMPTE stands for Society of Motion Picture and Television Engineers, who standardized the method). "Time-code" is really a set of numbers set out in hours, minutes, seconds, and frames, and can be laid down onto tape as both an audio signal and an image. The audio signal is used for synchronizing more than one tape (a process explained shortly), and the time-code numbers appear on the video screen to allow visual identification of any given point in a show. A time-code number would look like this: 01:22:34:26. Reading from left to right we would see the reading as 1 hour, 22 minutes, 34 seconds, and 26 frames (unlike film which runs at 24 frames a second, video runs at 30 frames a second). Assuming that the show containing this code started at 1 hour even, we are now 22 minutes, 34 seconds, and 26 frames into the show. The next frame of the picture would then be 01:22:34:27, and so on, with the seconds and minutes ticking over in exactly the same manner as a digital clock. As previously mentioned, these same numbers would be on an audio track of the videotape as an audio signal, as well as appearing in a "window" somewhere in the picture. Having the time-code in the picture is crucial as it provides the editors with a visual reference in their discussions with other people involved in the project. The audio signal with the identical time-code makes it possible to lock up more than one audio machine containing sound effects, music, etc., to the video picture. The tape on these audio machines has had time-code matching the picture recorded onto one of the audio tracks. This audio track is then "read" by what is called a "synchronizer" such as the "Q-Lock" or "LYNX." These devices read the time-code on various machines and then synchronize the tape machines so that they are all reading the identical time-code numbers at the same time. The videotape machine is known as the "master" and the audio machines which "chase" it are called "slaves" in that they merely follow the time code of the master, wherever it may go. By doing so, there is no longer a need for sprocketed systems as in film.

In order to create breakdown notes as well as stream and punch the picture for the scoring session in video, The Music Design Group developed a computer-based system called "VideoScore." By entering time-code drawn from the window in the picture the music editor creates the breakdown notes in much the same manner as before, only now the editor has all the advantages of a word processor at his or her disposal. One of the major headaches a music editor faces while creating breakdowns are changes in the picture after breakdown for a cue has been generated. A picture change in a spot where music is to be playing of course changes the length of that cue. The editor must then go into the affected breakdown notes and recalculate all of the timings from the point of change onward. With the computer-based system this is quite easy and fast as the computer executes all of the calculations and then prints out a new version. In film, the editor has to recalculate each timing entry to accommodate the change and then have the entire set of notes for that cue retyped.

In its ability to add streamers and punches to a video picture the Video-Score system is unique, although, as of 1989, several other systems have come on the market. In the past, in order for a music editor to accommodate a scoring session on video he would first have to stream and punch a 35mm print of the picture and have that print transferred to a videocassette which would then be used as a picture source at the scoring session. The major disadvantage of this procedure is that the editor is unable to make any quick changes in the streamers or punches on the videotape as they are imbedded permanently. VideoScore, on the other hand, overlays the streamers and punches on the video signal as it is sent out to the video monitors. This means that the streamers and punches are not a part of the original video picture but are, instead, added in real time as the picture is run for a recording "take." This also allows for rapid changes in the stream and punch information. In film, it would require ten or twelve minutes for an editor to change a streamer while he went to the projection booth, retrieved the reel of picture, and then made the change on the film itself. While this is all being done a very expensive orchestra sits and waits. With the computer-based video system changes are merely entered at the keyboard in a few seconds, and the picture, with the streamer changes incorporated, is ready for another take.

As with other aspects of video, the streaming and punching of picture is SMPTE time-code-based (see Figure 1). Figure 1 is a printout of stream and punch information for an individual cue. This sheet is provided to various recording studio personnel at the scoring session who need to know the start points for all of the cues to be recorded. Note that all of the information is indicated in time-code. In Figure 1 the information across the top of the page is as follows: The Project Name, "Simpsons 7F01 '3 Eyes' "; the cue number, 2M1; the Click Tempo, Time Code Type, and frame rate; the time-code start of the cue, 1 hour, 00 minutes, 00 seconds, and 00 frames; and, finally, the "rundown start point" which the computer always calculates as fifteen seconds before the actual start of the cue. This rundown start is needed so that all of the video and audio equipment has time to "lock up" in synch before the cue actually begins and the recording starts. The actual streamers and punches requested by the composer are listed in numerical order down the page. The "Line" entries are numbers assigned to each entry that allow easy accessibility to every individual entry in the event of changes. The "MM:SS:FF" (minutes, seconds, frames) indicates the actual synch point where an event should take place. The "Type" specifies the color streamer requested or a punch. The "Time" indicates synch points from the start of the cue. Note that streamer lengths can be varied. (See Chapter 8 for a complete discussion of the use of streamers and punches.) As in film, it is the

Figure 1. Print-out of stream and punch information for a visual cue.

```
Project Name:   Simpsons 7F01 "3 Eyes"
   Cue Name:    2M1.STR
Click Tempo:    24+0 with 4 free / Non-Drop Frame / 30 frames per second
Rundown Start:  00:59:41:00
```

NO.	TIME	HH:MM:SS:FF	TYPE	LENGTH	TEMPO
1		00:59:56:00	Red	2.0	
2	0:00.00	01:00:00:00	Start	2.0	24+0
3	0:03.10	01:00:03:03	White	2.0	
4	0:12.59	01:00:12:18	White	2.0	
5	0:17.16	01:00:17:04	White	2.0	
6	0:22.92	01:00:22:27	White	2.0	
7	0:30.19	01:00:30:05	White	4.0	
8	0:44.14	01:00:44:03	White	4.0	
9	0:50.25	01:00:50:06	Punch		
10	1:01.22	01:01:01:05	White	2.0	
11	1:13.70	01:01:13:19	Yellow	2.0	
12	1:21.21	01:01:21:04	White	2.0	
13	1:33.25	01:01:33:05	White	3.0	
14	1:50.27	01:01:50.05	White	2.0	
15	2:02.88	01:02:02:23	Punch		
16	2:10.89	01:02:10:23	Red	2.0	

music editor who enters all of this information based on the requests by the composer / conductor.

The overwhelming advantage to cueing a picture for a scoring session in this manner over traditional film techniques is the dramatic savings in time (hence, money). In addition, the ability to make rapid changes, if needed, on the scoring stage allows the composer far greater flexibility in an already inflexible situation.

Once the music has been recorded the cues need to be assembled in synch with the picture for the dubbing session. Here again the procedure is SMPTE time-code based. At present, four-track audio tape is used, pre-striped (or recorded) with identical time-code found in the picture. The recorded music tracks on the master tape from the scoring session are then "pre-layed," or transferred, onto that time-coded tape at those points where the music belongs in relation to the picture. This music "unit" is then taken to the dubbing session where it is "locked up," or synchronized, with other audio elements and then mixed into the final tracks. While four audio tracks for the music have been adequate in the past, the advent of stereo television is quickly creating the need for more tracks. As of this writing no multi-track format for the music units, aside from the existing four-track configuration, has been decided upon within the industry.

There is virtually no doubt that video post-production is the direction in which the film and television industry is moving. Because the television networks are now requiring that final product be on videotape rather than film, there is little reason left to produce a product entirely on film and then have it transferred to videotape, when the entire post-production process can be performed on videotape. This fact, coupled with the rather dramatic savings involved, virtually ensures that videotape will be the medium utilized well into the future. Feature films, on the other hand, will probably stay in the film medium for post-production for a bit longer, as the final product is exhibited as film. The growing size and influence of the commercial videocassette market, however, may alter that situation sooner rather than later.

11

Digital Audio

Digital audio is easily the most revolutionary development in the recording and reproduction of sound since the advent of magnetic tape recording in the early 1950s. Its value in the film post-production process, including music scoring, is that there is no noise buildup as one moves through the many generations away from the original master as a film soundtrack is assembled and dubbed. The first film ever produced using this process was *Digital Dream*, made in 1983 by Glen Glenn Sound, of Hollywood, as a demonstration of the technique of digital audio in motion pictures.

As *Digital Dream* was experimental in nature, a number of companies regarded as being on the technological "leading-edge" of the film industry were invited to contribute their talents and expertise to the project. One of the interesting aspects of the project for those involved was the very real uncertainty of the value of digital audio over traditional analogue techniques used for post-production sound and music. This was an extremely important consideration as there had to be a significant qualitative difference between the two techniques in order to justify moving motion picture audio post-production into the digital area. Since utilizing digital audio in the post-production process involves some entirely new technology where the filmmaker is concerned, it was hoped that the qualitative difference in the sound between digital and analogue would be so significant that producers would be able to overcome their inherent suspicion and fear of new technology. Film being one of the oldest forms in the entertainment industry which depends upon technology for its existence, it suffers from that typical human malaise of entrenchment where new techniques are concerned.

By describing the typical route of a sound effect as it passes through the film post-production process, the reader will quickly realize where the initial value of digital audio in motion pictures lies. A sound effect is first recorded by a sound effects editor on a specialized tape machine, called a Nagra, using quarter-inch audio tape. When that particular effect is called for in a picture, the quarter-inch master tape is then transferred to a piece of 35mm magnetic film which is subsequently cut into a sound-effects reel. We are now one generation away from the master. This sound-effects reel is then taken to a dubbing stage where it will go through a "pre-dub" process wherein it will be re-recorded, along with other tracks, from three to five times. By being generous and saying that this particular effect went through only three generations during the pre-dub stage, this sound effect is now four generations away from that original quarter-inch master—and it has yet to be mixed into the final track. At the final mix this sound effect will be mixed with all of the other audio elements onto a final dub master, and it is now five generations away from that original tape. The final dub master will then be used to create the optical track for the release print of the picture. The sound effect now stands six generations away from the original master. And herein lies, initially, the true value of digital audio for motion pictures. Contrary to analogue format, there is virtually no discernible qualitative loss or noise buildup as a sound moves through six generations in the post-production process. Twenty or more generations could be required and the same would be true. There is a broader, economic significance to this fact as well. Unlike other noise reduction systems such as Dolby, a producer can deliver an inherently quieter product to the film exhibitor without the exhibitor having to invest in upgrading his sound system. When the exhibitor projects a motion picture which has been produced with digital audio, he is, for all intents and purposes, running an audio track that is one generation away from the master.

The music for *Digital Dream*, by Ron Jones, was recorded at Record Plant's Stage "M" on the Paramount Pictures lot in Hollywood. The key piece of equipment used in the recording was the Sony 3324 digital twenty-four-track recorder. Because these tape machines, rather than film, were used for the scoring session, SMPTE time-code became the synchronization source for the post-production. This included the scoring session. The music editing was handled by The Music Design Group utilizing systems they developed in 1982–83, and continue to develop, which allow the composer and music editor to use film-style scoring techniques in the videotape medium. All of the recorded music was assembled and edited on the Sony 3324 by (at that time) Music Design Group editor Curtis Roush, using techniques he helped develop in the analogue format.

The final mix found the only analogue element to creep into the process. The mix was performed on Stage 1 at Glen Glenn Sound, and the mixing board at that facility is an ADM Technology customized analogue unit. Digital mixing boards were just beginning to appear at this time and were still experiencing difficulties, not to mention a prohibitive price tag. A standard three-mixer crew was used and two Sony 3324s were linked to a 35mm projector as a picture source. The tracks on both Sony machines were full and everything was mixed back to a final six tracks on one of the Sonys, creating a six-track stereo mix.

It is interesting to note that the mixers had to go through a small learning curve in dealing with digital audio. They had to make some adjustments for the wide dynamics and low noise factors inherent in digital audio, and they initially found it difficult to get a natural-sounding balance in the sound effects because everything was so clean and transparent. They also discovered the importance of "clean" tracks (no background or audio system noise) because, with so much transparency, any unintended noise appears on the soundtrack much as a spot of dirt does on an extremely white surface. In the end it was felt by the mixers that they had more complete and subtle control over the mixing process primarily because they were not constantly fighting the noise buildup problem associated with an analogue mix.

As a final test Glen Glenn Sound pre-dubbed duplicate analogue and digital tracks through five generations, with the analogue track being Dolby encoded for noise reduction. The results were that, by the third generation, the digital version was dramatically superior to the analogue, Dolby-encoded version. Almost everyone was surprised by the outcome of this test, having assumed that, by only the third generation, there would not be such a dramatic difference in the two formats.

As with any new technology there were some inhibiting factors surrounding digital audio for motion pictures. First, and most predictable, was the natural resistance of producers to incorporate the use of this new technology in their very expensive pictures. This has changed in recent years, however, and one sees more and more pictures being dubbed in the digital format.

Interestingly enough, another negative factor was the attitude of the mixers themselves. Because of the extremely clean nature of digital tracks, a mixer's skill—or lack of it—is naked before the world. The mixer doesn't have a noisy corner to hide in and the creative demands placed on the mixer are increased considerably.

The most positive and exciting result of digital audio in motion pictures is that it allows those working in the area of sound and music to expand the audio language of film in a way never before possible. The most subtle or quiet of sounds, which would have been lost in the noise buildup of an analogue mix, can now be used in ways that were not even considered previously. For example, in *Digital Dream* there is a scene where we see sugar granules falling into a cup of coffee. But we also *hear* those sugar granules falling into the cup while, at the same time, we hear an entire symphony orchestra tuning up. This sort of contrast in simultaneous sounds would be impossible in analogue without extreme exaggeration, which would destroy the effect anyway.

In digital audio, sound and music tracks are so clean that one can create tracks where the sound elements are mixed closer together in volume without one overpowering the other. In short, digital audio in motion pictures allows sound effects and music to be combined in ways never attempted before. Viewing the situation in 1991, there seems little question that the technique will be the standard for the next several decades.

12

The Music Synthesizer

Perhaps the most dramatic arrival in the creative palette of film music in recent decades is the music synthesizer. As the cost of professional versions of these instruments drops to a level that studio musicians can afford, their use in the studio setting in conjunction with acoustic instruments has proliferated. The most expensive versions, such as the Fairlight and the Synclavier, are being used by some of the more imaginative composers working in films. Cost alone, of course, is not the only reason for the introduction of synthesizers into mainstream film music. Just as the electric guitar was the foremost pop sound of the 1950s and '60s, the synthesizer has dominated the pop sound of the late 1970s and 1980s and into the 1990s. It is inevitable and quite correct that its influence would be felt in the film industry as well.

The synthesizer as a musical resource is perhaps one of the most revolutionary creations in instrumentation throughout the history of western music. This is even more provocative when one considers the relatively short period of time over which the technology (hence capabilities) of these instruments has been developed: about twenty-five years. It's as if someone invented the first orchestral instrument in 1950 and, by 1975, we had arrived at the full-blown modern symphony orchestra.

Just as opera was in the nineteenth century, film is the medium of our time and, as such, is constantly reflecting values and ideas from our popular culture. Familiarity with electronic sounds through Wendy Carlos's *Switched On Bach* album and the subsequent success of her score to the movie *A Clock-*

work Orange made the synthesizer sound more palatable and normal to the average listener. Pop music's use of the synthesizer and, indeed, the whole electronic / recording revolution have contributed to the acceptance of the synthesizer as a valuable musical resource. David Kurtz, a young composer working in Los Angeles has said, ''I'm twenty-eight now, and I believe my generation is the first to identify its music only as it sounds after having been electronically manipulated rather than 'live.' For example, I am very well versed in concert music, but I didn't learn it from live concerts, I learned it from recordings. The point of this is that, for me and probably most of my generation, going to live concerts is somewhat of a let-down sonically, particularly if acoustic instruments are involved. My musical beliefs were formed from hearing things from speakers within arm's length, controlled hearing, if you please.''

As for ''live'' rock concerts, Kurtz points out that, ''The audience already knew the music before they got there, and they learned it from a controlled, amplified presentation such as radio or records, so hearing familiar music being done 'live' was not so much a musical treat as it was a participation. In fact, since even the live concert is amplified, we might say that people today simply have not heard their music done 'live' as they think they have; from the stage they are hearing an electronic reproduction of even the voices. The only thing 'live' about it is that the performers are actually standing on stage, but they are delivering sounds that are electronically created, shaped, and enhanced. We must remember that at one time 'live' referred to acoustic sounds coming unaided from the instrument or the throat, as used to be common in chambers, theaters, and concert halls.''

The result of this is that ''. . . the *production* of the music has come to be its identifying factor rather than the more academic qualities of instrument identification, voice attributes, harmony, and orchestration.''

As film is a medium that can only be experienced through a reproductive process, the introduction of the synthesizer, from a technological standpoint, was a natural extension of its use in the pop field. The long-standing use of video synchronization techniques in the pop recording studio for purposes of overdubbing tracks has also been important in the use of the synthesizer in the film music recording studio. As more film (primarily for television at this point) utilizes video technology in the audio post-production process, synthesizer players have easily transferred the technology developed for the record studio onto the film music recording stage. Another recent, rapidly developing innovation important to the development of synthesizers as performance instruments has been MIDI (Music Instrument Digital Interface) which allows a performer to play any number of different synthesizers from a single keyboard source. This has been extremely valuable in the film music recording studio where the synthesizer is frequently being used in conjunction with other, acoustic, instruments.

The use of synthesizers in film music falls into two very distinct categories. First, the synthesizer is performance-oriented and is used as an additional instrument or sound resource in the recording session, and is generally incorporated into a texture involving traditional acoustic instruments. The second use is by a composer who utilizes a group of synthesizers as the sole sonic resource for a score. It is this second area where the most creative and imaginative (and, many times, boring) use of synthesizers in film is taking place. I say ''boring'' parenthetically because the synthesizer can be made to create sounds by just about anyone (engineer-types are especially enamored of them), regardless of their creative gifts or dramatic sense for motion pictures, with understandably dull results.

It is important at this point to make a significant distinction between those composers using the synthesizer to reproduce traditional instruments (a task synthesizers are becoming increasingly proficient in doing) as a way of saving musician's costs, and those who are utilizing the synthesizer for its limitless sonic capabilities. Merely replicating acoustic instruments on the synthesizer is, according to Kurtz, ''. . . wandering up a dead end. If you want the sound of trombones, you'll be far ahead of the game by hiring trombone players.''

Writing about synthesizer scores, in some respects, is more difficult than writing about acoustic scores in that there is no notation in the traditional sense that one can present as examples of the art. Of course traditional acoustic-type scores reproduced on the synthesizer could be examined but it is my feeling that such scores have made few original contributions to the genre and are, therefore, not within the bounds of this book.

The most pivotal synthesizer score was probably the Giorgio Moroder score for the 1978 film, *Midnight Express*. While there was actually very little music in this film, what was there was purely synthetic and, therefore, a significant departure from past tradition for major theatrical motion pictures. The creative, musical aspect of the score was fairly ordinary and did little to expand that particular element of film music language. Moroder's record producing background emerged through the use of ''fade-outs'' of the music at the end of scenes identical to the ''board fade'' at the end of many pop songs. I make this point only to raise the question of whether or not this was a conscious departure from film music tradition or merely a demonstration of the limits of Moroder's experience in creating music for films.

Another film, the 1982 *Chariots of Fire,* incorporated a synthesizer score by Vangelis. Again, there is very little music in this picture and very little imaginative use of the synthesizer as a dramatic resource. In fact, if one listens closely to this score, much of what it does achieve dramatically could have been just as effective with acoustic instrumentation. The score also suffers from the composer's lack of craftsmanship in knitting music into the fabric of a film scene. In the training sequence for the Olympic Games, for instance, the music is effective enough as a general wash of mood but it made no accommodation for the dialogue in either its volume or texture, which resulted in the mixer having to "dip" the level of the music whenever dialogue occurs in the scene.

In another scene, the first meeting of the two runners, Harold and Abraham, the music is almost naïve in its sensitivity for the scene, betraying the possibility that this particular cue may not have been written for this particular scene. It has been said that Vangelis composes his scores without reference to specific timings for scenes and merely delivers finished tracks to the music editor who is then expected to edit them to the appropriate length for a given scene. Much of his work, to the experienced ear, seems to indicate that this is, indeed, what is being done. All this aside, the score did win an Academy Award.

There are some advantages for the composer working alone in the electronic studio. Kurtz points out that, "When writing an electronic score you usually have much more freedom and you are more self-contained. You have a lot of time to experiment and you have fewer peripheral things to deal with and a lot fewer people to deal with. You approach budgets differently in that you're not having to say, 'I wish I had three more violins.' There are different considerations and, many times, the decision-making is more creative than financial. The negative of that is that the composer ends up working much harder in that you are doing the work of a lot of different people."

On this same subject, composer William Goldstein says that working alone in his studio allows him to ". . . personalize my music in a way that wouldn't be possible if I were writing a score for an acoustic orchestra and then going into a studio to record that score. The same principle would apply if I were writing the score for other synthesists to record. When you are composing music the colors you are working with are right there for you to hear; when you're discovering new and different colors and using signal processing to create certain delays and certain effects, etc., then those elements become part of the composition. Ideas then occur to you that wouldn't possibly occur to you if you were sitting alone with a pencil and paper at your desk.''

Because of the synthesizer's almost infinite palette of sonic possibilities the traditional creative dilemma of choice-making can be elevated to a level of refined torture for the composer. Goldstein says that, ''Because there are limitless possibilities [to synthesizers] it *can* slow you down. However, some things take longer to create and some things go much more quickly. When you stop and think that for an orchestral score you turn out, on an average, maybe three minutes of music a day or, if you are orchestrating, maybe two minutes a day, then it's quite reasonable that I am able to create pretty complex film music here in my electronic studio at a rate of a minute and a half a day—already recorded. On the other hand, because creating electronic music can be so complex and time-consuming, it can be as expensive as an orchestral score. If it's the kind of score that doesn't need a lot of layering or subtlety then it can go very quickly.''

On the negative side of this issue there is a ''. . . problem with having the ability to play a cue for a producer, against picture, here in my studio,'' says Kurtz. ''The problem created mainly has to do with indecisiveness and the fact that people think it's easy to create these scores. Sometimes what happens is that a producer takes advantage of the situation and wants a choice of more than one cue for a given scene. On the other hand, one of the reasons I've never made a producer unhappy is that I do invite him or her to my studio to hear the score in progress. In the old days that would have been the equivalent of playing the score on the piano. The problem with playing orchestrated music at the piano is that you are leaving so much to the imagination of the producer and that can be dangerous. Interestingly enough, in situations where producers wanted alternate choices, my first choice of a cue for a scene has always turned out to be the best choice.''

The practice of previewing scores for producers ''. . . hasn't created any problems for me and I like it.'' says Goldstein. ''If I'm not sure of something I ask the producer to come over and preview what I'm doing. I have very good communication with the people I work with and I think any successful composer probably does. I think its a prerequisite to get the next job. I don't mind making little changes but if the changes requested are major then it can be as rough as trying to make changes on the scoring stage with an orchestra. On the other hand sometimes the changes are quite easy. Working with a computer is very much like working on a word processor: you can edit very quickly. I actually think the magic of working right to picture, locking up to picture, is very exciting and I enjoy that aspect of working in my studio."

Two of the primary synthesizers in use as composition tools are the Synclavier and the Fairlight. These are then generally used to control, through a MIDI hookup, a bank of other synthesizers. Composers working with these instruments find, as with their acoustic cousins, that each synthesizer has a distinct quality to its sound. Kurtz observes that, "I will use my Roland for warm, string-like textures and my Oberheim for punchier, brass-like sounds. I'll never get rid of my Prophet 5, even though it's an older instrument, because it has its own distinctive sound I find useful. So those traditional values and qualities once associated with acoustic instruments still haven't changed in the electronic medium. My engineer, for instance, insists that there is a 'Japanese sound' to instruments produced there, and I think he's right. That particular sound, to me, is a colder, thinner sound."

Goldstein agrees, saying that, "You find certain kinds of synthesizers are better for producing certain kinds of sounds. However, unlike acoustic instruments, any one of the synthesizers is capable of producing a wide variety of sounds and has an almost endless palette to work with."

Overall, it is the vast sonic possibilities of the synthesizer which draws the more creative composers working in films to utilize them for their scores. Kurtz feels that "It's more exciting and challenging and more interesting to deal with the sounds I can create in my studio. It's very hard for me, and I can only speak for myself, to be creatively fulfilled in the orchestral world. Those instruments have been around for a long, long time. It's not that I don't enjoy working with an orchestra, it's just that now that those other, electronic instruments are out there, the potential is there for almost anything."

There is no question that synthesizers will continue to be a growing influence in film scores. With musical color being the predominant musical value expressed in film scores, the synthesizer is a natural and valuable new tool for the film composer. Goldstein observes, "I don't think the orchestra is going to disappear but I do think that synthesizers are going to become more and more capable and have more and more nuance. I think electronic music is going to be on an equal par with the orchestra and, in film scoring, it may have already reached that point. They are the sounds of our times, the sounds of this age. I find it very exciting."

Bibliography

1. MUSIC IN THE SILENT FILM

Borneman, Ernest J. "Sound Rhythm and the Film: Recent Research on the Compound Cinema," *Sight and Sound,* Vol. 3, no. 10 (1934), p. 66.

Eisenstein, Sergei. *Film Form.* New York: Harcourt, Brace & Co., 1949.

Eisler, Hanns. *Composing for the Films.* New York: Oxford University Press, 1947.

Huntley, John and Manvell, Roger. *The Technique of Film Music.* London: Focal Press, 1957.

Kriegsman, Alan. "A Fusion of Art," *The Washington Post,* March 24, 1972.

London, Kurt. *Film Music.* Trans. by Eric S. Bensinger. New York: Arno Press, 1970 (reprint of 1936 edition).

Peeples, Samuel A. "The Mechanical Music Makers," *Films in Review,* April 1973.

Winkler, Max. "The Origins of Film Music," *Films in Review,* December 1951.

2. MUSIC IN THE EARLY SOUND FILM

Borneman, Ernest J. "Sound Rhythm and the Film: Recent Research on the Compound Cinema," *Sight and Sound,* Vol. 3, no. 10 (1934).

Calvocoressi, M. D. "Music and the Film: A Problem of Adjustment," *Sight and Sound,* Vol. 4, no. 14 (1935).

Churchill, Douglas W. "Baghdad at Hollywood and Vine," *The New York Times,* August 1, 1937.

Grout, Donald J. *Short History of the Opera.* New York: Oxford University Press, 1965.

Goldner, Orville and Turner, George E. *The Making of King Kong.* New York: A. S. Barnes, 1975.

Huntley, John and Manvell, Roger. *The Technique of Film Music.* London: Focal Press, 1957.

Lawson, John Howard. *Film: The Creative Process.* New York: Hill and Wang, 1967.

London, Kurt. *Film Music.* Trans. by Eric S. Bensinger. New York: Arno Press, 1970 (reprint of 1936 edition).

Mast, Gerald. *A Short History of the Movies.* New York: Bobbs-Merrill, 1971.

Morton, Lawrence. Foreword to Clifford McCarty, *Film Composers in America: A Checklist of Their Work.* New York: Da Capo Press, 1972 (reprint, with minor additions and corrections, of 1953 edition).

"Florence Music Congress," *The New York Times,* June 4, 1933, sec. 9, p. 4.

Raybould, Clarence. "Music and the Synchronized Film," *Sight and Sound,* Vol. 2, no. 7 (1935).

Steiner, Max. *We Make the Movies,* ed. Nancy Naumberg. New York: W. W. Norton, 1937.

Toch, Ernst. Quoted in "The Cinema Wields the Baton," *The New York Times,* April 11, 1937, sec. 11, p. 3.

3. FILM MUSIC COMES OF AGE: 1935-1950

Antheil, George. All columns entitled "On The Hollywood Front" in *Modern Music,* Vol. 14, no. 1 through Vol. 16, no. 2 (1936–1939).

Applebaum, Louis. "Hugo Friedhofer's Score to 'The Best Years of Our Lives.' " *Film Music Notes,* Vol. 9, no. 5 (1947).

Bazelon, Irwin A. " 'The Heiress': A Review of Aaron Copland's Music Score," *Film Music Notes,* Vol. 9, no. 2 (1949).

Bernstein, Elmer. "What Ever Happened to Great Movie Music?" *High Fidelity and Musical America,* Vol. 22, no. 7 (July 1972).

Film Music Notes, Vol. 4, no. 2 (1944), p. 14.

Friedhofer, Hugo. Conversation with the author, May 1973.

Grout, Donald J. *A History of Western Music.* New York: W.W. Norton, 1973.

Herrmann, Bernard. "Citizen Kane," *Film Music Notes,* Vol. 1, no. 1 (1941).

Lawson, John Howard. *Film: The Creative Process.* New York: Hill and Wang, 1967.

Leibell, Judge Vincent L. *Civil Action Number 13-95.* Entered on March 14, 1950.

Mast, Gerald. *A Short History of the Movies.* New York: Bobbs-Merrill, 1971.

Morton, Lawrence. All columns entitled "Film Music of the Quarter" in *Hollywood Quarterly,* Vol. 1, no. 1 through Vol. 8, no. 3 (1945-1953).

Morton, Lawrence. "Composing, Orchestrating, and Criticizing," *Hollywood Quarterly,* Vol. 6, no. 2 (1951).

Morton, Lawrence. " 'Force of Evil' A Review of David Raksin's Score," *Film Music Notes,* Vol. 8, no. 3 (1949).

"Music in the Cinema," *The New York Times,* September 29, 1935, sec. 10, p. 4.

"Opera and Concert Activities," *The New York Times,* November 8, 1936, sec. 10, p. 7.

Pechter, William. "Abraham Polonsky and 'Force of Evil,' " *Film Quarterly,* Vol. 15, no. 3 (1962).

Raksin, David. Letter to Dr. Harold Spivacke, Music Division, Library of Congress, November 12, 1968.

Raksin, David. Conversations with the author, May 1973.

Rozsa, Miklos. Conversations with the author, May, 1973.

Seroff, Victor. *Sergei Prokofiev: A Soviet Tragedy.* New York: Funk and Wagnalls, 1968.

Steiner, Max. Quoted in "Music in the Cinema," *The New York Times,* September 29, 1935, sec. 10, p. 4.

Sternfeld, Frederick W. "Music and the Feature Film," *Musical Quarterly,* October 1947.

Sternfeld, Frederick W. "Copland as Film Composer," *Musical Quarterly,* April 1951.

Stewart, James G. Letter to the author, August 11, 1974.

Thomas, Tony. *Music for the Movies.* South Brunswick: A. S. Barnes, 1973.

Ussher, Bruno. "Composing for the Films," *The New York Times,* January 28, 1940, sec. 9, p. 6.

Williams, Ralph Vaughan. "Film Music," *Film Music Notes,* Vol. 6, no. 3 (1946).

4. FROM 1950 TO THE PRESENT

Bernstein, Elmer. "The Man With the Golden Arm," *Film Music Notes,* Vol. 15, no. 4 (1956).

Bernstein, Leonard. *The Joy of Music.* New York: Simon and Schuster, 1959.

Burton, Howard A. " 'High Noon': Everyman Rides Again," *Hollywood Quarterly,* Vol. 8, no. 1 (1953).

Canby, Vincent. "Music is Now Profit to the Ears of Filmmakers," *The New York Times,* May 24, 1966.

Giannetti, Louis D. *Understanding Movies.* Englewood Cliffs, New Jersey: Prentice-Hall, 1972.

Huntley, John and Manvell, Roger. *The Technique of Film Music.* London: Focal Press, 1957.

Kanfer, Stefan. *A Journal of the Plague Years.* New York: Atheneum, 1973.

Lees, Gene. "When the Music Stopped," *High Fidelity and Musical America,* Vol. 22, no. 7 (July 1972), p. 20.

Mast, Gerald. *A Short History of the Movies.* New York: Bobbs-Merrill, 1971.

Morton, Lawrence. "Rozsa's Music for 'Quo Vadis,' " *Film Music Notes,* Vol. 11, no. 2 (1951).

"Lights . . . Camera . . . Music!," *Newsweek,* July 24, 1967, p. 27.

Palmer, Christopher. "Music in the Hollywood Biblical Spectacular." Source of article unknown, but believed to come from publication of Performing Rights Society Ltd., London, ca. 1970.

Raksin, David. Conversations with the author, May 1973.

Raksin, David. "Raksin Raps State of Art," *Variety,* Vol. 275, no. 1, May 15, 1974, p. 59.

Rosenman, Leonard. Conversations with the author, May 1975.

Rozsa, Miklos. "Quo Vadis?," *Film Music Notes,* Vol. 11, no. 2 (1951).

Steiner, Fred. "Herrmann's 'Black and White' Music for Hitchcock's 'Psycho,' " *Elmer Bernstein's Film Music Collection,* Vol. 1 (Fall 1974), p. 31.

Thomas, Tony. *Music for the Movies.* South Brunswick, New Jersey: A. S. Barnes, 1973.

5. MUSIC IN THE CARTOON AND EXPERIMENTAL ANIMATED FILM

Bradley, Scott. Conversation with the author, May 1975.

Dahl, Ingolf. "Notes on Cartoon Music," *Film Music Notes,* Vol. 8, no. 5 (1949).

Jones, Chuck. "Music and the Animated Cartoon," *Hollywood Quarterly,* Vol. 1, no. 4 (1946).

Lamont, Austin. "An Interview with John Whitney," *Film Comment,* Vol. 6, no. 3, Fall 1970.

McLaren, Norman. "Notes on Animated Sound," *Hollywood Quarterly,* Vol. 7, no. 3 (1953).

"An Interview with Scott Bradley," *Pacific Coast Musician,* May 15, 1937, pp. 12-13.

Rosen, Charles. *The Classical Style.* New York: W. W. Norton, 1972.

Whitney, John. "Animation Mechanisms," *American Cinematographer,* January 1971.

Whitney, John. Conversation with the author, May 1975.

6. THE AESTHETICS OF FILM MUSIC

Bluestone, George. *Novels into Film.* Berkeley: University of California Press, 1966.

Copland, Aaron. "Tip to Moviegoers: Take off Those Ear-Muffs," *The New York Times,* November 6, 1949, sec. 6, p. 28.

Eisenstein, Sergei. *The Film Sense.* New York: Harcourt, Brace & Co., 1947.

Eisler, Hanns. *Composing for the Films.* New York: Oxford University Press, 1947.

Lawson, John Howard. *Film: The Creative Process.* New York: Hill and Wang, 1967.

Morton, Lawrence. "Film Music of the Quarter," *Hollywood Quarterly,* Vol. 5, no. 2 (1950).

Morton, Lawrence. "Composing, Orchestrating, and Criticizing," *Hollywood Quarterly,* Vol. 6, no. 2 (1951).

Raksin, David. "Talking Back: A Hollywood Composer States Case for His Craft," *The New York Times,* February 20, 1949, sec. 2, p. 7.

7. FILM MUSIC AND FORM

Applebaum, Louis. "Hugo Friedhofer's Score to 'The Best Years of Our Lives,'" *Film Music Notes,* Vol. 6, no. 5 (1947).

Bernstein, Elmer. "What Ever Happened to Great Movie Music?," *High Fidelity and Musical America,* Vol. 22, no. 7 (July 1972).

Steiner, Max.' Quoted in "Music in the Cinema," *The New York Times,* September 29, 1935, sec. 10, p. 4.

8. SYNCHRONIZING MUSIC TO PICTURE

Hagen, Earl. *Scoring for Films.* New York: Wehman, 1972.

ADDITIONAL SOURCES RECENTLY PUBLISHED

Gorbman, Claudia. *Unheard Melodies: Narrative Film Music.* London: BFI Publishing; Bloomington and Indianapolis: Indiana University Press, 1987.

Karlin, Fred and Rayburn Wright. *On the Track: A Guide to Contemporary Film Scoring.* New York: Schirmer Books; London: Collier Macmillan Publishers, 1990.

Palmer, Christopher. *The Composer in Hollywood.* London: Marion Boyars Publishers Ltd.; New York: Rizzoli International Publications, 1990.

The Cue Sheet: The Journal of the Society for the Preservation of Film Music. A quarterly journal available from the Society for the Preservation of Film Music, 10850 Wilshire Blvd., Suite 770, Los Angeles, California 90024.

Index

315

Acme Orchestra